HISTORY'S
NARROWEST
ESCAPES

HISTORY'S NARROWEST ESCAPES

JAMES MOORE AND PAUL NERO

The History Press

Front cover images: Authors' collection

First published 2013

The History Press
The Mill, Brimscombe Port
Stroud, Gloucestershire, GL5 2QG
www.thehistorypress.co.uk

British Library Cataloguing in Publication Data.
A catalogue record for this book is available from the British Library.

ISBN 978 0 7524 8987 2

Typesetting and origination by The History Press
Printed in Great Britain

CONTENTS

ACKNOWLEDGEMENTS

For all their advice and patience, as well as for helping us narrowly escape more inaccuracies than there might have been, we'd like to thank the following for their support in putting this book together: Tamsin Moore, Alexander Moore, Laurie Moore, Geoffrey Moore, Philippa Moore, Sam Moore, Dr Lana Matile, Dr Tom Moore, Dr Claire Nesbitt, Peter Spurgeon, Sarah Sarkhel, William Poole, Fiona Poole, Jim Addison, Daniel Simister, Felicity Hebditch, Jan Hebditch, Robert Smith, Mark Beynon, Yvonne Oliver, Angela Houghton, Vicky Green, Thomas Worsdale, Giusto Truglia, Bruno Ivini, Ken Robison, William Thiesen, William Neave, the Airey Neave Trust, Brian Best, the Victoria Cross Society, Nadine Linge, Samm Taylor, Brian Emsley, Fran Bowden, Hannah Reynolds, Ashley-Jane Steer, David Evans, Mike Hudis.

INTRODUCTION

'Nothing,' said British Prime Minister Winston Churchill, 'is more exhilarating than to be shot at without result.'

The pages of history are full of terrible disasters, shocking accidents, tragic incidents, death and destruction. But just sometimes, amid the carnage, the worst doesn't happen: wars are avoided, people cheat the Grim Reaper, masterpieces are saved. This book is dedicated to these incredible narrow escapes, the remarkable 'might have beens' of history, which prove, that however bad things are, there's always hope.

How exactly did the Nazis plan to assassinate Winston Churchill during the Second World War? Why was Abraham Lincoln lucky to be alive to free the slaves and so become an American icon? And what did it take for Prince Albert to help avoid a full-scale war from his deathbed? All these questions and many more are answered in the pages of *History's Narrowest Escapes*.

The tales in our book are studded with amazing feats of bravery and grim determination in the face of danger, as well as a good measure of sheer bloody-mindedness. But above all they reveal the importance of serendipity. No matter how famous the individuals concerned, or how big the nations involved, these stories reveal that luck always has a big role in the way history plays out. Sometimes the most trivial things can have a huge impact. And, of course, one person's bad roll of the dice can always be another's good fortune.

The narrow escapes we have chosen to include (there were many that we left out) broadly fall into five categories. There are the little-known stories of how famous people in history, such as Charles Dickens and Isambard Kingdom Brunel, narrowly avoided a sticky early fate. But we also meet ordinary folk, like 14-year-old Werner Franz, caught up in the destruction of the *Hindenburg* airship, who survived against incredible odds. Then there are souls who sacrificed themselves to save millions; characters like Edward Harrison, the inventor of the first practical gas mask. We also reveal how some of the world's best-loved buildings, including the Eiffel Tower, and artworks, such as the Bayeux Tapestry, avoided destruction. Lastly, we show how close whole countries, indeed humanity itself, came to disaster and how they, and we, were reprieved.

In common, all of the entries feature half-forgotten aspects of well-known episodes in history and different angles on momentous chapters from the past that you might never have considered. Most importantly, each offers a reason to feel uplifted. So, the next time someone says to you, 'Cheer up, it might never happen!', agree, and tell them one of these stories.

THE ASSASSINATION OF
WINSTON CHURCHILL

On the morning of 1 June 1943, the actor Leslie Howard, famed for his role in films like *Gone With The Wind*, boarded BOAC Flight 777 at Lisbon Airport, Portugal, bound for Britain. Beside him was another man, Alfred Chenhalls, Howard's financial agent, who enjoyed smoking cigars and, it is said, bore an uncanny resemblance to the then prime minister, Winston Churchill.

With Portugal and Spain still neutral in the Second World War, Howard, a popular heart-throb who was also a fervent patriot, had just completed a propaganda tour aimed at winning over hearts and minds in the region. Legend has it that his plane home was delayed after he went back to retrieve a package containing a pair of silk stockings for a lady friend. Howard had reportedly been reluctant to take the trip to the Iberian Peninsula at all and, as it turned out, with good reason. About 200 miles into his flight home, the Dutch pilot of the Douglas DC-3 radioed to say, 'I am being followed by strange aircraft. Putting on best speed ... we are being attacked. Cannon shells and tracers are going through the fuselage. Wave-hopping and doing my best.' At 11 a.m. radio contact was lost. The plane had been shot down over the Bay of Biscay by a force of eight German Junkers 88 aircraft. The lives of all seventeen people on board, including Howard and Chenhalls, were lost.

Within days, speculation was rife in the British press that the shooting down of the aircraft might well have been a botched attempt by the Nazis to assassinate Winston Churchill. While Howard's death was a much-mourned loss, Churchill's death would have been a huge coup for the Germans.

What made the theory more credible was that Churchill himself had been at a meeting in North Africa with American general Dwight D. Eisenhower, or 'Ike' as he was popularly known, then Allied commander in the region. Churchill actually flew back to England on 4 June, on a similar route to Flight 777, without incident. His flight had even been delayed due to bad weather. Rumours had been circulating, possibly put about by British intelligence itself, that Churchill might return on a civilian airliner such as the few that still plied the route from Lisbon to Britain. After all, in 1942, he had flown back to Britain from Bermuda on a Boeing flying boat. The theory goes that poor Alfred Chenhalls could have been mistaken for the portly prime minister by German agents monitoring these flights. It's certain that German spies were watching such airfields.

In his memoir *The Hinge of Fate*, Churchill said he believed that the Bay of Biscay attack was indeed intended for him. But he noted that the Nazis were idiotic to think he would be on a civilian airliner, saying, 'The brutality of the Germans was only matched by the stupidity of their agents.' When the Second World War was brewing Churchill had known he would be a target for assassins. As early as August 1939, before he was even prime minister, he had re-employed Detective Inspector Walter H. Thompson, paying him £5 a week to be his bodyguard. In an earlier period of service, Thompson had thwarted an attempt by IRA shooters to kill Churchill in Hyde Park. And, in June 1940, during a dash over to France before the nation fell to the Nazis, Thompson had managed to stop a crazed lunge on Churchill by the French countess Hélène de Portes, who was armed with a knife.

Other theories sprang up about Flight 777. The most plausible was that the Germans had actually planned to kill the anti-Nazi campaigner Howard, thinking he was a British spy. Even today, the truth behind the episode remains mysterious.

A few months before the demise of Flight 777 there was a very definite and carefully planned bid by the Nazis to end Churchill's life.

While one of the more bizarre German ploys uncovered by British intelligence – to kill Churchill via exploding chocolate bars served to him in London meetings – was highly unlikely to succeed, in February 1943, spies prepared to do away with him via one of the old campaigner's better known vices – alcohol.

Churchill travelled 200,000 miles during the war and it was probably during these foreign trips, which gave his government and military chiefs nightmares, that he was most vulnerable. The poison plot emerged as Churchill toured North Africa following a visit to Turkey in January, in which he met President İsmet İnönü to persuade the nation, which had remained neutral, to come in on the side of the Allies.

After the negotiations, which proved fruitless, Churchill flew on to Cyprus and then Cairo before landing in Tripoli to celebrate with the Eighth Army, who, after their success at the Second Battle of El Alamein, in November 1942, had all but cleared the North African deserts of German resistance.

Then the alarm came. There had been some kind of leak. Immense amounts of planning always went into disguising the prime minister's location when he was on a foreign trip, but now Churchill's route home to Britain had somehow become known to the Germans. Thankfully, code-breakers at Bletchley Park, the secret wartime intelligence headquarters, had discovered the lapse in security. But what they discovered spread fear amongst the British Cabinet as they awaited Churchill's homecoming. The intercepted messages, between Nazi agents in the field and Berlin, showed that the knowledge of Churchill's travel plans would be used to try and kill him.

On 4 February 1943 Britain's deputy prime minister, Clement Attlee, sent a 'clear the line' message marked 'Most Secret' to the Western Desert, for the prime minister's eyes. It read:

> Attempts are going to be made to bump you off. We have studied possibilities very carefully and I and my colleagues, supported by the Chiefs of Staff, consider that it would be unwise for you to adhere to your present programme. We regard it as essential in the national interest that you cut out visits to both Algiers and Gibraltar and proceed to England.

Analysis showed that Algiers was the most likely place where the assassination attempt would be made. The intercepted messages had

British Prime Minister Winston Churchill visiting North Africa during the Second World War. (Imperial War Museums © IWM E15299)

The Big Three: Stalin, Roosevelt and Churchill at the Tehran Conference in 1943. (Courtesy of the Library of Congress)

been sent from an agent called Muh, based in Tangier, Morocco. This was actually Hans-Peter Schulze, a man working undercover as a German press attaché. According to his communiques to Berlin, four assassins were on their way to Algeria with an 'assignment against Churchill'. He had asked high command to 'dispatch urgently 20–50 machine pistols with ammunition, magnetic and adhesive mines. Also poisons for drinks.' According to the wires, by 4 February, the killers – recruited from the ranks of local, disaffected nationalists – were already on their way to ambush the PM.

It's unclear what Churchill's reaction to the message was. What is not in question, however, is that by the morning of 5 February Churchill was already on his way to Algiers to meet Eisenhower and the British admiral, Sir Andrew Cunningham. In fact, the prime minister seems to have enjoyed the chance to let his hair down in Algiers, saying to his aides, almost playfully, 'There is no reason why we should hurry on from here. No-one knows we are here.'

Eisenhower had been informed of the assassination threats and had given the prime minister his own car, with bulletproof windows. But as Churchill was finally ready to fly home that evening, something strange happened. His Liberator plane developed a fault. Not a serious one, but enough for Churchill to decide to stay another day. Ike was furious, desperate to get Churchill back to London where he was 'worth two armies' but a 'liability' anywhere else.

After the war there was a theory that Churchill had ordered Thompson to tamper with the aircraft on purpose by removing a rotor arm. Thompson denied the fact publicly but, apparently, once admitted to his son that this was true. Was Churchill playing a dangerous game of bluff with his movements, in order to outwit Nazi agents who might target his plane? Had he wanted it to look like the aeroplane had mechanical trouble, to cover the fact that he had been tipped off about an assassination attempt? After all, making sudden changes to his plans might signify that British intelligence had cracked the Germans' codes, putting the war effort at risk. Much more likely was that Churchill was simply enjoying his trip and saw the chance for a few more drinks. As it turned out, on the evening of 6 February, Churchill finally flew back to Britain in the Liberator via a more direct route than originally planned. Nothing more was heard of the would-be assassins.

Later the same year there was another scheme, code-named Operation Long Jump, to kill not only Churchill but also Stalin and Roosevelt at the Big Three's conference in Tehran in November 1943. Ordered directly by Hitler, after German intelligence had found out about the conference, and masterminded by Nazi superspy Otto Scorzeny, the plot involved six German radio operators being parachuted into Iran to plan the attack. But the Soviets knew the conference was a likely target and a 19-year-old Soviet agent called Gevork Vartanyan led a team working tirelessly to track down the German group. He found them 'travelling by camel and loaded with weapons' and began monitoring their dispatches back to Berlin. Discovering that a second wave of German agents were on the way he had the first group arrested, then forced them to report the failure of their mission by radio back to Berlin leading to the cancellation of the attack.

Thankfully for the British people, and perhaps the rest of the world, Winston Churchill survived all the wartime attempts on his life. We can only speculate as to what would have happened had he been successfully 'bumped off', as Attlee put it. By 1943 the tide of the war had definitely turned in favour of the Allies. But there was a long way to go before peace, including the thorny question of Allied landings on the Continent of Europe. Then there was Churchill's value as a cog in the personal relationships between the leaders of the Big Three and his influence on post-war planning. Most importantly, no doubt, there was his ongoing value to British morale. Roosevelt certainly had no doubt when he told Churchill's bodyguard, Thompson, to 'Look after the Prime Minister. He is one of the greatest men in the world.' Whatever Churchill's personal worth, it was certainly fitting that he was there on the balcony of Buckingham Palace on VE Day in 1945, along with the Royal Family, to celebrate the Allied victory over Hitler.

There was no doubt that the wily old man had always embraced the dangers of his position with a degree of sangfroid. On the way back to England in February 1943, having eluded the assassins of North Africa, he ruminated, 'It would be a pity to have to go out in the middle of such an interesting drama, without seeing the end.'

2

WHEN BRITAIN ALMOST MADE PEACE WITH HITLER

During early May 1940 it was clear that Neville Chamberlain, the prime minister who had once promised 'peace for our time', could no longer continue to lead the country. Some eight months into hostilities with Hitler, the war was going badly for Britain. Poland had already been defeated and then there had been a disastrous campaign to Norway, in which 4,000 troops and a large number of ships had been lost, in a failed bid to stop the Germans overrunning Scandinavia. It was this military debacle that precipitated a fierce debate in the House of Commons on 7–8 May, culminating in a confidence vote in Chamberlain's government.

The prime minister won the ballot, but only by eighty-one votes. A war leader needed better backing. Embattled and worn out, with his past as an appeaser of Hitler a millstone round his neck, Chamberlain was finished as PM. The Labour leader, Clement Attlee, refused to offer his party's participation in a national government led by Chamberlain. In the debate over Norway, Attlee even noted that the prime minister and others were leading 'an almost uninterrupted career of failure.' It was time to find a successor.

Winston Churchill, then First Lord of the Admiralty, was not the favourite of the two main candidates who emerged. Already 65 years old, he had spent much of the 1930s in the political wilderness, noisily criticising the policy of appeasement from the sidelines. His past wartime experiences in government did not instil great confidence. Churchill's reputation had been left in tatters after he had masterminded the calamitous Gallipoli campaign during the First World War. Now his fingerprints were all over the Norwegian campaign too. Even Churchill's own former private secretary, Sir James Grigg, warned that he would 'bugger up the whole war'.

The obvious person to be prime minister, agreed most of the establishment, was Lord Halifax, then foreign secretary. He had experience, gravitas and seemed a safe pair of hands compared to Churchill, a man who had switched political parties twice. Born into a sickly family and fourth in line to inherit the family seat, Halifax attained his title when his three older brothers died in childhood. With extraordinary wealth and the best of educations, Halifax was an unprepossessing man with an attuned political instinct. Nicknamed 'the Holy Fox' he had worked his way up through Tory ranks during thirty years in Parliament before giving up his job in the Commons on becoming Viceroy of India. Then, in the late 1930s, he had returned to government, serving in a number of roles, even meeting Adolf Hitler in 1937 in Germany. The fact that he had almost handed the Führer his coat, mistaking the dictator for a footman, was not auspicious.

With Chamberlain set to resign it appeared that Halifax had the backing of the majority of the Conservative party as well as the Royal Family. The press baron Lord Beaverbrook, one of the few to want the bombastic Winston to take the role, wrote, 'Chamberlain wanted Halifax. Labour wanted Halifax. The Lords wanted Halifax. The King wanted Halifax. And Halifax wanted Halifax.'

On the afternoon of 9 May Chamberlain met with Churchill and Halifax, the main contenders for his job. Churchill initially stayed quiet in the meeting – quite out of character. But by this stage it seems that Halifax was wavering. Beaverbrook was mistaken. Halifax, it appeared, did not want to be prime minister, not at this juncture at any rate. With defeat by Germany a distinct possibility, perhaps he felt the premiership was a poisoned chalice. In fact, on the morning of the crucial meeting, he was already suffering from a 'stomach ache' at the prospect of being PM.

And, as Chamberlain seemed set to recommend him to the king, Halifax himself pointed out that as a peer, unable to sit in the House of Commons, it would be tricky to serve as prime minister. Undoubtedly this obstacle could have been overcome. Yet Halifax clearly felt it would be difficult to have Churchill serve under him in a War Cabinet where Winston would inevitably lead military policy. Halifax intimated to Chamberlain that Churchill was the better choice as leader. And Winston, recalled Halifax, 'did not demur'.

Churchill certainly hadn't pushed to be prime minister. He had originally expected to merely be in a new Cabinet led by Halifax. And for some Tories, who loathed the idea of Churchill in charge, the fight to make Halifax PM wasn't over. One senior minister, 'Rab' Butler, rushed to see him, trying to get Halifax to change his mind. He was told that the foreign secretary had gone to the dentist. On 10 May Chamberlain went to the king and recommended that Churchill be made prime minister. By 6 p.m. Churchill had got the job.

Three days later Halifax was already carping. He confided to a friend, 'I don't think WSC will be a very good PM ... though the country will think he gives them a fillip.' Churchill himself admitted to the people, a few days after taking office, that he had 'nothing to offer but blood, toil, tears and sweat', but vowed to achieve 'Victory. Victory at all costs. Victory in spite of all terror. Victory, however long and hard the road may be, for without victory there is no survival.'

Within days, however, it was looking like Halifax might be right. The war didn't seem to be going much better with Churchill at the helm. On the very day Chuchill came to power, Hitler ended the so-called 'phoney war' and invaded the Low Countries. Soon the British Expeditionary Force on the Continent had been pushed back to the sea and France was on the verge of surrender.

Halifax remained foreign secretary in Churchill's new government. And he was soon lobbying Churchill to be allowed to sue for peace through the Italian ambassador Giuseppe Bastianini (he'd already sounded out the diplomat), Italy not yet being at war with Britain. The Holy Fox had form in this area. Earlier in the conflict Halifax had helped organise a travel permit to Germany for a fellow Old Etonian, John Lonsdale Bryans, who, at first, believed he could promote a coup in Germany, and then later tried to contact Hitler hoping to broker a peace settlement. Halifax accepted intelligence reports from Lonsdale Bryans who appears to have passed himself off as an unofficial envoy.

By 26 May Britain was desperately trying to extricate the 200,000 strong British Expeditionary Force from the beaches of Dunkirk, after they had been beaten back to the English Channel by Hitler's blitzkrieg. The Battle of France was now lost and Halifax felt it was time to explore the 'possibilities of mediation' using Mussolini as a go-between with the Germans. His belief was that if Britain negotiated while still unbeaten, then something could be salvaged from a situation that would otherwise lead to a possible invasion and further hardship for the nation. Hitler would remain undefeated but at least a vestige of the British Empire would survive. Chamberlain, interestingly, backed Halifax.

On 28 May Churchill narrowly persuaded government members around to his point of view – that Britain should maintain its course – with an impassioned speech in which he said:

> I am convinced that every man of you would rise up and tear me down from my place if I were for one moment to contemplate parley or surrender. If this long island story of ours is to last, let it end only when each one of us lies choking in his own blood upon the ground.

Inspired by his words, enough Cabinet members rallied to Churchill's side and the decision was taken to fight on.

Fortunately for Churchill, while Dunkirk had been a defeat, hundreds of thousands of troops had, at least, been successfully evacuated back to Britain. By 10 June Italy, the nation that Halifax felt might help Britain come to terms with Hitler, had declared war on the Allies. In January 1941 Churchill dispatched Halifax to Washington to see out the war as ambassador.

It's certain that had Halifax become prime minister in May 1940, he would have sued for peace. Whatever the eventual terms, Hitler would have been dominant in Europe and Britain crippled as a world power. Yet, had Halifax wanted to, he certainly could have led the country. According to Churchill's biographer, Roy Jenkins, 'We owe much to the fact that Halifax, who on 9 May could have become prime minister, wisely declined to do so.'

We'll never know if Rab Butler could have persuaded him to change his mind, but, certainly, in getting Churchill instead of Halifax, Britain got a wartime leader determined to win. As one of the boys in Alan Bennett's play *The History Boys* says, 'If Halifax had had better teeth, we might have lost the war.'

3

HOW ST PAUL'S SURVIVED THE BLITZ

'The church that means most to London is gone. St Paul's Cathedral is burning to the ground as I talk to you now.' It was with these words that American reporter Ed Murrow announced the destruction of St Paul's in a radio broadcast on the evening of Sunday 29 December 1940. Fortunately he was premature in giving Christopher Wren's great masterpiece the last rites. Though the cathedral was indeed alight, it would survive the onslaught of the Luftwaffe's bombers. Some called it a miracle, but saving St Paul's was a close-run thing and it took more than divine intervention to ensure its survival. The church had famously risen from the ashes of the old St Paul's burned down in the Great Fire of London in 1666. But on a chill Sunday evening during the Second World War came the biggest threat to Wren's iconic structure, in what was dubbed 'the second great fire of London'.

As early as September 1940, with the Battle of Britain still raging in the skies above, St Paul's had been in danger of total destruction. On the 12 September an 8ft-long, 1-tonne bomb landed in the road a few feet in front of the cathedral and became buried some 27ft down. A disposal team headed by Lieutenant Robert Davies of the Royal Engineers was dispatched to try and diffuse it. The sappers dug furiously for three days, while more bombs rained down around them, and even had to be temporarily confined to hospital when they hit a gas main. Eventually a cable was attached to the time-fused device – which could explode at any moment – and Davies and his team gingerly winched the monster out and lowered it onto a lorry. Then they drove the truck, with its deadly cargo, through the streets of London to the Hackney Marshes on the outskirts of the capital and, in a controlled explosion, blew it sky high. The bomb left a crater 100ft wide. Had it detonated outside St Paul's, the cathedral wouldn't have stood a chance. Davies and fellow sapper George Cameron Wyllie won the George Cross for their efforts. Then, a month later, a 500lb bomb hit the cathedral itself, leaving a 20ft by 10ft hole above the choir and destroying the high altar, though not endangering the edifice as a whole.

By Christmas 1940, London had already been pulverised by Hitler's bombing campaign – suffering more than 100 air raids. The Battle of

Britain might have been won several months earlier, fending off the threat of invasion, but the German bombers were still carrying out huge night-time raids on the metropolis. After a pause over Christmas, bombing resumed and on the night of 29 December came one of the most sustained attacks London would endure during six years of war.

In just over three hours, 127 tonnes of high explosive fell, along with 22,000 incendiaries designed to start firestorms. Before long the city around the cathedral was ablaze, the streets thick with smoke. Firemen struggled in vain to quell the fires with buildings collapsing all around them. With the Thames at a low ebb many of the fire crews ran out of water. Wren's chapter house to the north of St Paul's was burned out, and eight of the great architect's churches fell victim to the flames. By this stage of the war Coventry had already lost its cathedral in a bombing raid. And, knowing what a blow to morale it would be if the country's most famous cathedral was now lost too, Winston Churchill himself telephoned an urgent message to London's fire brigades: 'St Paul's must be saved at all costs.'

The dome of St Paul's Cathedral, hit by an incendiary bomb in December 1940.
(© James Moore)

Yet the cathedral, which had been standing sentinel over the capital for 230 years since its completion in 1709, now looked like it would succumb. Both inside and on its roof, brave members of the St Paul's Watch, a group of some 300 volunteers who vowed to save the cathedral from aerial assault, were working furiously. Some forty of these heroes, many of whom were members of the Royal Institute of British Architects, stood guard each night. They knew the building inside out and just where to be to tackle the flurry of incendiary bombs, establishing tanks, baths and buckets full of water at strategic points. At the higher levels of the cathedral they were armed only with stirrup pumps and sandbags, smothering the incendiaries as they landed.

An incendiary that hit the cathedral library was quickly dealt with. Then at 6.39 p.m., with more waves of bombers passing overhead, Cannon Street Fire Station reported that the 365ft high dome was ablaze. An incendiary bomb was lodged in the lead of the dome and burning furiously, giving rise to Murrow's report as he surveyed the scene from the top of the Press Association building in nearby Fleet Street. The bomb was melting the lead, sending drops hundreds of feet to the nave floor below. The fire, though small, threatened to engulf the wooden rafters supporting the dome. Members of the Watch, holding their tiny pumps, bravely endeavoured to climb along the beams towards the bomb to try and put out the flames. Then, suddenly, almost magically, the incendiary fell from the lead outwards on to the stone viewing gallery which ran around the dome. Watch members ran to it and extinguished the still burning bomb before it could do any more damage.

That same night, on the top of the *Daily Mail* building, photographer Herbert Mason took what became a famous photograph of St Paul's showing it wreathed in smoke and surrounded by gutted buildings, yet still standing tall. He recalled, 'Suddenly, the shining cross, dome and towers stood out like a symbol in the inferno. The scene was unbelievable. In that moment or two, I released my shutter.'

By early morning the raid was over. Fires still burned, but the immediate threat to the cathedral had passed. That night twenty-eight incendiaries had fallen on or around the cathedral. Thanks to the efforts of the firefighters – and a good measure of luck – it had come off relatively unscathed. As dawn broke, the smouldering ruins around St Paul's demonstrated just how lucky the church had been. An area larger than that levelled in the Great Fire of London had been lost. Nineteen other churches had been wrecked; London's Guildhall was gutted and hundreds of other buildings, including the whole of Paternoster Row, the

The National Firefighters Memorial near St Paul's, London, showing fire fighters at work during the Blitz. (© James Moore)

centre of Britain's publishing industry, had gone up in flames. Sixteen firemen lost their lives and more than 160 civilians perished.

It wasn't the last close shave for St Paul's. The bombing of London went on in earnest into 1941, and on the night of 16 and 17 April a bomb came through the cathedral's north transept blowing glass out of the windows and smashing through the floor, destroying the vaulted roof of the crypt, but not threatening the main structure. After that spring the bombing of London continued, but was never quite as intense.

Following the war much restoration was needed to St Paul's. Sadly no one could quite salvage the reputation of Lieutenant Robert Davies, who had undoubtedly helped save the cathedral but had a weakness for easy money. Though he had been decorated for his action, later in the war Davies would spend time in prison for fraud and dishonesty.

In total during the London Blitz, more than 28,000 people were killed. And on VE Day, 35,000 people took part in a series of thanksgiving services held at St Paul's to mark the end of the war. The cathedral's survival had certainly given heart to the British as they endured the pounding from the bombers, and services there had been kept up throughout the conflict. The cathedral's dean, Walter Matthews, spoke of a woman who, at a local Underground station, had acknowledged that she was not herself religious, but summed up the feeling of millions about the church: 'It's meant something that it was there and people praying in it. It's kept us going.'

Ernie Pyle, another American journalist, was amazed that St Paul's had withstood the terrible night of 29 December reporting:

> St Paul's was surrounded by fire, but it came through. It stood there
> in its enormous proportions – growing slowly clearer and clearer,
> the way objects take shape at dawn. It was like a picture of some
> miraculous figure that appears before the peace-hungry soldiers on
> a battlefield.

4

THE SHIP THAT NEARLY SANK NEW YORK

On 11 September 2001, New York suffered its worst tragedy when nearly 3,000 people were killed in the terrorist attacks on the World Trade Center. It is an event that no one in the city, or around the world, will ever forget.

Few, however, know that a very different kind of disaster could have destroyed a portion of the city and claimed thousands of lives during the dark days of the Second World War. The forgotten drama centres around a humble ship called the SS *El Estero*. On 24 April 1943, the Panamanian-registered freighter was tied up at Caven Point Pier in Bayonne, New Jersey. On the other side of the Hudson River, just a few miles away, the skyscrapers of Manhattan and the Statue of Liberty could clearly be seen. The ship was being loaded with the last of some

Ordnance being loaded into a ship like the SS *El Estero*, overseen by the US Coast Guard. (Courtesy of William Thiesen/US Coast Guard)

1,400 tonnes of explosives, including the feared 4,000lb 'blockbusters' – fearsome conventional weapons each with the power to level a whole city block. The ordnance was bound for the Allied forces fighting in Europe. And the dilapidated, 325ft *El Estero* was due to join a convoy crossing the Atlantic. It was tied to other freighters, full of similar deadly cargos. Railroad cars along the dockside were packed with more bombs. In all, it

Last resting place of the SS *El Estero*. Had the ship exploded it could have devastated parts of New York. (Courtesy of William Thiesen/US Coast Guard)

is estimated that 5,000 tonnes of bombs, ammunition and depth charges were in the immediate vicinity. And it wasn't just the ammunition and bombs at risk; any explosion could also take out huge fuel tanks nearby.

That evening, at 5.20 p.m., a US Coast Guard loading party on the docks, where the *El Estero* was berthed, were finishing up their work. The next day was Easter Sunday and they were no doubt looking forward to a day off. Suddenly a bell sounded in the nearby barracks. The ship had caught fire. A boiler flashback had ignited oil floating in the ship's bilge and the blaze had quickly spread. Within the next hour, and with growing horror, the port authorities realised that the ship now posed a threat to New York and the surrounding area as big as any enemy attack.

There was already a chilling precedent from history. In 1917, during the First World War, a French ship called the SS *Mont-Blanc* had blown up after a collision in the port of Halifax, in Nova Scotia, Canada. The blast had been so powerful that it devastated thousands of homes and buildings, caused a mini tsunami and left 2,000 dead, with some 9,000 more injured. By 1943 it was still the biggest man-made explosion the world had ever known.

If the *El Estero* went up, the cataclysm in Halifax might look trifling by comparison. The blast would certainly be much bigger – perhaps enough to flatten everything within a 5-mile radius, the same as a small nuclear weapon. Lower Manhattan, Brooklyn, New Jersey, Bayonne and Staten Island were all threatened. Thousands would be killed. A million people would be affected; even the city's iconic skyscrapers were likely to be damaged.

Within half an hour of the fire being reported by the ship's crew, five fire trucks from Jersey City Fire Department and sixty volunteers from the Coast Guard were battling the blaze. The Coast Guard men and firefighters used hoses and axes while two fireboats, the *Fire Fighter* and *John J. Harvey*, arrived pouring thousands of gallons of water and foam onto the ship to try and snuff out the flames. However, their efforts appeared to be in vain; by 7 p.m. the fire was out of control.

On land, hospitals and police precincts were being warned that a massive explosion was imminent. Radio stations told residents to stay away from their windows and keep them ajar. Industrial plants were cleared.

Back at the *El Estero*, Arthur Pfister, a retired fire chief, managed to oversee the removal of some of the red hot ammunition boxes onto the pier via a greased plank, but the Coast Guard realised the only way to save the city would be to tow the ship to a safe distance and scuttle it. A site in Upper New York Bay was quickly identified and two tugboats tied to the craft, hauling the *El Estero* away from the dockside and the main shipping channel. Because the ship's seacocks were inaccessible, she would have to be sunk by pumping water into her cargo holds. Sailing alongside the vessel the firefighting boats pumped thousands of gallons of water onto the *El Estero* in a desperate battle against the clock.

In charge of the operation, Lieutenant Commander John Stanley asked for twenty Coast Guard volunteers to remain aboard and to attempt to assuage the fires. Those that stayed knew their odds of survival weren't good. They speedily exchanged their personal effects with those leaving. Seaman Seymour Wittek, then aged 22, was one of those who had to be ordered off, as he was due to be married in a matter of weeks. In an interview for the *New York Times*, he recalled a fellow serviceman handing him his wallet saying, 'If it blows, at least they'll know I was here.'

Inside, the fire was still raging and anti-aircraft ammunition above deck was also at risk. By now the heat on deck was singeing the shoes of those firefighters still aboard. But, between them, the fireboats and the Coast Guard volunteers appeared to be doing enough to stop the bombs detonating. Eventually the ship reached the target area near Robbins Reef Lighthouse. And, as water washed over the deck, the remaining hands were ordered off.

At 9 p.m. the *El Estero* slowly sank in 35ft of water, belching smoke, but not exploding, as the seawater poured in and cooled the ship down.

The few remaining fires were put out and by 10 p.m. the all-clear was given. Incredibly not one person had lost their life.

Civilian defence authorities later said it had been the biggest threat the city had faced during the war. Had the *El Estero* exploded, New York's harbour would have been devastated and the US war effort would have been severely dented. For directing the battle against the flames on board, Commander Stanley was awarded the nation's Legion of Merit. Amazingly, it had been his first day in the job. Pfister was also honoured and the city of Bayonne laid on a parade for the Coast Guard heroes.

On Easter Sunday New York's mayor, Fiorello La Guardia, went on local radio revealing to the region's residents how close they'd been to a major disaster. He said, 'We felt that at any minute we might be gone and thank God we got through it safely.' Certainly, few would refer to the Coast Guard men by their nickname, 'bathtub sailors', ever again.

A few months after it had been sunk, the *El Estero* was raised and floated out further to sea to be used as target practice by the military. But, some fifty-eight years later, on that fateful day in 2001, there was an apt postscript: the two fireboats that had been key to averting the wartime disaster, the veteran *Fire Fighter* and the *John J. Harvey*, by then officially decommissioned, helped pump water and fight fires at Ground Zero following the destruction of the Twin Towers.

5

THE FEMALE SCHINDLER

At 3 a.m. on 20 October 1943, there was a loud and insistent knock on the door of Irena Sendler's first floor flat in Warsaw. There was no time to lose. Sendler, an operative in the Polish resistance, knew that she was about to be captured by the Gestapo. Of more concern than her own safety, was the fear that a vital roll of paper she carried with her at all times would fall into the enemy's hands.

For a moment she thought about throwing the papers out of the window into the yard below, as she had planned to do if this day ever came. But the building was now surrounded by Germans and they might see what she had done. Instead, Sendler hurriedly gave the roll to a female colleague – with whom she shared the flat – to hide, and went to answer the door. Over the next two hours, eleven Germans ransacked the apartment, even pulling apart the beds and pillows, but found nothing incriminating. Sendler's co-conspirator, Janina, had put on a dressing gown and stuffed the precious roll of paper into her underwear. Fortunately, she was left unsearched. Sendler was bundled away for interrogation but, even as the Germans marched her off, she felt a sense of relief that her vital documents remained undiscovered.

The pieces of paper Sendler had been trying to hide were lists containing the names of 2,500 children who had been secretly smuggled out of the city's Jewish ghetto. They were the product of her remarkable work in organising the escape of youngsters who might otherwise have shared the fate of their other family members, most of whom would be gassed at notorious concentration camps like Treblinka. Irena Sendler hoped that her secret list, which noted the original names of the children beside the new non-Jewish names they were to adopt, as well as their new addresses, might one day enable the children to be successfully reunited with any parents who survived the war.

A similar story of Jews narrowly escaping the Holocaust, that of the industrialist Oskar Schindler, who helped rescue over 1,000 people by employing them in his factories, is well known thanks to Steven Spielberg's movie *Schindler's List*. Irena Sendler's efforts remain much less well known, yet her story is arguably even more remarkable.

A Polish Catholic and doctor's daughter, Sendler was 29 years old when war broke out and was working as a social worker in Warsaw's welfare department. She had always had a strong affinity with Poland's large Jewish population and wanted to help when she saw what was happening to them after the Nazis occupied her homeland. After the invasion and defeat of Poland in 1939 half a million Polish Jews had been imprisoned in the city's ghetto, an area in the city which covered little more than 1 square mile. Ultimately, Sendler would join an underground movement called Zegota, code-name for the Polish Council to Aid Jews. The organisation had been formed in 1942 after the deportation of 280,000 of Warsaw's Jews to the Treblinka death camp, and Sendler became the head of its children's section.

Helping the Jewish community was an extremely dangerous business, punishable by death, and thousands of non-Jewish Polish citizens were executed for trying. Yet Sendler was determined to do what she could, once it became clear that the ultimate fate of the Jews in the ghetto was extermination in the death camps. Working under her code-name, 'Jolanta', she and a group of colleagues obtained special passes to gain access to the ghetto, aiming to get as many youngsters out and into hiding as they could. Dressed as a nurse, and wearing the Star of David, she was ostensibly there to deal with outbreaks of typhus, with the Germans worried that the disease could spread outside the ghetto's perimeter. However, Sendler's real aim was to try and persuade Jewish families to part with their children, in order that they at least might be given new non-Jewish identities and saved. While whole families were difficult to get out, children could be spirited away more easily and, once out, fewer questions would be asked about their identity. When Sendler spelled out her plan to the parents many simply refused to part with their children, while others sought a guarantee that they'd see them again – a guarantee she couldn't give. Sendler later recalled how she would sometimes leave a family to consider their options only to return the next day to find that they had disappeared, having been taken to the camps.

Many families did, however, realise the danger they were in and agreed to deliver their children into Sendler's care. Her team of twenty-five people then worked around the clock to get them away. There were drivers for vehicles and forgers working to produce false documents. Priests were recruited to issue false baptism certificates. Others assisted in providing homes for the children once they were out.

The means of getting hundreds of children of all ages out of the ghetto, which was walled off from 1940, varied enormously. Some very small children were hidden in blankets or carried out in potato sacks. Others were even given a sedative or put in coffins, with Sendler pretending they had succumbed to disease – it helped that a cemetery adjoined the ghetto. A mechanic who worked with Sendler even smuggled babies out in his toolbox; an ambulance driver used by the team carried a dog which was trained to bark when German guards came near, drowning out any noise from the children concealed underneath the vehicle's floor.

Once out, the children were given new identities and found places in orphanages and convents or with non-Jewish families. All correspondence had to be in code. For instance, to alert the nuns at one convent that she had children ready to be picked up, Sendler would write a note saying, 'I have clothing for the convent.'

When that fateful knock on the door came for Sendler in late 1943 she was taken to the notorious Pawiak prison. Here, over the course of three months, she was tortured by her captors. Her legs and feet were broken and she was left permanently scarred. When she still refused to inform on other Zegota members she was sentenced to death by firing squad. Sendler only managed to escape after the organisation bribed one of her guards who, on the day her sentence was due to be carried out, marked her down as already having been executed.

Once out of prison, Sendler was forced to adopt a new identity, though she continued working for Zegota. From then on, for safety, her list of the children who had been rescued was buried in a jar under an apple tree in a friend's garden. Sendler survived the war and, after hostilities had ended, went to the tree where the list had been buried. She passed on the information to those trying to reunite as many Jewish children as possible with their parents. Sadly, most of them were already dead, having perished in the camps.

After liberation, Irena carried on in social work but, with a new Communist government in place, received few plaudits for her wartime role. It was only in 1983 that she was allowed to travel to Israel, where a tree had been planted in her honour. Finally, in 2003, she received Poland's Order of the White Eagle, the nation's highest honour, for her heroics. Before her death in 2008, Sendler said, 'Every Jewish child who survived due to my efforts has justified my existence on this Earth.'

One of those she helped escape was Elzbieta Ficowska who, at 6 months old, was placed in a carpenter's box and put in a lorry under a pile of bricks to be driven to safety outside the ghetto, before being adopted by a Roman Catholic midwife. Elzbieta later said, 'It took a true miracle to save a Jewish child ... Mrs Sendler saved not only us, but also our children and grandchildren and the generations to come.'

6

CAUGHT IN THE BLAST OF TWO ATOMIC BOMBS

On a clear, sunny morning at 8.15 a.m. on 6 August 1945, Tsutomu Yamaguchi was making his way through a flat landscape along a track verged with potato fields when he heard the faint noise of an aircraft in the sky above. Yamaguchi, a naval draftsman working for Mitsubishi Heavy Industries, had just alighted from a tram and was walking towards the shipyard in the Japanese city of Hiroshima where he had been working as part of a three-month-long posting. The job was coming to an end and Yamaguchi was looking forward to getting back to his wife, Hisako, and baby son, Katsutoshi, at their home some 260 miles away. Earlier that morning, as Yamaguchi was preparing to leave the city with two co-workers, Akira Iwanaga and Kuniyoshi Sato, the 29-year-old realised that he had forgotten a vital travel document and returned to his digs to get it. Leaving his workmates to go on, Yamaguchi retrieved the official stamp and was hurrying to the shipyard for a final farewell with his colleagues when, at the sound of the plane, he looked up and saw a tiny object fall from it.

The plane Yamaguchi had seen was an American B-29 bomber called the *Enola Gay*. Its crew was tasked with dropping the first nuclear bomb ever to be used in anger. At exactly 8.15 a.m., from a height of 31,000ft above Hiroshima, the aircraft's bomb bay door was opened and a 13-kiloton uranium atomic weapon, nicknamed 'Little Boy', slid out. Forty-three seconds later, at just under 2,000ft above the city, the bomb detonated.

Down below, Yamaguchi was suddenly blinded by what he later described as a 'great white flash in the sky' accompanied, moments later,

Mushroom cloud over Nagasaki after the second atomic bomb, dubbed 'Fat Man', was dropped over the city on 9 August 1945. (Public domain)

by a deafening roar. Trying to dive down, as he had been trained to do in air raids, he was instead sucked up several feet into the air, then violently flung back down to the ground. A few moments later he came to, lying in the mud of one of the potato fields. At first, as Yamaguchi opened his eyes, he could see little. Slowly, as the dust began to clear, he could make out the singed leaves of the potato plants around him. Then, with a mixture of horror and bewilderment he saw a huge mushroom cloud rising into the now dark and menacing sky. Later he would describe what he saw as 'a tornado that did not move' and told of strange ethereal lights that seemed to dance around it. Then the pain hit him, a searing heat on the left side of his face and down his arms.

The first thing Yamaguchi did was to make sure his legs were still intact; then made his way to an air-raid shelter 200yds away. There, two students told him that he had been badly burned. His left eardrum had also been ruptured and his hair completely burned off. He would later tell *The Sunday Times*, 'My left ear swelled and blood oozed out ... the skin on my face was like it had been burned with a blowtorch. The skin not covered by my clothes was charred.'

Two hours later Yamaguchi decided there was no point in lingering and stepped outside once more, making for the shipyard. Once there he found that his two colleagues, Iwanaga and Sato, had also survived; the office at the shipyard, where they had been when the blast hit, had been partially protected by a low hill.

Badly shaken and still unsure exactly what had happened, the trio decided to try and return to their lodgings, get their possessions and leave the city as quickly as possible. Commandeering a motor launch, they headed into Hiroshima by river. Yamaguchi and his colleagues encountered a scene of total devastation. Those that were not dead were limping or walking in a state of utter bewilderment, many stripped of their clothes, others with skin hanging off them 'like gloves'. That night the three co-workers huddled together in an air-raid shelter listening to the moaning of the dying all around them. At dawn they made their way to the train station where, incredibly, the railway was still operating. Yamaguchi and his two friends boarded the first train out and headed west.

Yamaguchi had been 2 miles from the epicentre of the Hiroshima blast. Those nearer were not so fortunate. Some 78,000 had been killed by the immediate effects of the explosion. Within months the death toll would hit 140,000 thanks to the effects of radiation. Some 69 per cent of the city's buildings were flattened. Yet Japan did not immediately surrender as the US Government had expected.

The aftermath of the bombing at Nagasaki. (Public domain)

For the young engineer, heading back to the bosom of his family, that might have been the end of the story. Except for the fact that Yamaguchi's home city went by the name of Nagasaki. After arriving back in the city Yamaguchi went to the hospital for treatment. Japan had been losing the war for some time and there were few resources or doctors. Eventually an eye surgeon operated on his burns, covered him in ointment and sent him away covered in dressings.

Incredibly, despite his injuries and still swathed in bandages, Yamaguchi reported for work as usual on 9 August. At precisely 11.02 a.m. he was busy telling his boss what had happened in Hiroshima. His superior was incredulous that a single bomb could flatten a whole city, feeling that Yamaguchi's mind must have been affected and telling him that he ought to go home and rest. At that very moment came another blinding flash. The second atomic weapon to be deployed over Japan had been detonated. As the United States stepped up its ploy to force Japan to capitulate, a bigger, 25-kiloton plutonium bomb, this time dubbed 'Fat Man', was exploded in the sky above Nagasaki, one of the country's most important industrial centres. The resulting blast shattered Yamaguchi's office, hurling him to the ground all over again.

Once again Yamaguchi had been 2 miles from the epicentre. His bandages were torn off, but he was otherwise unhurt, thanks partly to the protection of a nearby steel stairwell. Yamaguchi got out through a window and plied his way through the ruined streets in search of his family. Ultimately, 70,000 people died in the Nagasaki attack although, thankfully, Yamaguchi's wife and son were safe. Their home, however, was half ruined and the beleaguered family took refuge in a makeshift shelter behind it. The hospital, where Yamaguchi had been treated, was now itself in ruins, so he simply lay in the dug-out, suffering with a fever while, as he later learned, chickens picked maggots from his skin. Then, on 15 August, he heard the sound of nearby residents crying. Japan had finally surrendered.

Yamaguchi eventually recovered. His hair grew back, but he lost the hearing in his left ear, suffered from weakness in his legs and had to undergo countless operations on his wounds. His daughter Naoko, born after the bombs, remembers her father in bandages until she was 12 years old.

Incredibly, Yamaguchi's former colleagues, Sato and Iwanaga, had also survived again. Sato, working in Nagasaki's shipyard, had immediately jumped off the quayside into the water when he saw the second flash, knowing what it meant, while Iwanaga, on a suburban train at the time, also escaped unhurt.

After Japan's surrender Yamaguchi worked as a translator for the American army of occupation, and then as a teacher, before finally returning to work for Mitsubishi. He battled ill health for the rest of his life, but lived until the age of 93, finally dying of stomach cancer in 2010 in a rebuilt Nagasaki. The blasts left a legacy upon his family too: his wife suffered with liver cancer and Yamaguchi's son died of cancer, aged 59, in 2005.

Yamaguchi was one of 250,000 *hibakusha*, the survivors of the atomic explosions who were entitled to government support and medical benefits. And, in 2009, the Japanese Government finally officially acknowledged that he was a survivor of both explosions, the only person to be so recognised. In fact, there were around 160 people present at both explosions, though none had been as close to the epicentre of both atomic blasts. Before his death, Yamaguchi became a vociferant opponent of nuclear weapons. In 2006 he addressed the General Assembly of the UN, telling them, 'Having been granted this miracle it is my responsibility to pass on the truth to the people of the world.'

7

OPERATION UNTHINKABLE – A THIRD WORLD WAR IN 1945?

As the Allies advanced into Germany in the final months of the Second World War the race was on for influence in a post-conflict Europe without Hitler. And, by VE Day on 8 May 1945, British Prime Minister Winston Churchill felt that Stalin was winning the contest. While the rest of Britain took a moment to revel in a hard-won victory over the Nazis, Churchill seems barely to have taken a breath before contemplating a new war, one with a now rampant Soviet Union. Unknown to the millions of Britons looking forward to peace, Winston's plan, code-named Operation Unthinkable, might see the Second World War morph almost seamlessly into the Third World War.

In February 1945 Franklin D. Roosevelt, Joseph Stalin and Churchill had met at the Yalta Conference to discuss the reorganisation of post-war Europe. Among other things, they had decided to divide Germany into four occupation zones run by Britain, the USA, Soviet Union and France, while Stalin had agreed to hold free elections in the Eastern European countries his forces now occupied. As the war with Germany entered its final stretch, the Red Army reached the German capital, Berlin, first, much to Churchill's chagrin. He wanted the British and Americans to press on to the city, but the Soviet Union was in a better position to take Berlin and the other Allied forces eventually agreed to stop at the River Elbe.

That spring Churchill felt that Stalin was preparing to break the promises made at Yalta. The PM worried that the Russians were installing puppet Communist governments, ones that would be loyal to Moscow in Eastern Europe. The idea that these would become mere satellite states of the USSR was anathema to Churchill, making a mockery of the fact that the whole war had been sparked by the British commitment to defend Poland. Roosevelt, meanwhile, seemed happy to give ground to the Russians if it meant their backing in the Pacific theatre where Japan remained undefeated.

Later, in 1946, Churchill would make his famous speech about an 'iron curtain' descending across Europe. But he was already using the same language on 12 May 1945, when he cabled the new US President, Harry S. Truman, complaining about the behaviour of the Soviets:

'An iron curtain is drawn down upon their front. We do not know what is going on behind. There seems little doubt that the whole of the regions east of Lübeck-Trieste-Corfu will soon be completely in their hands.'

Six days later Churchill summoned the Soviet ambassador, Feodor Gousev, to a meeting where he lambasted the official for his country's behaviour in Eastern Europe, even warning him that Britain was prepared to postpone the demobilisation of the RAF. Churchill also told his foreign secretary, Anthony Eden, 'A tide of Russian domination is sweeping forward ... it is to an early and speedy showdown and settlement with Russia that we must now turn our hopes.' After a War Cabinet meeting on 13 May, the Chief of the Imperial General Staff, Field Marshal Alan Brooke, noted, 'Winston gives me the feeling of already longing for another war!'

Churchill wasn't just sounding off – he wanted something done. Anglo-American armies were still on the Continent in force. Was there a way, he wondered, of stopping Stalin and showing him who was boss before the Soviet grasp over Eastern Europe was complete? If the Russians did not back down, could the former German army, he mused, even be recruited by Britain and re-armed to help take on Stalin?

On 14 May 1945 Churchill told Field Marshal Bernard Montgomery, commander of British troops in Germany, to stockpile captured German weapons for possible future use. And Churchill now ordered his military chiefs to draw up a plan for Operation Unthinkable, a study, subsequently kept secret for decades, on how Britain and America might wage war on the Russians. He asked the planners to consider whether there were sufficient means, 'to impose upon Russia the will of the United States and the British Empire. Even though "the will" of these two countries may be defined as no more than a square deal for Poland, that does not necessarily limit the military commitment.' Churchill wanted to know the options, based on the assumption that public opinion would be in favour of an attack and that the British and Americans would be able to 'count on the use of German manpower and what remains of German industrial capacity'. There was even a notional start date for hostilities: 1 July 1945.

On 22 May the planners duly produced their dossier: 'Russia: Threat to Western Civilisation.' It imagined a surprise attack by forty-seven Anglo-American divisions starting at Dresden in the middle of the Soviet front line. Fourteen of these would need to be tank divisions and another forty divisions would need to be kept in reserve – a total of 2.5 million men. It might be possible to recruit 100,000 German troops but they would be war-weary and unlikely to make much difference in the outcome of any conflict. The report noted that the Allied navies and bomber squadrons were strong, but that the Red Army would outnumber the Anglo-American force by four to one and had twice as many tanks. An offensive against the USSR, it concluded, would have to be a 'total war', which would be long and costly.

Reviewing Unthinkable on 24 May Brooke was certain that victory would be quite impossible, writing, 'There is no doubt that from now onwards Russia is all powerful in Europe.' This sentiment was expressed further in a note included with the report when it went to Churchill on 8 June which stated that the odds of winning a war, if the Americans did not take part, would be 'fanciful'.

Faced with such a verdict Churchill realised that an attack on the USSR would be hopeless. But he wasn't quite done. He asked for another assessment, this time for how Britain, in the absence of American support, might tackle a Soviet invasion of Western Europe pushing to the English Channel as Hitler had done. The follow-up study reckoned that a rocket attack in the style of the German V-1 and V-2 offensive would be Stalin's most likely option. The position would be pretty hopeless. Britain would need 230 squadrons of fighters and 300 squadrons of bombers to tackle the threat. In ordering the second study Churchill admitted that the war scenarios were 'highly improbable', before changing his words to 'purely hypothetical'.

The Unthinkable file was closed. In one sense it had been useful, focussing minds about the strategic realities of the new global balance of power and Britain's relative weakness in it. But Churchill was playing a dangerous game. It's likely that the Russians had got wind of what he was up to thanks to their spy network in London. After his May meeting, Gousev had reported back to Moscow, 'We are dealing with an unprincipled adventurer: he feels more at home in wartime than in peacetime.' Stalin had always been suspicious of Churchill, once saying to his military commander, Marshal Georgy Zhukov, 'That man is capable of anything.' In June 1945 Moscow ordered units in the West to dig in defensively.

When the big powers met at the Potsdam Conference in July 1945 Churchill now thought that the American atomic bomb would solve his Russian problem. Stalin didn't yet have the bomb. Churchill told Brooke, 'We can tell them that if they insist on doing this or that, well we can just blot out Moscow, then Stalingrad, then Kiev and so on.' The British PM urged the Americans to keep up a significant military presence in Europe. In fact, the Americans wanted little to do with Churchill's plans. They weren't going to go head to head with the Russians to save democracy in Poland. General Eisenhower summed up their policy when he said, 'We're going to get along with the Russians.' At the end of Potsdam it was clear that Poland and the rest of Eastern Europe would remain under Soviet domination. By that time Churchill had been resoundingly beaten in the British general election and was out of power, having left the Potsdam Conference halfway through.

Over the next few months, as the disagreements between the United States and the USSR increased, it didn't take long for the Americans to think again. Operation Unthinkable now seemed less ridiculous, and in the summer of 1946 new joint discussions between the US and Britain began planning scenarios for how a war in Europe might play out. In opposition Churchill would continue to warn that there was going to be a 'war with Russia'. But it was not the kind of war he expected; the Cold War had begun in earnest.

8

HOW A BEAR NEARLY STARTED ARMAGEDDON

Lieutenant Dan Barry steeled himself in the cockpit of his state-of-the-art F-106A interceptor plane and switched on the engine. The aircraft, readied on the runway, was armed to the teeth with weapons that included infrared heat-seeking missiles, two radar-guided missiles and a rocket tipped with a nuclear warhead. Just minutes earlier, at his snowbound base at Volk Field, Wisconsin, Barry, already wearing his flight suit, had been woken by the sound of an ear-piercing klaxon. Along with the rest of his squadron he had quickly pulled on his flight boots and plunged into the icy cold night towards his plane, a thirty-second dash away. He had been told that in this situation there would be no drill. This was the real thing.

It was just after midnight on 26 October 1962 and the Cuban Missile Crisis was at its height. Earlier in the month the United States Government announced that it had gathered photographic evidence of Soviet missile silos in Fidel Castro's Cuba, lying 100 miles from the Florida coast. With the Soviet leader Nikita Khrushchev refusing to back down, America had launched a naval blockade of Cuba to stop Soviet ships from getting to the island. On the day before the alarm at Volk rang out President Kennedy had written to the Soviet leader stating that he considered that the USSR bore responsibility for the situation that had brought the two superpowers to the brink of conflict. American forces were at DEFCON 2, the highest state of alert since the start of the Cold War. The Soviet Union seemed equally determined. The world held its breath.

By October 1962 B-52 bombers and air interceptors like Barry's had been dispersed across the USA to bases such as Volk, with all of them maintaining a fifteen-minute alert status. As he taxied down the runway, the 27-year-old knew that tensions between his country and the Soviets were at breaking point. As second in line to take off he assumed that nuclear war had begun and expected to see incoming Soviet bombers flying in the skies over Canada towards US cities. It was his job to shoot them down.

Earlier that night, in the neighbouring state of Minnesota, an air force guard had been patrolling the perimeter at Duluth Sector Direction Center when he saw a movement in the dark. It appeared to be a figure climbing the fence. He had been trained for just such an eventuality. During the Cold War the US authorities believed that special Soviet sabotage forces known as *Spetsnaz* units would be activated as a precursor to an all-out attack. Their aim would be to cause disruption at airfields and thereby thwart the military's capability of responding to a first strike. These units had been included in war-gaming scenarios and exercises. And, as part of the defence against them, an alarm system had been set up to warn other bases about the impending threat if saboteurs were intercepted at any installation.

On this particular night the guard fired off his gun, activating the alarm system and automatically dispatching anti-saboteur units at other bases across the region, where they found nothing untoward. But at Volk Field something went wrong. The base had only recently become a station for the F-106A planes and their pilots. It had no control tower and only rudimentary alarm systems, and the pilots were bunking down in the hospital dispensary. Instead of the saboteur alarm going off, a klaxon sounded – the one which directed the pilots to scramble to their aircrafts. In this situation it was assumed a nuclear attack on the US had already begun and the plan was to get as many aircraft in the air as quickly as possible.

Waiting in his plane, Barry suddenly saw a truck speeding towards the aircraft from the command post, with its lights flashing and an officer frantically signalling at the pilots to stop. Checks had been made – it was all a false alarm. No saboteurs had been discovered. It had only taken four minutes for the mistake to register, but just a minute more and the aircraft would have been launched.

Over the coming weeks theories abounded as to what the mysterious 'intruder' could have been. Some said it was a drunken member of the military trying to smuggle himself back into the base. Finally, on inspection of the fence at Duluth, the conclusion was made that the shadowy figure had been a rogue bear – and not a Russian one.

According to defence experts such an incident, though almost comical, could have posed a real threat. Soviet forces were monitoring the movements of US forces and with the political situation on a knife-edge any action that looked provocative could spark an immediate and catastrophic response. Also, in the confusion, the nuclear-equipped aircraft might shoot down a friendly bomber or crash, causing a nuclear incident that might also unleash a chain of events in which the US could imagine it was under attack. The incident at Volk led to changes in the alarm system but it was just one of a host of false alarms and technological failures that, in the climate of the Cuban Missile Crisis, could have sparked an accidental confrontation. The bear incident showed that in a context of fear and high stakes, and with a dependence on untested technology, no system was fail-safe. Scott Sagan in *The Limits of Safety* concluded, 'The bizarre incidents that actually did occur during the crisis should serve as a reminder however, that unlikely events, even highly improbable events, do happen.'

There were a string of other near misses that October as the thirteen-day crisis gripped the world in terror. Just twenty-four hours after the Volk incident, on 27 October, a Soviet Foxtrot-class sub, *B-59*, was hemmed in near Cuba by a group of US warships led by the aircraft carrier USS *Randolph*. The Soviet submarine was forced to dive and found itself trapped. The Americans, having tipped off the Kremlin, began to rain down practice depth charges to try and force the submarine to the surface. They might not have been so antagonistic had they known that it was armed with a single nuclear-tipped torpedo. More worryingly, their message had not been passed on by the Russians to the craft in the deep with its nervy crew. Believing his submarine was under attack and unable to contact headquarters for technical reasons, the captain, Valentin Savitsky, concluded that a war had probably already begun above them. He was all for launching the nuclear torpedo. One crew member recalled how Savitsky had said, 'We're going to blast them now!

We will perish ourselves, but we will sink them all! We will not disgrace our navy!' Fortunately, also on board, was the cool-headed Commander Vasili Arkhipov. Although technically only second in command of the *B-59* he was also commander of the wider Soviet submarine force in the area, making him of equal rank. It would need both men to agree if the torpedo was to be fired. After a heated discussion Arkhipov refused to back the launch and eventually persuaded Savitsky to surface and try contacting Moscow for further orders. When the *B-59* emerged from beneath the waves one of the American ships even had a jazz band playing on deck in order to show they weren't about to attack. The submarine refused assistance from the Americans and slowly headed east and home, escorted to a safe distance by the US ships. As an American security academic Professor Thomas Blanton concluded in 2002, 'The lesson from this is that a guy called Vasili Arkhipov saved the world.'

Again, what could have provided an accidental trigger to war in an atmosphere of paranoia and high tension was averted. In the end, and at the last minute, both Kennedy and Khrushchev stepped back from war. The US agreed not to invade Cuba if the Soviet Union removed its missiles from the island. In return the Americans removed their missiles from Turkey. The crisis was over. But, as the Cold War went on, there would be more frightening near misses.

9

THE MAN WHO CANCELLED DOOMSDAY

Inside the concrete underground bunker it appeared to be just another ordinary, uneventful night for duty commander Stanislav Petrov. The 44-year-old Soviet army software engineer had settled down in front of his computer and the banks of monitoring equipment as he had countless times before, expecting a vigilant but quiet shift. It was just after midnight.

Suddenly the screen in front of him turned red and an ear-piercing alarm shattered the quiet murmur of the room. Then a second, identical alarm went off; then another. Around him were flashing electronic maps and on his screen was a message. It read, in Russian, 'Start!'

On that early morning of 26 September 1983 only a handful of people knew what was happening deep beneath the ground at the nuclear early warning station in the military installation of Serpukhov-15, just south of Moscow. The world was preoccupied with other matters. There was the outfall from the bombing of Gulf Air Flight 771 in the United Arab Emirates which had killed 117 people. In Britain debate raged about the mass escape of Irish Republican inmates from the MAZE prison. And, after a balmy summer recess, there was anticipation in Westminster that Neil Kinnock was on his way to being elected the new leader of the Labour Party. Tony Blair and Gordon Brown were getting to grips with being new MPs following the 1983 election which had seen Margaret Thatcher win by a landslide.

As they went about their business, most of the globe's population were unaware that 26 September 1983 had almost become the most infamous day in history. Armageddon had been avoided by the narrowest of margins. In fact, the presence of mind of just one person, Petrov, had prevented the USSR and the USA unleashing their formidable nuclear arsenals against each other. His heroic actions, which were to remain unknown to the world for another fifteen years, had stopped the Cold War turning hot.

Yet Petrov, a lieutenant colonel in the Soviet Union's Strategic Rocket Forces and deputy head of the combat algorithms department, wasn't even supposed to be at his post on that potentially fateful day. It was his night off, but he had ended up filling in for another man who had rung in sick.

Petrov later described the alarm which jolted him out of his seat as 'loud enough to raise a dead man from his grave'. According to the information on his screen – and the flashing lights on the bunker's huge map of the USA – a Minuteman nuclear missile was inbound to Soviet territory having been launched from Malmstrom Air Force Base in Montana. Five minutes later the system was reporting the launch of another missile, then another. In total, five intercontinental ballistic missiles, each 100 times more powerful than the Hiroshima bomb, were hurtling towards Soviet territory. The screen was now reading 'Missile Attack'.

Petrov could have been forgiven for thinking the attack was real. Cold War tensions were at their highest level since the Cuban Missile Crisis of 1962. In March, US President Ronald Reagan had branded the Soviet Union an 'evil empire'. NATO had been undertaking major military manoeuvres in Europe, which would have been well known to the Soviets. The USSR had also recently rolled out their SS-20s, nuclear missiles on mobile launchers. There was even a potential trigger. Just three weeks before the incident, the USSR had shot down a civilian South

Korean airliner, Korean Air Lines Flight 007, which, they maintained, had invaded their airspace and had been on a spy mission. All 269 people on board had been killed, including a sitting US congressman.

Back in his hot seat Petrov hesitated. Initially, he and his 120 staff reeled, in a state of shock. Yet protocol called for him to act fast. There would only be about twelve minutes before the missiles hit their targets inside the Soviet Union. The concept of Mutual Assured Destruction held that the nuclear deterrent worked because both sides would, in the event of a first strike, unleash their own weapons, therefore annihilating the other. It was Petrov's duty to report up the chain of command to the general staff, who would pass the information of the attack to the Politburo and the hard-line Soviet leader, Yuri Andropov. They would have only minutes to decide what to do and would almost certainly order a full-scale retaliation, launching the USSR's missiles against the USA before they were destroyed in what seemed to be a pre-emptive act on the part of the Americans.

As he held an intercom in one hand and a phone in the other, Petrov knew that the fate of not only his own country, but also the world, was in his hands. He himself had written the procedure that he was supposed to follow, pressing the button to notify Yuri Votintsev, commander of the Soviet Air Defence's Missile Defence Units. Petrov later told a TV news station, 'I was the one with the information and my reaction would determine the course of action. I'll admit it, I was scared. I knew the level of responsibility at my fingertips.'

The system that was giving him the information about the American missiles was called Oko. It used satellites to monitor any launches of ballistic missiles. It was relatively new and had only come on stream fully in 1982. Petrov knew this. And he knew that he didn't entirely trust the information it gave. The system had generated reports of lone missiles being launched before that had turned out to be false alarms. But this time there appeared to be multiple weapons on their way.

As the minutes ticked by ground radar stations reported nothing untoward. Yet they couldn't see what was going on beyond the horizon. An attack could still be on. But why were there only five missiles if the USA really was going to order an all-out attack? Petrov called the Kremlin. He reported that the attack was a false alarm. It was a big call. If wrong he would be responsible for the destruction of his homeland. More vital time ticked by: fiteen minutes; twenty minutes. No missiles had arrived. There were no explosions, no nuclear Armageddon. Petrov, following his instincts rather than the millions of roubles worth of technology in front of him, had been proved right. Doomsday had been cancelled.

He later said, 'I had a funny feeling in my gut. I didn't want to make a mistake. I made a decision. That's it.' But he also knew how close he came to making a different decision, later telling the *The Daily Mail*, 'A nuclear war could have broken out. The whole world could have been destroyed.' It was later concluded that one of the system satellite's infrared sensors had been confused by the sun's rays reflecting off high altitude cloud near the American base.

Petrov was quickly forgotten, even reprimanded for not keeping proper notes. For ten years he didn't even tell his wife and simply slipped into quiet retirement on a paltry pension. In fact, the affair did not come to light until the 1990s when General Votintsev published his memoirs. He commended Petrov's actions.

What is certain is that while the Cuban Missile Crisis may have been an exercise in international brinkmanship, experts acknowledge that the Petrov incident was the closest the world came to an accidental nuclear war. Had someone else been in command that night would they have made the same judgement call? Consider the pilot of the Soviet SU-15 fighter which shot down the Korean airliner, Major Gennadi Osipovich. In an interview years later he revealed that he had known at the time that the plane was a Boeing, a civilian aircraft, but felt that it could have been on a military mission. He had shot it down regardless.

In 2004 Petrov himself was finally given a World Citizen Award and received a cheque for $1,000. He is said to have spent it on his grandchildren and something he had always wanted, a vacuum cleaner. It subsequently turned out to be faulty.

10

BEATING THE IRON CURTAIN IN A HOT AIR BALLOON

After the Berlin Wall was built in August 1961 it's estimated that as many as 1,000 people died attempting to escape across it. Many more simply tried, failed and were imprisoned. It wasn't just the 96 miles of wall in Berlin that formed a seemingly impenetrable barrier; the 866-mile border between East and West Germany – part of what Churchill had dubbed the Iron Curtain – extended from the Baltic Sea to what was then Czechoslovakia and was fortified with high walls, barbed wire fences, watchtowers and minefields, all patrolled by dogs and heavily armed guards, some 50,000 in all. There were orders to shoot at anyone who tried to make an illegal crossing.

The wall was built in a bid to combat the emigration of East Germans; between 1949 and 1961 some 3.5 million people who wanted out of the post-war socialist state had left the country. After the wall's construction, as the Cold War went on, many of the 17 million people living in East Germany felt trapped behind the formidable barrier and vowed to escape. In 1957 the German Democratic Republic had even invented a special crime for those who tried to flee: *republikflucht* or 'flight from the Republic'. Some people, it transpired, would do almost anything to get across the frontier. Escape methods included digging tunnels and driving modified cars underneath the barriers at checkpoints, and one man even built his own miniature submarine, making it across the sea to Denmark. It's estimated that in the years until the wall fell in 1989, the equivalent of seven people a day attempted to escape East Germany, despite the threat of around three years in prison and subsequent social death.

Perhaps the most incredible of all the escape stories features two brave families who, in 1979, attempted to fly over the heavily fortified border in a homemade hot air balloon. Their story began in the mid-1970s when two men, Peter Strelzyk, an electrician and former aircraft mechanic in his early thirties, and Günter Wetzel, a bricklayer and truck driver in his twenties, struck up a friendship. The pair, both technically minded, liked meeting for a beer and discussing engines and cars. Both their families, living close to the border in the town of Poessneck in Thuringia, were relatively well off by East German standards but had slowly realised that they wanted to escape from an 'hermetically sealed world'. Peter and Günter had long toyed with the idea of escaping but with two young families they knew that an overland escape – involving eight people in all – was impractical. Then, one day, they happened to read a newspaper article about a balloon festival. Peter and Günter now believed they had a method that might just work. In March 1978 they agreed that they would fly out – by building their own, homemade, balloon.

They began borrowing library books on ballooning but had to largely second guess the technology needed to construct such a craft, learning by trial and error. They understood the basic physics, but to lift the estimated weight of 1,700lb, including a gondola, equipment and eight people, they would need thousands of yards of fabric. They also realised that they would need some way of heating the air to a temperature at which the balloon would rise. It seemed a mammoth task, but if they could get the balloon off the ground from the right launch location it would take them just half an hour of flying to cross the border into West Germany.

Amassing the fabric needed without alerting the authorities wasn't going to be easy. They began scouring shops in different towns, pretending they needed the material to line tents. Then, using an old sewing machine and helped by their wives, Petra and Doris, they worked up to twenty hours a day, painstakingly piecing their balloon together, experimenting with different materials as they went – umbrellas, nylon jacket liner and shower curtains – eventually plumping for taffeta.

The balloon's burner would be made from modified propane gas cylinders fixed to the base of a gondola, itself constructed from sheets of steel welded into a 4.6ft by 4.6ft frame. It would have steel posts at each corner and clotheslines strung together as guard rails. From each of the corner posts lines were tied to secure the balloon bag. All of this had to be hidden in the cellars of their houses, for fear of being discovered.

By April 1978, they were ready to test their 50ft by 66ft balloon. After initial experiments they decided they needed to test the inflation by hanging it vertically and drove out to an old quarry with a high cliff. But while setting up they got spooked, sure that someone was peering at them while they worked. Stuffing the balloon into the boot of their car they drove back to town, and fearful of immediate arrest, burned the whole thing.

When no one seemed to be on their trail after all, they started building a second balloon and soon learned some valuable lessons. They came up with a blower made from an old motorcycle motor, which would fan air into the balloon, helping it to inflate, and used a mini burner to get the heating process started before switching to the main burner. They needed hundreds of yards of further material, and clocked up many more miles in search of it. Despite their efforts, once completed in May 1978, they were disappointed with the results of their new balloon. The burner simply failed to provide the lift they needed. A dejected Günter temporarily withdrew from the project.

Peter tinkered on alone for months and, finally, perfected the burner. On 4 July 1979 he managed to launch the balloon from a deserted spot with his wife and two children aboard. The balloon quickly rose to around 6,000ft. But they lost their bearings. Suddenly the balloon hit a cloud. The material it was made from became sodden and the craft began to descend fast, crashing into some woodland. Amazingly, the family were unhurt, but as it began to get light Peter realised with horror that they had landed on the eastern side of the border, just yards from the so called 'death strip', and were surrounded by alarmed tripwires. Somehow he managed to lead his family back through the woods and fields unseen, to where they had parked their car. But the remnants of the balloon had been left behind.

By the time Peter turned up at Wetzel's door, Günter had already heard rumours about a mysterious balloon found near the border and knew his old friend must be behind the attempt. Knowing the authorities were now on to them there was no time to lose. They began to work together again, this time on a third, bigger balloon, some 82ft high and 66ft in diameter. Over the coming weeks they would drive 2,500 miles buying up nylon fabric and taffeta. Finally, at the start of autumn 1979, it was finished.

On the evening of 15 September they decided the weather conditions were perfect – a clear cold night with the right wind direction to blow the balloon to the west. Driving out to a clearing in some wooded hills which they'd carefully chosen for the launch, they began laying out their multi-coloured balloon, then knocking the iron pins and nylon lines into the ground which would hold it fast. At 1.30 a.m. they were ready, and started filling the balloon with hot air using the blower and burners.

Soon the flame extended high into the night sky and the balloon began to lift. Peter, along with his wife Doris and their children, Frank, aged 15, and Andreas, aged 11, and Günter, with his wife Petra and their children, Peter, aged 5, and Andreas, aged 2, jumped onto the gondola. With Peter at the burner, Frank and Günter cut the guide ropes and they were aloft. It was 2.20 a.m. They huddled together as the balloon rose fast and within nine minutes their altimeter, converted from an old barometer, was telling them they were at 6,500ft ... then 8,500ft.

Suddenly there was a ripping sound from the top of the balloon – a hole had appeared, then the burner went out. Frantically Günter managed to relight it with some matches and somehow they drifted on through the chill night air. Then they saw searchlights strafing the night sky below. They could only be from the border. Fortunately, by now, the balloon was out of range of the beams and they sailed on through the darkness.

Below, two policemen near the town of Naila, inside West Germany, 6 miles from the border, were doing their patrols when they saw a light flickering in the sky. They estimated that it was around 5,000ft up, but descending. They rushed to the point where they felt it might hit the ground.

Back in the balloon, the burner went out again and finally the gas ran out. They were coming down, first brushing the top of some trees, then coming to Earth in a field with a loud thud, still in the dark. The flight had lasted just twenty-eight minutes. But were they in the West? Doris and Petra, with the children, took cover in some bushes, while Peter and Günter (overcoming the pain from a broken leg) went to investigate a nearby barn. Inside they found some strange looking farm machinery and began to feel hopeful. Minutes later an Audi 80 drew up and two policemen got out. The men rushed up to them. 'Are we in the West?' they asked.

When the policemen gave them the good news Peter and Günter let off a firework to signal to the rest of the party to come out from their hiding places. But, before they left with the police, Petra rushed back to the balloon crash site. They had brought no belongings with them from the East, but Petra had brought a bottle of champagne, purchased at great cost. They cracked open the fizz – after all, she had heard it was what all pioneering balloonists did when they landed.

The two families had travelled just 15 miles in their makeshift balloon but within twenty-four hours their achievement was being toasted by news organisations across the world. The balloon escape had been particularly galling to the authorities in East Germany as it took place on the eve of the celebrations being planned for the state's thirtieth anniversary. The country would officially cease to exist when it became unified with the Federal Republic on 3 October 1990.

11

ESCAPE FROM THE *HINDENBURG*

The *Hindenburg* is remembered not so much for being a state-of-the-art airship, which exuded glamour as it ferried passengers across the Atlantic, but for the dramatic way in which it crashed on 6 May 1937. As it came in to land at the Lakehurst Naval Air Station in the United States, the huge German Zeppelin was suddenly engulfed in flames, with the shock of its spectacular destruction captured both on camera and in a gripping radio broadcast by reporter Herbert Morrison:

> It burst into flames! It burst into flames, and it's falling, it's crashing ... Oh, my, get out of the way, please! It's burning and bursting into flames ... and it's falling on the mooring-mast and all the folks agree

that this is terrible, this is the worst of the worst catastrophes in the
world ... it's smoke, and it's flames now ... and the frame is crashing to
the ground ... oh, the humanity!

At 804ft in length and 135ft wide the *LZ 129 Hindenburg* was the largest
man-made object that had ever flown. Yet it had been reduced to cinders
in just thirty-seven seconds. Zeppelins, named after the German Count
Ferdinand von Zeppelin who had pioneered them, had already been used
to drop bombs on London in the First World War. But in the 1930s the
Germans led the way in the construction of lighter-than-air dirigibles
to be used as passenger aircraft. Powered by diesel engines and steered
by rudders, the *Hindenburg*, launched in 1936, was the latest model.
Its massive metal skeleton was covered in a cotton skin, treated with
reflective materials, and it was fitted with sixteen enormous bags holding
some 7 million cubic feet of gas to keep the airship afloat. Buried in the
belly of the *Hindenburg* were the passenger quarters, with a separate
control gondola towards the bow.

Airships had already begun to rival the big liners in carrying
passengers across the Atlantic, slashing the travelling time from around
a week to just two days. The *Hindenburg* was able to fly at 80mph and
cross the ocean without refuelling, something planes still couldn't do.
Indeed, by 1937, the *Hindenburg*, which was even larger than the *Graf
Zeppelin* that famously circumnavigated the globe in 1929, had made a
total of sixteen successful flights from Germany to both Brazil and the
United States, carrying more than 2,500 passengers. Airships, it seemed,
were the future of long-distance travel.

A one-way ticket across the Atlantic on the *Hindenburg* cost $400,
and some of the 1930s big name celebrities travelled on it, including
American actor Douglas Fairbanks and German boxer Max Schmeling.
Over two decks the airship was kitted out in a style befitting its well-to-do
clientele. Cabins came with private showers, chefs served up gourmet
food and there was a bar and a plush lounge. There was even a specially
pressurised smoking compartment.

As the Nazis rose to power in Germany they were eager to cash in
on the kudos offered by this engineering marvel. But when notorious
propaganda minister Joseph Goebbels demanded that the *LZ 129* be
called the *Adolf Hitler* not the *Hindenburg* (after the German president
of the 1920s), the Zeppelin Company chairman, Dr Hugo Eckener,
bravely refused.

The *Hindenburg* airship bursting into flames as it arrived at Lakehurst Naval Air Station, New Jersey, US, in May 1937. (Public domain, courtesy of Thomas Worsdale, US Navy)

Despite its majesty, when the *Hindenburg* left Frankfurt on 3 May for the first of its scheduled flights to America that year, the airship was potentially hindered by the type of fuel it carried. The Zeppelins were originally designed to be filled with non-flammable helium, but because of US trade restrictions, which limited the global supply, the *Hindenburg* was filled with flammable hydrogen instead. To this day no one knows quite why the *Hindenburg* burst into flames, though a brief official investigation into the crash concluded that a spark from static electricity had ignited leaking hydrogen.

Of the ninety-seven people who boarded the airship, comprising thirty-six passengers and sixty-one crew, thirty-five were killed in the crash, with another member of the ground crew also perishing. This was actually fewer than in the crash of the British airship *R101* in 1930, which killed forty-eight people on its maiden overseas voyage, and a death toll smaller than the seventy-three lives lost when the US Navy airship, the *USS Akron*, was downed in a storm in April 1933.

In fact, what was remarkable about the *Hindenburg* crash, given how it had turned into an enormous ball of flame within moments, was how many people escaped with their lives. Many had jumped from the windows, which opened, as the crippled airship sank to the ground, managing to run to safety as it collapsed behind them.

Among the sixty-two who made it out was a 14-year-old cabin boy called Werner Franz. Back in 1936 Franz landed what must have been every young boy's dream when he got his job aboard the *Hindenburg*. His brother had heard about the post whilst working as a waiter at a luxury hotel in Frankfurt, where passengers stayed before airship flights. With his father ill and jobs in Depression-era Germany scarce, Franz jumped at the chance.

Franz's role saw him working in the crew mess, washing dishes, setting tables, making the beds in the cabins and carrying out other sundry tasks. Sometimes he would have to traverse the precarious catwalks that criss-crossed the hull. In October 1936 Franz made his first, thrilling flight on the airship to South America, later reprising the journey three times. And, in the spring of 1937, Franz was excited about making his first journey to the United States aboard the *Hindenburg*, not knowing that it would be his beloved craft's final voyage.

On the afternoon of 6 May, Franz was working in the officers' mess when he saw the skyscrapers of New York pass below. Then, after waiting for bad weather to clear at Lakehurst, the *Hindenburg*'s destination in New Jersey, the airship's commander, Captain Max Pruss, ordered the craft to start its landing procedure. It was just after 7 p.m. Franz continued with his duties in the galley, putting washed china away in a cupboard. In the past he'd joined crew members who were required to move to the bow of the airship to act as ballast during the landing process, but on this occasion Franz was too busy with his mess tasks.

As the *Hindenburg*'s engines were reversed, bringing it to a stop, lines were dropped from the airship to the ground crew so that they could tether the dirigible to a mooring mast. But, at 7.25 p.m., with the *Hindenburg* still 200ft from the ground, flames were spotted at the stern of the airship, near its fins. As hydrogen rushed out, the tail of the airship dropped to the ground and the craft was quickly overtaken by the growing inferno.

Franz had just been putting away the last of the crockery when he felt the airship shudder. Then, as the *Hindenburg* lurched violently, all the china Franz had put away flew out of the cupboard, crashing to the floor. The airship began to tilt alarmingly upwards and Franz ran into the passageway. Flames leapt towards him and he edged backwards along the walkway, holding on to its handrails. Just then a water ballast tank burst somewhere above Franz's head, drenching him and putting out some of the fire. Franz realised that near him was a cloth-covered hatch in the starboard side of the airship through which provisions were loaded. As the fire overwhelmed the ship its nose now fell towards Earth, giving Franz his chance. Diving for the hatch he punched his way through and jumped. Fortunately, he timed his leap to perfection, with the airship now less than 20ft from the ground. Once on the airfield, Franz got up and ran as fast as he could as the airship's ghostly frame, consumed with fire, plunged down behind him. Incredibly Franz made it clear, his soaking clothes protecting the youngster from the burns suffered by many others. Franz barely had a scratch on him.

At first, knowing his duty, Franz went back to see if he could help anyone else out. But by now the *Hindenburg* was already a pile of ashes and twisted metal. He was soon bundled away from the airfield. He knew how lucky he had been. Most of the crew who had gone to the nose of the airship had died in the blaze. Captain Pruss, abandoning the airship at the last moment, survived, but suffered bad burns after trying to rescue some of the passengers.

The day after the disaster Franz got permission to go back to the smouldering crash site to look for his grandfather's pocket watch, which had been in his bunk aboard the airship. Amazingly, he found it – still ticking amid the wreckage. Fourteen days after the disaster, Franz returned to Germany aboard an ocean liner where he was feted as a celebrity. Four years later, during the Second World War, he would join the German air force, surviving the conflict to go on and become a skilled machinist.

Rumours persist that in the fevered international situation of the late 1930s foul play was responsible for bringing down the *Hindenburg*. The actual evidence is scant. Whatever the truth, the disaster dealt a blow to the passenger airship industry from which it would never recover. After the end of the Second World War and the development of the jet engine, it would be the aeroplane that would take centre stage in transatlantic travel.

12

THE WRIGHT BROTHERS AND THE WORLD'S FIRST FATAL PLANE CRASH

Orville and Wilbur Wright have gone down in history as the men who achieved the first successful powered flight in a manned aircraft that was heavier than air. But back in the early 1900s their incredible achievement, later seen as defining a whole new era, did not appear so clear cut.

It was at 10.35 a.m. on the cold, windy day of 17 December 1903 that the Wrights' flimsy *Flyer* took to the skies at Kitty Hawk, North Carolina, with Orville at the controls. The plane flew just 120ft at an altitude of around 10ft, and covered the distance in twelve seconds before landing safely, if bumpily. But the two brothers, who had been tinkering with gliders and aircraft for several years, knew they had done something special, even newsworthy, claiming a few days after the event that 'the age of the flying machine had come at last'. There was even a photograph to prove what had happened.

However, a whole host of other pioneers around the world had been experimenting with embryonic aeroplanes, and there were many who were sceptical that two brothers, whose day jobs involved running a humble bicycle shop in Ohio, could have mastered the required technology and thereby opened up the prospect of a new age of human aviation. Even the newspaper in their home town, the *Dayton Journal*, refused to report the flights, saying they were simply too short to carry any merit.

So it was that the Wrights' first flight, in a wooden and cloth biplane fitted with a homemade petrol engine, turned out to be only the beginning of a campaign to convince the world they had done something truly momentous. Over the next few years they would travel thousands of miles as they aimed to show that their planes could not only fly but were a practical proposition – and even of use to the armed forces.

The brothers had actually made four flights on that December day in 1903, with the last – flown by Wilbur – covering an impressive 852ft. However, rebuffed by an incredulous world, the pair now worked to improve their plane, focussing on honing aircraft controls, knowing this would be vital to the future of successful manned, powered flight. It was an area in which they would soon stand out from other pioneers.

The Wrights' initial efforts at getting airborne had been dangerous enough. Orville seemed to be the most accident prone. In 1902, flying a glider, the younger Wright had nearly been killed, ending up in 'a heap of flying machine, cloth, and sticks in a heap, with me in the centre without a bruise or a scratch'. Then, in 1904, he survived two more near misses flying powered craft while testing in the Huffman Prairie, outside Dayton. He got away with no more than a cut hand and a sprained shoulder. On 14 July 1905, during another test flight, there was a problem with the controls and the plane hit the ground at around 30mph. Orville was catapulted through one of the wings, but again walked away unscathed.

By 1905 the Wright brothers, without fanfare and few funds, had built two more versions of the *Flyer*, and in October Wilbur made a thirty-nine-minute, 24-mile circling flight. Spurred on by their success, they decided the time had come to try and sell their now fully controllable aeroplane and to bring it to the attention of the wider world.

It was during the following years, as the brothers attempted to convince officials of their aircraft's credentials, that Orville would have his nearest brush with death in the air in what became recognised as the first fatal plane crash in human history.

There was still much cynicism and lack of understanding about the Wrights' aviation efforts. A Paris newspaper asked if the Wrights were 'fliers or liars', with others branding them 'bluffers'. At home, in the US, the reaction was lukewarm. The American Government had already been involved with failed flying experiments, including those by renowned scientist Samuel Langley. Initially, the Wrights' attempts to sell their aircraft to governments, both domestically and in Europe, got nowhere, perhaps hindered by the fact that they refused to demonstrate what it could do without a contract. But in 1906, the Wright Brothers finally got a patent for their machine and a year later, both the US Army and a French company began to show interest. Each was determined to see it fly before they would agree to buy.

At this point the Wright brothers decided to split up for the make or break public demonstration flights that the deals demanded. Wilbur crossed the Atlantic to France with one modified *Flyer*, now called the *Model A*, and Orville prepared for tests in front of the US Army with another at Fort Myer, Virginia. On 8 August 1908, during a demonstration at a horse racing track near Le Mans, Wilbur finally put any doubts about their aircraft to bed with a startling display of flying skills which included 'figure eights'. It was clear to all who witnessed the demonstration that the Wrights had achieved mastery of three-axis control, able to deal with the pitch, roll and yaw of a plane. Even other pioneers of flight had to admit they were ahead of the game.

Part of the agreement with the US Government was that any aircraft they purchased should be able to carry two people. The Wright brothers had successfully included this modification and, in France, Wilbur carried around sixty people aloft during flights that summer. Back in the US, Orville started his demonstrations on 3 September and was soon stunning people with his flying ability, setting nine new world records. Then, on 17 September 1908, as the trials continued, Orville took off with a passenger, Lieutenant Thomas Selfridge, a member of the army's assessment team. They climbed to 150ft and down below some 2,000 spectators marvelled as the aircraft circled the base's parade ground. Everything seemed to be going well, but on the fourth circuit, at around 5 p.m., Orville heard a strange sound from the back of the plane. Looking round he could see nothing, but thought it wise to prepare to land anyway.

Suddenly, Orville recalled later, there were, 'two big thumps, which gave the machine a terrible shaking'. A propeller had broken and snapped the rudder wire. The plane made a sudden lurch to the right. Orville lost control of the levers and remembered 'a most peculiar feeling of helplessness'. He turned off the engine and tried to glide down. But, at about 75ft, the machine simply nosedived towards the ground. Selfridge grabbed one of the framework's wooden struts and let out an 'Oh! Oh!' as the plane plummeted down, smashing into the Earth in a cloud of dust.

The crowd ran towards the mangled wreckage where both Selfridge and Orville were trapped. Once disentangled, the pair were stretchered away. Selfridge had a fractured skull and died three hours later in hospital, the first victim of a powered plane crash. He was buried in Arlington National Cemetery with full military honours. Somehow, however, Orville had survived again. But this time he was badly hurt, with a broken left leg, smashed ribs and cuts to his head. He spent more than a month in hospital but fractures to his hip were missed by the doctors, and these would plague him for the rest of his life.

Despite his injuries, Orville was determined to fly again. Legend has it that when a friend visited him in hospital he asked, 'Has it got your nerve?' 'Nerve?' repeated a bemused Orville. 'Oh, do you mean will I be afraid to fly again?' He then replied, 'The only thing I'm afraid of is that I can't get well soon enough to finish those tests next year.' Orville did indeed take to the skies again just months later. In fact he went on to have three more accidents in the air, this time without sustaining any further, major injury.

Finally, in July 1909, the Wright brothers completed the trials and sold the *Flyer* to the US Army for $30,000. They also formed a commercial company. They had proved they could fly with a passenger for an hour at an average speed of 40mph. President Taft came to see them fly and they were both awarded the Congressional Medal for their services to aviation. In October Wilbur celebrated with a flight that circled the Statue of Liberty. In the meantime a French company had also bought the aircraft. The brothers' place in history was secure.

However, until that point, Wilbur and Orville had never flown together, because their father, Milton, had made them promise not to. But, on 25 May 1910, back at Huffman Prairie, they took off in the *Flyer* together for a short flight. Both landed safely. Then it was their 81-year-old dad's turn. The clergyman was clearly thrilled as he lifted off with Orville at the controls. Leaning in close to his son he shouted, 'Higher, Orville, higher!'

Wilbur died in 1912 from typhoid fever and Orville gave up flying, partly because of the injuries sustained in the 1908 crash. However, he lived until 1948, long enough to witness the invention of the jet engine and modern airliners. Two weeks after the end of the Second World War, having recently turned 74 and just days after US planes had dropped nuclear bombs on Hiroshima and Nagasaki, he told a friend, 'I once thought the aeroplane would end wars ... I now wonder whether the aeroplane and the atomic bomb can do it.'

13

THE FOREIGN 'FEW' WHO HELPED TURN THE TIDE IN THE BATTLE OF BRITAIN

The plucky British pilot in his Spitfire taking on the might of Hermann Goering's Luftwaffe, the only thing standing in the way of Hitler's invasion during the Second World War – it's the traditional image that springs to mind when we think of the Battle of Britain, the critical conflict in the skies over southern England that led Churchill to utter the immortal lines, 'Never in the field of human conflict was so much owed by so many to so few.'

In the high summer of 1940 Britain famously stood alone against the Nazi threat. France had surrendered on 22 June, the Soviet Union was not yet at war with Germany, and America and Japan were more than a year away from entering into hostilities. To defeat the British Navy and achieve their aim of invasion across the Channel, code-named Operation Sea Lion, the Germans knew they would need air superiority.

Ordering his invasion plans, on 16 July 1940 Hitler wrote, 'The English air force must have been beaten down to such an extent morally, and in fact, that it can no longer muster any power of attack worth mentioning against the German crossing.'

His plan was never realised. Ultimately, Britain would escape invasion thanks to the efforts of a few thousand fighter pilots and ground staff who fought tooth and nail to thwart the German landings. But, contrary to the myth, they did not rely entirely on the Spitfire to do so. The fact that the invasion never materialised was thanks in good measure to another fighter aircraft, the Hurricane. Nor were the pilots who took to the air solely British; and the foreign airmen who flew with the Royal Air Force proved to be some of the most brilliant fighter aces of the war.

It has been fashionable in recent years to play down the importance of the Battle of Britain. Some historians don't think Hitler possessed the wherewithal to carry through his invasion plan. Even without the air force, they say, the British Navy would still have been too strong. Of course, we'll never know, but defeat of the RAF may have forced the nation to the negotiating table. The fear of invasion was also very real at the time. In the autumn of 1940, the nation's military chiefs bit their fingernails, expecting to receive reports of landings at any moment. On 3 October General Alan Brooke wrote in surprise, 'Still no invasion!' and after the war explained, 'I considered the invasion a very real and probable threat and one for which the land forces at my disposal fell far short of what I felt was required to provide any degree of real confidence in our power to defend these shores.'

The odds facing the RAF at the start of the Battle of Britain were not overwhelming, but the British were outnumbered. Fighter Command had suffered serious losses in the Battle of France – 280 pilots and more than 400 planes. By July 1940, as the waves of German planes began to sweep over Britain, the RAF had 650 fighter aircraft compared with the Luftwaffe's 2,500 planes, of which two-thirds were bombers.

Over the coming weeks and months the Germans tried to neutralise the RAF. There was a large death toll on either side but over the whole course of the battle, which lasted from mid-July until the end of October, the Luftwaffe was unable to replace aircraft and men as quickly as the British. The most intense phase of the Battle of Britain took place in late August and early September, and the date of 15 September, now marked as Battle of Britain Day, proved critical. Over those twenty-four hours, the Luftwaffe lost about sixty aircraft while Britain's Fighter Command had twenty-six of its planes shot down. The scales were tipping and the Germans were losing. Unknown to the British it was at this point that Hitler postponed his invasion. One of the reasons for the defeat had been the Führer's decision to switch his strategy from concentrating on attacking airfields to bombing London. By the end of October the Luftwaffe had lost 1,900 aircraft, with more than 2,500 aircrew killed. Fighter Command had lost 1,000 fighter aircraft and 544 pilots.

It was not just the iconic Spitfire that had made the difference. R.J. Mitchell's Supermarine Spitfire was an incredible aeroplane that had great firepower and was lightning fast, but the older and slower Hawker Hurricane, designed by Sydney Camm, was the workhorse of the battle in 1940. With its thick wings and wood and fabric construction it would be difficult to argue that the Hurricane had the elegance of the dashing metal Spitfire. But at 340mph it was no slouch. The Hurricane was a very manoeuvrable fighter and the design of its frame meant it could soak up plenty of damage during dogfights. Douglas Bader, the British fighter ace who flew despite having lost both of his legs, thought it had a 'marvellous gun platform'. The Hurricane was easier than the Spitfire to repair and there were more of them too. In July 1940, at the start of the Battle of Britain, there were twenty-nine Hurricane squadrons and nineteen Spitfire squadrons. Hurricanes would eventually account for 55 per cent of German losses, while the Spitfire notched up 42 per cent.

The success of the unsung Hurricane is linked to the forgotten foreign airmen of the Battle of Britain, for many of them flew the plane. This crack international contingent were crucial in swelling the ranks of a fighter force that badly needed well-trained pilots who could throw themselves into action with fervour.

A leading ace in the Battle of Britain, by some estimates the most successful pilot of all, was a Czech man called Josef František. After Czechoslovakia had been annexed by the Germans in 1938 František escaped to serve with Polish forces. When Poland was then overrun too he made his way via Romania and North Africa to France and then Britain, flying with the No. 303 Polish Squadron during the Battle of Britain. In September 1940, flying a Hurricane, he shot down a staggering seventeen enemy planes, receiving the Distinguished Flying Medal for his efforts.

František was just one of a large number of foreign pilots, 574 in total, who flew alongside 2,353 British pilots in the battle. These foreign 'Few' made up 20 per cent of the airmen who took on the Luftwaffe in those vital days. They came from a variety of countries including Poland, Czechoslovakia, New Zealand, Canada, the United States, France and Belgium.

At the forefront of these international forces were the Polish pilots, many of whom had escaped from Poland after its conquest by the Nazis and already had experience of fighting the Luftwaffe. The RAF had two Polish fighter squadrons in 1940, and Squadron 303, to which František was attached, was the most successful in the Battle of Britain, downing 100 German planes in just a month. During the whole course of the battle 12 per cent of enemy aircraft were shot down by Polish pilots, out of all proportion to the 145 men who took to the skies. The Polish had honed the skill of firing on the enemy at less than 200yds and went into battle with a bravado that reflected what had happened to their country. Yet the Polish weren't reckless. The death rate in Squadron 303 was almost 70 per cent lower than the rate in other RAF squadrons. Even so, thirty-one Poles were killed during the Battle of Britain along with twenty airmen from Czechoslovakia. These included František, who died in a crash landing on 8 October. More than 150 other foreign souls also lost their lives.

As 1940 drew to a close, the British breathed a collective sigh of relief. Bombing continued but the threat of a German invasion had receded.

The Battle of Britain had been narrowly won and the international and Commonwealth pilots had played a pivotal part in making sure that happened. The boost to morale from the victory was huge and by 1941 Churchill was so sure that the threat of invasion had passed that he boasted, 'We are waiting for the long promised invasion. So are the fishes.'

It was sad, then, when the war ended in 1945, that the contribution of the Polish armed forces to the Allied war effort was not properly recognised. Thanks to pressure from Stalin, Polish units were not asked to take part in the victory parade held in London in 1946.

14

THE MIRACULOUS SURVIVAL OF THE *LAST SUPPER*

Tucked away in the Dominican convent of Santa Maria delle Grazie in Milan, Italy, is an artwork that has captivated millions of visitors down the centuries. That Leonardo da Vinci's *Last Supper* survives at all, however, is miraculous given how and where it was painted, the ravages of time, the destruction wrought upon it by misguided 'restoration' and, above all, by the effects of Allied bombing in the Second World War.

The *Last Supper* is a large mural measuring 15ft high by 29ft long, covering the northern wall of the convent's refectory. Commissioned by Ludovico Sforza, the Duke of Milan, it was begun in 1495 and depicts the moment at that Biblical celebration of the Passover where Jesus reveals that one of his disciples is to betray him. Christ is seated in the middle at a table, with six apostles either side. Each takes on an animated pose as they react to what Jesus has told them. Judas, the apostle who will ultimately betray Christ to the Romans, is featured to Jesus' right, symbolically tipping over a salt cellar and looking a good deal shadier than the rest.

The genius of da Vinci's work lies not only in the indulgent and vivid detail but also in his clever use of perspective, which makes the painting appear to be an extension of the room itself, drawing the eye towards Christ and bringing the whole scene to life. Its realism is helped by the fact that da Vinci drew on the faces of the friars around him as inspiration for the figures in his painting.

When the *Last Supper* was finally revealed, after three years in the making, it was immediately considered a triumph and has since been acclaimed by art critics and historians down the centuries. In 1788 the great German writer Goethe said, 'It is a unique picture of its kind and one can compare nothing else with it.' The art historian Sir Kenneth Clark thought the *Last Supper* a marvel of the High Renaissance, calling it the 'keystone of European art'. When King Louis XII of France saw the painting in its prime he was so enthralled that he asked if it could be taken down and sent home to France.

Over the years the *Last Supper* has also become notorious as the subject of a number of mysteries and controversies. Some believe, for instance, that the apostle to the right of Jesus is not John, as is usually interpreted, but actually Mary Magdalene – the closest of Jesus' female disciples. It's a claim which is heavily played on in Dan Brown's thriller *The Da Vinci Code* but refuted by most serious experts. However, recent restoration work has thrown up fascinating new insights into the content of da Vinci's painting, revealing many long-forgotten details.

The fact that it can still be studied at first hand by scholars is rather surprising when you consider the *Last Supper*'s turbulent 500-year history. Even by 1517, two years before da Vinci died, the *Last Supper* was already suffering. It was just two decades old but was starting to flake and the bright colours beginning to fade. Antonio de Beatis, secretary to the cardinal of Aragon, wrote that the mural was 'beginning to deteriorate, I know not whether owing to the damp which the wall exudes or to other carelessness'. Another visitor, Giorgio Vasari who saw the *Last Supper* in 1556, reckoned there was, by then, 'nothing visible except a muddle of blots'. By the time the critic Francesco Scannelli saw it in the middle of the seventeenth century he reported that the apostles could barely be made out and that the painting was falling off the wall.

Part of the reason for the speedy demise of the *Last Supper* was the way da Vinci had created it in the first place. To form a traditional fresco he would have had to paint quickly on damp plaster. But the great man didn't like to rush his work. Instead, he decided to use a different technique, using oil and tempura over dry plaster. This enabled da Vinci to spend longer finessing the piece and making changes as he went along, yet also meant that the painting was never really properly fixed to the surface, leaving a time bomb for those who, in the following centuries, attempted to preserve one of the world's artistic wonders.

Da Vinci's method of painting had nothing to do with the work's next calamity. In 1652, while carrying out a bit of monastic remodelling, some unenlightened friars decided to have a door put through the middle of the wall supporting the painting, entirely obliterating Christ's legs. As time went on humidity was also a big problem in the busy refectory, which was, of course, near the kitchens. So, while the lucky friars were able to enjoy their meals gazing on the great work, the painting was, in fact, slowly disintegrating in front of their eyes. From the middle of the eighteenth century, as it began to deteriorate even further, there were a series of well-meaning, if farcical, attempts to try and save it using everything from wax to alcohol and caustic soda. A journeyman painter called Michelangelo Bellotti was hired to fill in missing sections, which he did crudely. Then a curtain was put across the whole painting in a bid to protect it. All this did was trap more moisture in the wall and scratch off more paint. In 1770 Giuseppe Mazza was hired in another botched restoration that saw him paint over many of the faces in the *Last*

Damage at Santa Maria delle Grazie in Milan after an Allied air raid in August, 1943. Da Vinci's *Last Supper* on the convent's refectory wall narrowly avoided destruction. (Courtesy of the Church of Santa Maria delle Grazie, Milan)

Supper in his own hand. When his vandalism was discovered the prior was sacked but the harm was already done.

In 1796 Napoleon marched triumphantly into Milan and French troops were billeted at the convent. When the general saw the painting he apparently ordered that the refectory be made off limits. However, the space was soon in use as a stable, with soldiers using the painting for target practice, amusing themselves by lobbing bricks at the heads of the apostles. Some of their eyes were even scratched out. Then, in 1800, a flood left the painting covered in green mould. In these years the refectory was also said to have been used as both a prison and a makeshift fire station.

The nineteenth century saw further attempts – and yet more failures – to secure the painting for future generations. In 1821 one Stefano Barezzi, under the illusion that the *Last Supper* was a fresco, came up with the idea of taking all the paint off and mounting the whole thing on canvas instead. When he realised that he was destroying the thing as he went along, Barezzi gave up and haplessly tried to glue the pieces back on.

More sensitive attempts to stabilise the *Last Supper* in the twentieth century did little good. Then, when Mussolini's Italy entered the Second World War, the biggest threat of all emerged. As an important industrial centre, Milan was targeted by Allied bombers on around fifty occasions during the conflict. And, on the night of 16 August 1943, a 10-tonne bomb landed on the convent, blowing out the east wall and roof of the refectory. Amazingly, the end wall, which sported the *Last Supper*, emerged from the dust and rubble intact. It had been sandbagged, which meant that the work was largely protected from shrapnel. But, roughly covered with a tarpaulin, it was left dangerously exposed until the refectory could be rebuilt after the war.

In 1951 yet another restoration was attempted but this only succeeded in trapping more damp and mildew within the work. Finally, in 1978, a mammoth new effort was started which was to last more than twenty years. Original sketches and a 1520 copy of the *Last Supper* by the painter Giampietrino, as well as state-of-the-art infrared technology, were used to identify da Vinci's original vision. Layers of dirt and bodged restoration work were removed, while some parts which proved impossible to salvage were repainted in watercolours. But the work was incredibly difficult. The woman who oversaw it, Pinin Brambilla Barcilon, sometimes despaired at the task, telling the *New York Times* that, in comparison, restoring the Sistine Chapel was a simple window wash. Finally, in May 1999, the restored painting was put back on view to the public with just a few visitors permitted to enter at any one time. In order to combat the humidity problem the room ceased to be a refectory and became an empty, climate-controlled space.

Some have been critical of the style of the restoration work, complaining that much of the painting is not now da Vinci's at all. But the *Last Supper* is certainly no longer the sorry sight that the writer Henry James once encountered, and which led him to describe it as the 'saddest work of art in the world'.

15

THE CHARMED LIFE OF THE *MONA LISA*

In 1911 the artist Pablo Picasso was in a pickle. Just as his cubism period was getting under way he found himself brought in for questioning over the stealing of a painting called *La Gioconda* – or the *Mona Lisa* as English speakers know it – by Leonardo da Vinci. Picasso was one of many quizzed over the theft as he had been caught up in the robbery of two miniature statues stolen from the Louvre museum in Paris two years before which, unwittingly, he had bought from a friend. Fortunately, Picasso's movements on the morning of Monday 21 August 1911, the day the *Mona Lisa* went missing, put him in the clear. Picasso was off the hook but investigations into the disappearance of the *Mona Lisa* would continue.

Even before the theft, da Vinci's masterpiece had been in the news, raising both its own profile and that of the Louvre where it was displayed. By reframing it in reflective glass, the gallery had upset art lovers, who said they could now see themselves peering back as they viewed the work. So could ineffective glazing be at the root of its theft? If so, why just this particular painting? After several acts of vandalism, the Louvre had reframed several works behind thick panes over the preceeding weeks and at the time the *Mona Lisa* was no more famous than some of the other masterpieces around it.

In fact, so relatively unimportant was the *Mona Lisa* in 1911, no one actually noticed that it was missing for a while. On Tuesday 22 August, when an artist called Louis Béroud decided he would cash in on the glazing controversy by painting a girl brushing her hair in the reflection of the painting's new glass, he was surprised to come across four nails on the wall where the da Vinci had hung for five years. Abandoning his easel to ask a guard where the painting had been moved to, he was irritated by the vague answers from the guard, who told him the painting was possibly down at the photographers and would probably be back soon. Anxious to get his parody under way, Béroud passed the time in other parts of the gallery before checking back with the guard several hours later. Only when further enquiries were made did it begin to dawn: more than thirty hours after it was last seen, the *Mona Lisa* was missing.

The police were called in, the museum closed and the hunt began for clues, of which very few could be uncovered. One worker remembered seeing the picture in its normal position on the Monday morning at 7 a.m. and when he walked past a blank wall an hour later he assumed it had been removed legitimately. That narrowed the theft to an early hour on a day when the museum closed for cleaning, administration and, if necessary, moving pictures around. The duty guard that morning had gone for a cigarette at one point, leaving a gap of about half an hour; time enough for the painting to be snaffled.

Theft was now a certainty. With the *Mona Lisa* missing, ports were closed and even clairvoyants consulted. Fingerprint pioneer Alphonse Bertillon was summoned. Although the *Mona Lisa*'s frame, together with the controversial piece of glass, had been found in a stairwell, his work proved fruitless. Every indication was that the thief knew the Louvre intimately, but this didn't help much. Eight hundred people had access to the *Mona Lisa* that Monday morning. The number of suspects grew larger still when the entire German nation was blamed, accused of demoralising the French by plundering their treasured art. Germany hit back, saying it was more likely to be an inside job by the French Government to distract attention from its own inadequacies.

After nine days in which an expected blackmail letter failed to arrive, investigators allowed the Louvre to reopen to brisk business as visitors flocked to admire the blank space where the picture used to be. As weeks turned into months there were doubts that it would ever be seen again. Art historians warned that unscrupulous private collectors who coveted da Vinci's works might keep them discreetly forever. Some voiced the worst-case scenario: a painting now world famous would be impossible to offload – it would be burned or buried.

And so two years passed, with frequent sightings that all turned out to be false. Then, on 10 December 1913, an Italian art dealer received an intriguing visitor. Having placed an advertisement saying he would pay good money for interesting works, Alfredo Geri's usual trickle of enquiries led, as always, to responses of varying quality. What he hadn't been expecting was a mustachioed man saying he had the *Mona Lisa* wrapped in a pair of his underpants and concealed in a trunk. In the two weeks since placing his advertisement, correspondence between the mysterious art collector with the suitcase, Leonardo Peruggia, and Geri had gone back and forth – the former covering his tracks by using a post box address. Peruggia was in little doubt of the provenance of his painting. He knew for a fact that it was the original da Vinci, because, Peruggia admitted he had taken it from the Louvre himself. And this, he implied, was not a theft so much as a kidnapping – he intended no harm to the painting. If Geri would come to Paris, he would see that his intentions were honourable: the *Mona Lisa*'s true home was Florence, the city where da Vinci had started his seminal work, and together Geri and Peruggia could arrange its repatriation. They would be heroes.

Geri couldn't believe his luck. It's not every day you get to discover a stolen da Vinci. But clearly the police would have to know. Bluffing that he could not make it to Paris, Geri invited Peruggia to Italy instead. Meeting in the thief's hotel room, Peruggia explained again that as an Italian art lover, he had rescued the painting for his country. Oh, and to show that his motives were entirely a matter of national pride in restoring an artwork stolen by Napoleon for the French, all he asked was half a million lire and a promise that the picture would return to its rightful place in the Uffizi, Italy's most famous gallery.

Sensing that Peruggia was more conman than art historian, not least because the Napoleon link was a complete fabrication – the artist having taken the picture to France himself when he moved to the court of King Francois I – Geri indicated his interest in acquiring the painting. Fixing a time to return the following day, Peruggia showed Geri to the door happy, the money finally in sight.

The next morning Geri, accompanied by Uffizi director Giovanni Poggi, stood, goggle-eyed, as Peruggia pulled out a trunk, discarded various items of clothing from the top and revealed a small wooden panel. Unmistakably this was the *Mona Lisa*. The buyers prevaricated a little. They explained that they would need to check its provenance against other da Vincis, although the Louvre's seal on the panel left them in no doubt. If they could just check it in daylight, rather than in the dark hotel room, they would be clearer. As they stepped into the street, several police officers took hold of Peruggia's shoulder. He'd fallen for the oldest trick in the book. For him, this was the end of the heist. Prison beckoned, but, for a while, so did fame.

Joy at the news of the painting's safe return turned to confusion when a Franco-Italian spat broke out. Wasn't Peruggia right? The true home of the *Mona Lisa* was surely Italy? The Louvre was having none of it. Having gone through one scandal by losing the picture in the first place, there was no way they were conceding the *Mona Lisa* to the Italians. They would, however, allow it a two-week sojourn so that the Italian people could view it. After a gap of nearly two-and-a-half years, the painting returned to its pegs in the Salon Carré at the Louvre. Fifty thousand people a day filed past it during its first few days home. It has been revered at the gallery ever since.

In court, Leonardo Peruggia made two confessions. First, his name wasn't Leonardo, but Vincenzo. And second, yes, he had stolen the *Mona Lisa*. As a former Louvre employee he had walked around unchallenged on a day the gallery was closed. Picking the painting off the wall, and releasing it from the awful reflective glass and heavy frame, he had left the building with the panel stuffed up a painter's smock. Sympathetic to his unlikely story about repatriating the painting to its true home, the court sentenced him to time served, just eight months. The art world considered its good fortune. As of 4 January 1914, thanks to a talented thief, a Renaissance icon was safely back at the Louvre, behind much tighter security and propelled to the status of 'most famous painting in the world', a position it has held ever since.

16

HOW THE BAYEUX TAPESTRY SURVIVED THE FRENCH REVOLUTION AND THE NAZIS

The Bayeux Tapestry depicts the Norman conquest of England in 1066 in thrilling and vivid detail. More properly called an embroidery, it is made using eight colours of wool worked into sections of linen and is an incredible 230ft long. Historians tend to agree that it is from the late eleventh century, with many reckoning that it was commissioned by

Bishop Odo of Bayeux, William the Conqueror's half-brother. Some say that it was created in England, perhaps at Canterbury, as Odo was also Earl of Kent. Others say that it was made in France, where it is sometimes referred to as *La Tapisserie de la reine Mathilde*, or Queen Matilda's Tapestry, after William's wife.

As well as its mysterious origin, controversy has always surrounded the version of events which the tapestry charts. Unsurprisingly, the story within the tapestry is told from the perspective of the Normans, the victors at the Battle of Hastings on 14 October 1066, in which King Harold of England was killed, to be replaced on the English throne by William the Conqueror, who became William I. The tapestry seemingly shows Harold swearing an oath that he will back William's claim to the English throne when Edward the Confessor dies. According to the tapestry, Harold broke this oath after seizing the Crown, eventually leading to William's invasion of England and the events at Hastings, in which Harold is killed by an arrow in the eye. Much debate has surrounded whether Harold ever made such an oath or whether he was indeed killed by an arrow in the eye (critics point out that the arrow was probably added during a later repair). That William won at Hastings, or that Harold died at the battle, is not in dispute.

The mystery and myths surrounding the Bayeux Tapestry are partly due to the fact that the first mention of the work didn't appear until 1476, when it was listed in an inventory of the items owned by Bayeux Cathedral in Normandy. Many think it was made to decorate the cathedral on its consecration in 1077 and it is believed to have been hung in the nave each year to celebrate the Feast of the Relics.

What certainly isn't in question is the Bayeux Tapestry's importance as one of the finest existing artworks of the medieval period. It has given us some of the most abiding images of the Norman Conquest and what we imagine life to have been like in the eleventh century. Perhaps most remarkable of all is the fact that such a fragile and rather impractical relic has survived, more or less complete, for nigh on 1,000 years. Indeed, the tapestry has had a life almost as turbulent as the historic events which it attempts to chronicle.

By 1476 it had already somehow survived the burning of Bayeux in 1106 by King Henry I of England, as well as a bad fire in 1159. It appears to have gone on to survive the destruction wrought in the city in 1562 by the Huguenots, keen to trash Catholic buildings. There is a theory that for many of these years it was locked in a cedarwood chest, which at least had the benefit of protecting it from the moths, if not the damp.

The tapestry only began to attract serious attention again in 1724 when a sketch of it came to light. Investigations by the Benedictine scholar Bernard de Montfaucon led to the tapestry being identified at Bayeux, and complete drawings and recordings of it were subsequently made and circulated among scholars. It was soon recognised as something unique and started to attract the attention of English enthusiasts too. Then, in 1789, the French Revolution broke out. Preserving Norman works of art was not high on the priority list of those trying to sweep away the old institutions and create a modern France. All church property was soon placed in public hands thanks to a decree by the National Assembly. But for several more years, while the *Ancien Régime* was swept away, the tapestry lay safe in its chest, kept, by some accounts, in the bishop's study.

In 1792 France was at war and a fevered defence of the nation began as a Prussian army invaded the new republic. Patriotic volunteers in Bayeux rushed to form a battalion and waggons were readied with equipment. Those organising the new force decided they needed something to cover their weapons and ammunition with, protecting them from the elements. Some bright spark mentioned that there was a handy piece of linen in the cathedral that could be cut up and used as makeshift tarpaulins. The local authority decreed that this was a good idea and the tapestry was duly removed for the purpose. When local police commissioner Lambert-Leonard le Forestier got wind of the plan he was outraged. Realising the historical importance of the tapestry, he immediately issued an order for its return and rushed to where the historic cloth was about to be savaged. Waving his piece of paper in front of a crowd he demanded that the tapestry be handed back. Grudgingly, those preparing the waggons agreed to use pieces of sacking instead and le Forestier seized the tapestry, storing it in his own home until the emergency had passed, eventually handing it over to the city.

Two years later, there was a second revolutionary threat to the tapestry. By now King Louis XVI's head had been chopped off and some locals had decided that the tapestry should meet a similar fate, being cut up to decorate a festival float devoted to the new 'Age of Reason'. In April 1794 local art commissioners, appointed across France to protect the nation's public monuments, intervened, demanding that the local mayor hand over the tapestry for safe keeping, as the 'conquest of England by the Normans has contributed to our national pride'.

A wilier revolutionary, Napoleon would soon put the tapestry to a better use than mere colourful bunting. France was now immersed

A section of the complete replica of the Bayeux Tapestry made by thirty-five women of the Leek Embroidery Society in 1885. (Reading Museum & Town Hall, www.readingmuseum.org.uk)

in a long conflict with Britain and, like the Norman duke before him, Napoleon planned an invasion. Realising that the tapestry was useful propaganda to rouse the country and his troops for the quest, he brought it to Paris in 1803, where it was exhibited at the Louvre (then called the Musée Napoléon) to serve as a curtain-raiser to his own proposed conquest. When the invasion was subsequently abandoned, the tapestry went back to Bayeux where it was kept in the city hall and the municipal library before being moved to a special museum in 1913. During this time its fame advanced further and there was even a complete copy made in the 1880s by thirty-five women from Staffordshire.

The tapestry's dangerous passage through history would, however, continue. When the Second World War broke out in September 1939 it was sprayed with insecticide, rolled up and locked inside a zinc-lined case in an underground concrete bunker. But it wasn't just bombs or the invading German army that were to prove a threat to the tapestry. Once France had been occupied, a sinister organisation called the Ahnenerbe began to take an interest. The group was a research body led by Heinrich Himmler, also head of the Gestapo and SS. It had been created in the 1930s to provide historical evidence of Aryan superiority. Himmler pointed to the fact that the Normans were essentially Nordic, not French, and believed that the wonder of the Bayeux Tapestry somehow represented the superiority of Nordic peoples, among whom he included the Germans. In June 1941 the tapestry was moved to a local abbey for study by the Ahnenerbe's 'academics'. It was then ordered that, along with other great French works of art, it should be put in the Chateau de Sourches, near Le Mans, for safe keeping. The job of getting it there was left to the city authorities and the tapestry ended up making the 100-mile journey in a rickety, charcoal-driven charabanc, which broke down on the way and nearly ended up in a ditch.

Following D-Day, on 6 June 1944, Himmler became even more determined that the tapestry remain in Nazi hands. Interestingly, Bayeux was the first city to be liberated by the Allies. In late June 1944 Himmler had the tapestry moved to the Louvre, in case it too should fall into enemy hands. By August it was clear that Paris would soon fall to the Allies, yet Himmler still seemed more obsessed with the tapestry than the growing threat to Germany's ultimate victory. Code-breakers at Britain's Bletchley Park even intercepted a message on 18 August, a few days before the German army withdrew from Paris, in which Himmler reminded his operatives not to forget the tapestry when they retreated. He wanted it taken to the Fatherland where it would be 'important for our glorious and cultured Germanic history'. On 22 August, two of Himmler's SS officers arrived at General Dietrich von Cholitz's office demanding that the tapestry be handed over to them from its shelter at the Louvre. Cholitz, commander of the German Armed Forces in Paris, told them that the Louvre was already in the hands of the French Resistance. The SS officers left for Berlin without it.

At the end of the war, in 1945, the tapestry was exhibited in the Louvre for a time, before finally being returned to Bayeux, where it is exhibited today in the Musée de la Tapisserie de Bayeux. Despite its survival, the tapestry has certainly suffered down the years. During the nineteenth century it was displayed on a winding apparatus of two cylinders, which is thought to have caused damage. And it has undergone a total of 518 repairs at different times, including a major restoration in 1842. Not all of the restoration has been done sensitively. Some of it has altered the original and several yards have probably been missing from the end of the tapestry for centuries. Experts believe that the tapestry would originally have shown the Coronation of William rather than the English simply fleeing the battlefield at Hastings as it does today. With debate continuing to rage about the story of the tapestry and the insights into the past that it gives us, the history of the tapestry itself also remains incomplete.

17

THE FRENCH ADMIRAL WHO THWARTED NAPOLEON'S INVASION OF BRITAIN

During the course of the eighteenth and early nineteenth century French leaders seemed to be consumed with a passion for invading Great Britain. In 1744 a large invasion fleet actually sailed before being forced back by bad weather; a detailed plan to land 100,000 troops in 1759, during the Seven Years War, was put on hold; and a huge joint French and Spanish Armada was almost launched against Britain in 1779, during the American War of Independence. None of these plans, however, matched the magnitude of the threat posed during the wars which raged between Britain and France from 1793 to 1815. At the height of British invasion fever between 1803 and 1805 the country was on constant alert, with ordinary folk believing that, at any moment, they might be woken by the sound of French troops marching down the streets outside their homes.

In 1793, four years after the French Revolution began, war broke out between the two nations following the execution of Louis XVI. There was a feeling in France that reformists and disgruntled sectors of society across the British Isles merely had to be roused into action and the old regime would fall. In 1796, with this in mind, the French, under General Hoche, attempted to land an army of 15,000 in Ireland with the idea of supporting a nationalist revolt, to be led by Theobald Wolfe Tone, against their British rulers. Once again, bad weather came to Albion's rescue, forcing the invading French fleet back. In early 1797 there was another small-scale invasion attempt at Fishguard, in Wales, which was foiled with the help of locals, including a woman called Jemima Nicholas who single-handedly rounded up twelve French soldiers with a pitchfork after they had celebrated their victory too soon by getting drunk.

A bigger threat to the realm came as the successful general Napoleon Bonaparte began to assert his power within France. The Royal Navy had certainly not covered itself in glory during the failed French raids and the ambitious Corsican felt that it was possible to land forces on the British mainland. In late 1797 he declared that France 'must destroy the English monarchy, or expect itself to be destroyed by these intriguing and enterprising islanders ... let us concentrate all our efforts on the navy and annihilate England. That done, Europe is at our feet.'

In the same year the French created the 'Army of England' with Napoleon as its commander. It boasted thirty vessels and 50,000 men. But Napoleon, who two years later seized the reins of power in France, realised he would need command of the sea before launching an attack across *La Manche*. At war with Austria and Russia, as well as Britain, he postponed an invasion and instead largely concentrated on land campaigns. In March 1802 the Treaty of Amiens brought a shaky peace between Britain and France and the danger of invasion seemed to have passed. But it was only an interlude. By May 1803 Britain was back at war with France facing an even stronger Napoleon, now determined to invade.

His preparations to do so were at least as impressive as those drawn up by the Germans for Operation Sea Lion, the planned invasion by Hitler's forces in 1940. Napoleon set about assembling a massive army of some 150,000 men at camps in Northern France. All along the Channel coast a huge flotilla of 2,000 barges was built to transport all the men, artillery, horses and supplies that would be needed to overwhelm the British defences. The port of Boulogne, which was extended in order to launch the main body of invasion craft, became the army's headquarters. For almost two years the army was kept on a constant war footing while Napoleon, now Emperor, made repeated visits to inspect his troops. In 1804 he wrote, 'I want only for a favourable wind to plant the Imperial Eagle on the Tower of London.'

In typically confident fashion Napoleon created a medal for the campaign before it happened, and even commissioned a triumphal column in Boulogne celebrating his victory over the British. There was even an idea to use troop-carrying balloons to ferry soldiers across the Channel. English newspapers took the threat from the air very seriously, as well as the possibility that the French might tunnel under the Channel as part of their takeover.

Napoleon planned to land his army at Sheerness and Chatham in Kent, reckoning that, with overwhelming numerical superiority, he would be able to take London within four days. Once there, he believed the English lower orders, long oppressed, would soon rise up in revolution, recognising the French 'not as victors but as brothers'.

From 1803 the British Government were in no doubt about the seriousness of the situation facing them. Fortifications, called Martello Towers, were constructed all along the south coast, while Dover Castle was strengthened. And while there was indeed agitation domestically for reform, the threat from the French actually sparked a wave of loyalist hysteria which saw one in five able-bodied men enlist in the armed forced or local militias. For two years Britain stood on the brink, with invasion panic at fever pitch. Even the king, George III, vowed to take up arms in the event of an invasion, writing that he was 'in daily expectation that Bonaparte will attempt his threatened invasion'. In 1805 waggons were even readied to carry away the gold from the Bank of England in London if the French landed.

A cocky Napoleon had declared, 'The channel is a mere ditch, it will be crossed as soon as someone has the courage to attempt it.' However, he also knew that he had to control it, adding, 'Let us be masters of the Channel for six hours and we are masters of the world.' So Napoleon devised an audacious plan to trick the British navy into leaving the English Channel unprotected. Most of his own navy and that of the Spanish, his ally, were blockaded in their home ports by British ships. But Napoleon's idea was for two squadrons of ships to attempt to break out from Brest, on the French Atlantic coast, and Toulon, in the Mediterranean, and to make for the West Indies, taking the British with them. Once there, Napoleon's ships were to shake off the British, link up and double back to Europe. They would head for the Channel, overwhelm the remaining British naval forces and provide cover for the invasion. It was a highly ambitious scheme, but it came close to working.

The man who would be vital to the successful execution of this plan, and ultimately pivotal in its failure, was Vice Admiral Pierre Villeneuve. In 1805 he was in charge of the French fleet at Toulon and in that spring he did indeed break out of the Mediterranean with eleven ships of the line, linking up with a group of Spanish ships on the way. When he realised what had happened, Vice Admiral Horatio Nelson gave hot pursuit with his fleet. Although failing to link up with the still trapped fleet from Brest as planned, Villeneuve captured some British ships in the Caribbean and was soon heading back towards the Bay of Biscay and the English Channel.

By 22 July Villeneuve's force, now of twenty-two ships of the line, was off Cape Finisterre, on the north-western tip of Spain, when they ran into a British force led by Sir Robert Calder. In fog there was an indecisive clash and Villeneuve was able to retire to the nearby port of Ferrol. He now had an impressive combined Franco-Spanish force at his disposal. There was still time for Villeneuve, with a fleet of twenty-nine ships, to break through the smaller British force blockading Brest in Brittany, link up with the French ships trapped inside the port and bear down on the Channel where they would rendezvous with Napoleon's invasion force. At this point Nelson was still giving chase, but in the middle of the Atlantic. It was the height of summer and conditions were good for a French invasion. There was no time to waste. Yet Villeneuve lingered.

Napoleon wrote to Villeneuve urging, 'Get to sea, lose no time, not a moment and enter the Channel with my united squadrons, England is ours!' But for some reason Villeneuve ignored Napoleon's orders and left port, heading south, taking his fleet to Cadiz, arriving there on 21 August. Hearing what Villeneuve had done Napoleon declared, 'What a Navy ... what an admiral. What sacrifices for nothing!' Once in Cadiz Villeneuve was, as Napoleon predicted, blockaded by the British once again. Napoleon's chance to deceive and crush the Royal Navy had passed. By the start of September Napoleon had called time on his invasion plans, renaming his force the Grand Army and marching them east to fight the Austrians instead.

That October, Villeneuve got wind that the Emperor was to replace him for his failures and hurriedly ordered his fleet to sail, where it was quickly intercepted by Nelson resulting in a full-scale engagement at the Battle of Trafalgar. The Franco-Spanish fleet was destroyed, dealing a fatal blow to Napoleon's naval power and effectively ending the chance of any new invasion plan for the rest of the Napoleonic Wars. Nelson was, of course, killed at the battle and carried back to Britain in a vat of brandy in order to preserve his body. Villeneuve was captured alive and also brought back where, instead of being clamped in irons, he was quartered in The Crown Inn at Bishop's Waltham in Hampshire. In January 1806 Villeneuve was even given leave to be able to attend Nelson's funeral. Perhaps it was not surprising; according to a defeated Napoleon, writing in 1815 after the Battle of Waterloo, the British had reason to be thankful to Villeneuve: 'If Admiral Villeneuve, instead of entering Ferrol, had contented himself with rallying at the Spanish squadron, and had sailed for Brest to join Admiral Gantheaume, my army would have landed; it would have been all over with England.' In early 1806 Villeneuve was set free by the British and allowed to go back to France. On 22 April he was found dead at the Hôtel de la Patrie in Rennes, stabbed six times. The official verdict was suicide but rumours persisted that a vengeful Napoleon had ordered his murder.

18

THE HUMBLE SAILOR WHO SAVED NELSON FOR TRAFALGAR

When news arrived back in Britain that Vice Admiral Horatio Lord Nelson had been killed at the Battle of Trafalgar grown men are said to have wept in the streets. For Nelson was already a famous and much-loved figure by the time a musket shot felled him during his fleet's triumph over the combined French and Spanish navy. Some of the enemy ships were already surrendering when Nelson passed away aboard the HMS *Victory* and the battle, fought off the south-west coast of Spain on 21 October 1805, saw Nelson's fleet achieve a decisive victory. The enemy lost twenty-two out of thirty-three ships, while the British lost none. From that moment, Britannia really could claim to 'rule the waves'.

Despite Nelson's demise during the fray, his place in the history books was firmly established and was only bolstered by the fact that he had heroically died during the battle. Some thirty monuments, including the column in Trafalgar Square, were erected in his honour during the following years. But Nelson was extremely lucky to have been at Trafalgar at all. Before the action he famously sent a signal to his fleet: 'England expects that every man will do his duty.' The message was apposite. It was only because one particular brave soul had already shown his absolute loyalty to Nelson some years earlier, that the great man was actually present on the day for his chance to destroy Napoleon's power at sea.

By 1805 Nelson had become a household name with victories at the Battle of the Nile in 1798 and Copenhagen in 1801. But it was back in 1797, when he was only just establishing his reputation, that an incredible act of heroism saved Nelson's life. Without the actions of humble seaman John Sykes the name of Nelson might today mean nothing to the average Briton.

Nelson in Conflict with a Spanish Launch, 3 July 1797 by Richard Westall, painted in 1806. (National Maritime Museum, Royal Museums Greenwich, www.rmg.co.uk)

Nelson was never a shy or retiring type. After taking part in the American War of Independence, followed by a period of inaction, he was itching to make his mark when hostilities broke out between France and Britain in 1793. By 1795 Nelson reckoned that he had been in '140 fights in two wars'. He had also lost the sight in his right eye during a siege of French forces in Calvi, Corsica, in 1794.

By 1796 the war with France was not going well for Britain. Spain had entered the conflict on the French side and the British had been forced to withdraw from the Mediterranean. The nation was in need of heroes who could raise spirits. On to this stage stepped Nelson. At the Battle of St Vincent, in February 1797, he distinguished himself when, in command of HMS *Captain*, he led boarding parties and captured two ships. He had actually disobeyed orders by directly attacking the Spanish line and the battle had ultimately achieved little, but Nelson's gallantry was awarded with a knighthood and he was promoted to rear admiral.

In May, handed command of the HMS *Theseus*, Nelson was given the job of blockading the Spanish fleet at Cadiz and with mutinies breaking out on some British ships, more stirring deeds were called for. At around 8 p.m. on 3 July, under direction from the fleet's commander-in-chief, Lord St Vincent, Nelson attempted to provoke the Spanish out of their refuge by launching a daring attack. A bomb vessel, the *Thunder*, was towed in close to the harbour walls in order to shell the city. Nelson said, 'I wish to make it a warm night in Cadiz.' Supporting the *Thunder* were a number of other small British craft and Nelson, always wanting to be in the thick of things, joined the attack in a barge.

Inevitably, the Spanish came out in their own group of small boats aiming to force the bomb vessel back and defend their city. It was a moonlit night and the commander of the Spanish boats, Don Miguel Irigoyen, identified Nelson's smaller barge as his target, heading straight for it in the *San Pablo*. As the two boats came alongside there followed a hand-to-hand battle, of which Nelson would say two years later, 'my bravery has never been so conspicuous.' In fact, as Nelson also acknowledged, it had been the courage of his coxswain, Sykes, that was most remarkable that night. As cutlasses were brandished and pistols fired the bloody tussle saw around thirty officers and men on the Spanish barge take on just thirteen British including Nelson. In an account by an eyewitness, told to the *Guiana Chronicle* in 1836, we learn that:

John Sykes was close to Nelson on his left hand and he seemed more concerned for the admiral's life than his own. He hardly ever struck a blow but to save his gallant officer. Twice he parried blows that must be fatal to Nelson for Sykes was a man ... who never knew what fear was any more than his admiral. It was cut, thrust, fire ... the Spaniards fought like devils ...

Twice had Sykes saved him and now he saw a blow descending which would have severed the head of Nelson. In that second of thought which a cool man possesses, Sykes saw that he could not ward the blow with his cutlass ... he saw the danger; that moment expired and Nelson would have been a corpse: but Sykes saved him – he interposed his own head. We all saw it – we were witnesses to the gallant deed and we gave in revenge one cheer and one tremendous rally.

Nelson and his men were victorious, killing eighteen of the Spanish and taking Irigoyen prisoner, though they had been helped by another British barge which attacked the Spanish craft from the other side. Somehow Sykes, though sustaining injuries to his head, shoulders and back, was still alive. Nelson is said to have caught Sykes in his arms vowing, 'I cannot forget this.' For his part, Sykes replied simply, 'Thank god sir you are safe.'

The action achieved little apart from the capture of two boats and 120 prisoners. The full Spanish fleet was not tempted to leave Cadiz. But Nelson was safe to fight another day. He wrote to St Vincent praising Sykes by name and recommended him for promotion. Nelson told how, 'his manners and conduct are so entirely above his station that Nature certainly intended him for a gentleman.' However, Sykes hadn't served long enough to be made up to lieutenant as Nelson wanted. That September, Nelson wrote to Sykes' mother, Hannah Huddlestone, saying, 'Your son John Sykes is now completely recovered from his wounds and is now on board Lord St Vincent's ship the *Ville de Paris*, by whom he will be made a Gunner and, if he is not, before he comes to England I will take care and provide for him.'

Nelson would never forget what Sykes had done, arranging for him to be given a commemorative silver watch and writing of the action in a short sketch of his own life in 1799: 'This was a service hand to hand with swords, in which my coxswain, John Sykes, twice saved my life.' Sadly, by this time, Sykes was already dead. He had been killed aboard the HMS *Andromanche* when, manning a gun, it had exploded in his face on 1 May 1798. Yet the tale about how Sykes had saved the navy's finest asset soon filtered back to England. In fact, Lincolnshire-born Sykes became so famous that, years later, some men fraudulently claimed to be the humble hero.

In the same summer of 1797 there were others who would protect Nelson from harm, not least of whom was his stepson, Josiah Nisbet. Nelson had cultivated his stepson's career, taking him to sea with him as a midshipman, but later became disappointed with his poor performance within the navy and unsuitability for life at sea. Yet on 22 July, at the

Battle of Santa Cruz de Tenerife, an ill-fated amphibious attack on a Spanish port in the Canary Islands, Nisbet's presence proved invaluable. Just 17 years old, but already a lieutenant, he was standing beside Nelson just as their boat came ashore to engage the enemy when his stepfather was shot in the arm. The bullet had severed an artery and blood pumped out of Nelson's shattered limb. Nisbet hurriedly applied a tourniquet in the form of his own silk necktie, no doubt preventing Nelson from bleeding to death. As Nelson grew faint at the sight of all the blood Nisbet also put a hat over the wound. Another bargeman tore off his shirt to make a sling. Then Nisbet ordered the sailors to row Nelson back to HMS *Theseus*, keeping close underneath the fire of the Spanish guns which were strafing the harbour. Nelson managed to climb back onto the *Theseus* and was brought below where he was delivered to surgeon Thomas Eshelby. Nelson was lucky to have such an experienced surgeon tend to him; his arm was successfully amputated, though without any form of anaesthetic. Nelson said later that he owed Nisbet a great debt, though the pair became estranged, not least because of Nelson's infamous affair with Lady Hamilton.

Defeated in the Tenerife battle, which ended up turning into a rout, and now minus his right arm, Nelson sunk into depression, writing mournfully as he returned to England, 'I am become a burden to my friends and useless to my country ... when I leave my command I become dead to the world. I go hence to be no more seen.' Little did Nelson realise that, thanks to the dedication of those who had served under him, his greatest achievements still lay ahead.

19

THE ENGLISH ARMADA OF 1589: SIR FRANCIS DRAKE'S FORGOTTEN FAILURE

In 1588, with the Armada defeated against the odds, the battle against Spain was won, but not yet the war. After seeing surviving Spanish ships scuttle away to circumnavigate England, Scotland and Ireland, scattering vessels and bodies along the way, Sir Francis Drake surveyed his work.

And he was disappointed. Although the Armada's defeat was a cause for celebration, the reality could not be overlooked; many of the Spanish ships and 10,000 men had escaped and could be expected to seek revenge. The subsequent counter-attack by way of an English Armada sent to Spain and Portugal in 1589, in which thirty ships were lost, led to Sir Francis Drake being hauled over the coals; Elizabeth suggested his actions could be treasonable. And for treason, Drake could lose his head. Yet Drake's eventual escape from the axe – and from the disease, battle and pestilence that saw 11,000 men die around him – had all been down to a mission the queen wanted in the first place.

Almost immediately after the remaining Spanish ships had escaped from the English Channel in 1588, the queen's thoughts turned to revenge. Spain, weakened in the water but far from on its knees, needed putting in its place. Whilst the Spanish licked their wounds, tired and demoralised, they might be vulnerable. A quick attack would take advantage of the situation and would be of strategic benefit too; this was the opportunity to help Portugal reclaim its sovereignty from Spain's King Philip II.

Surprisingly Drake, generally the first to take up arms, especially if there was money in it, urged caution. Her majesty should tread carefully, he warned, for the English fleet was in a poor state of repair. The queen's instructions, however, were unambiguous. This mission, led by Drake and his fellow Armada veteran General Sir John Norris, would go ahead. In the event, it would become an unmitigated disaster with the joint commanders lucky to avoid the chopping block.

To show her commitment to this new venture, the normally miserly monarch contributed tens of thousands of pounds, stating the 'first and principal action should be to take and distress the King of Spain's navy and ships where they lay'. If her commanders acted otherwise, they would be 'content to be reputed as traitors'.

The stakes were high. Spain remained a threat. So Elizabeth's plans went further than sinking Spanish ships in port. If Drake could also start an uprising in Portugal, which had accepted Philip as its monarch in 1581, that would help all round. A pretender to the Portuguese throne, Don Antonio, would be waiting and, with Drake and Norris' help, he could defeat Philip and ally with England.

Drake may have wavered initially, but Elizabeth knew she had appointed England's finest commander. In 1587 he had led a notable raid on Cadiz, doing so much damage that Philip had to delay the 1588 Armada's attack on England. His reputation for thrashing Spaniards was unrivalled but the joint military command in 1589 caused a problem. Drake and Norris would soon be arguing fiercely over differing strategic objectives that would hinder the queen's goal. For Drake, destroying Spanish ships would only be part of the job; piracy could be part of the action too. If he captured ships in the Azores before sailing to Lisbon to incite the intended uprising, he could recover losses incurred on earlier ventures.

These treasure-hunting ambitions, though, displeased the queen, for whom destroying Philip's fleet was paramount. She warned, 'Whilst we attempt an uncertainty, we shall lose a certainty, and to seek for a bird in a bush and lose what we have in a cage.' To ensure Drake and Norris were not distracted by a chase for booty, she placed cuckoos in the crow's nest, sending a trio of trusted advisers with the fleet of 150 vessels, 19,000 soldiers and 4,000 sailors. Although they had no operational authority, their very presence rattled Drake and Norris.

To make matters worse, before they sailed in April 1589, court favourite, the dashing Earl of Essex, joined the fleet, attracting the queen's further anger. Not only did she prefer to have Essex around her palaces, she believed the practice of young gentlemen pulling rank to serve whenever and wherever they liked risked military discipline. Essex had disobeyed her orders and Drake and Norris, together with their low-born captain Sir Roger Williams, had contrived in his rebellion. This was an offence so serious an execution was required. Following a series of increasingly agitated messages, Elizabeth wrote to the joint commanders: if they had not hanged Sir Roger already, he was to be kept securely to face his fate later.

If Drake and Norris were irritated at the queen's interference, they were careful enough to keep their misgivings from her. Happily for Sir Roger, Elizabeth, being in London, was far enough away to be ignored safely for the present. The commanders read her ranting call for Sir Roger's head and decided that rather than hang him he would be much more use if they promoted him to a higher rank. And so the adventure continued.

On 20 April, the Armada landed in north-west Spain at Corunna, where Drake and Norris sacked the town, capturing munitions and destroying a galleon in the process. The first notable spat then broke out between them. Corunna's Upper Fort was well manned and adequately armed. The guns could not be taken without risking further English resources. Norris wished to press on to Lisbon right away and although this had some appeal to Drake, whose eye, as ever, was on treasure, it was a fatal mistake. As Elizabeth had feared, the primary mission was compromised by the quest for glory and gold. Hacking 50 miles through unknown terrain in the Iberian heat after weeks at sea proved so arduous that many of the men died. Most suffered disease of one sort or another. Drake and Norris argued again. Should they mount their attack on Lisbon or not – the queen's instructions were not to besiege the city unless 'the party that Don Antonio hath there is great'. As there was no evidence of that, before deciding upon Lisbon, Drake took the opportunity to attack the city of Vigo, capturing grain ships sailing from Poland – a cargo that bagged him £30,000, far less than the cost of the expedition.

In Lisbon, usurper Don Antonio's appeals to rise up and help the English subsequently fell on deaf – and quiet often dead – ears, thousands of his supporters having been hanged or tortured by Philip's second in command, Cardinal-Archduke Albert. The Portuguese part of the expedition proved disastrous, the result of quibbling and the strategic mistake of landing 50 miles from Lisbon and marching to the capital. On 26 May 1589, to Spanish gunfire, English troops began withdrawing from the city, the wounded abandoned to their fate. Two thousand men were killed. Drake and Norris then wantonly defied the queen; with the Portuguese coup dead in the water, they tried to sail to the Azores to recoup their investments by raiding ships, but the weather put paid to that. Drake's ship, *Revenge*, sprang a leak on the way home and almost sank before limping into Plymouth.

The English Armada had mirrored the Spanish attack on England, failing spectacularly. Drake and Norris would now have to answer to Elizabeth at a sitting of the Privy Council. Their major crime, for which Elizabeth had warned at the outset that they would be 'content to be considered traitors', was making not the least attempt to attack Santander or sink the Spanish fleet. Only two-thirds of those English gentlemen who set sail for Spain returned: more than 600 died, including two colonels and thirty captains. Of the men, more than 10,000 perished. Even those who survived didn't have it good. Discovering they wouldn't be fully paid, those who did manage to make it back to England took to the streets to protest. Five hundred descended on Westminster, planning to attack Bartholomew Fair. For this, four men were executed.

Many blamed the penny-pinching queen. She had stumped up insufficient cash. She had appointed Drake, who didn't want to go when told and whose stage was the sea, not land expeditions. Yet Elizabeth had been right about acting swiftly; Drake and Norris' delay hindered rather than helped, and the multiple objectives, caused confusion. Although they had captured 150 guns and destroyed some vessels, the pair had failed in the goal set by their monarch. Like all naval commanders, she lamented, they had 'gone to places more for profit than for service'. In this case, ships at Santander and San Sebastian remained unsunk, and whilst Spain may have been temporarily disabled, Philip II went on to rebuild his navy, providing a base strong enough to prolong the English–Spanish war by seven years.

Outwardly supporting the returning adventurers, Elizabeth was neither surprised by the outcome or the outcry. Norris faced three charges and Drake four, but both escaped with their lives. Drake in particular was one of her favourites. Putting her irritation aside, the queen was graceful. 'We do most thankfully accept of your service and do acknowledge that there hath been as much performed by you as true valour and good conduction could yield,' she proclaimed.

Drake's adventures, though, were over. With most of the blame attributed to him, he was given a land post. He was not to return to sea for five years, and when he did, it was the death of him. Five months into an expedition to intercept treasure on its way from Peru to Spain, he perished, buried at sea in the Caribbean in a lead coffin. In later centuries his reputation escaped the disaster of 1589, Drake becoming remembered as the man who had been so confident of victory in 1588 that he had time to finish a game of bowls.

20

MUD AND THE MYTHS OF AGINCOURT

In Shakespeare's *Henry V* the famed English monarch is the hero of the Battle of Agincourt, rousing English archers to victory against the French despite overwhelming odds. So stirring is the play that during the Second World War it was made into a morale-boosting film starring Laurence Olivier in the title role. What story could be better to show how England, as the plucky underdog, could take on and beat her foes? Few could fail to be inspired by Shakespeare's words when Henry, before the battle, cries, 'We few, we happy few, we band of brothers.'

There is no doubting that, in reality, Henry was a brave, if cruel, sovereign who did win a remarkable victory over the French at Agincourt in 1415. It was an incredible, narrow escape for an army which was hugely outnumbered, exhausted and far from home. But the idea that it was Henry's strategic acumen alone that had won the day at Agincourt is a myth. The fact that his army was able to turn what looked like being inevitable disaster, into a triumph that would inspire generations, owed just as much to luck as the king's magical military touch.

The Battle of Agincourt was part of the Hundred Years War, a protracted tussle between the kings of England and France. Henry V came to the throne two years before the battle, in 1413, already holding a reputation as a tough fighter who, as a teenager, had led an army against the Welsh rebellion of Owain Glyndŵr. At the Battle of Shrewsbury in 1403 he had nearly been killed when an arrow hit him in the face. Now, as king, he was determined to regain England's 'lost territories' in France, such as the Duchy of Normandy, and take the French crown in the bargain. The French were in a weak state, riven by internal strife and led by the sickly King Charles VI, who suffered from bouts of madness.

On 13 August 1415 Henry landed in France with an army of 12,000 men and laid siege to the Norman port of Harfleur, which the king intended to conquer before marching on Paris. Henry had expected to take Harfleur quickly but the siege dragged on for five weeks as the garrison put up stiff resistance behind the town's strong walls. Meanwhile, hundreds of the English troops died from dysentery. By the time Harfleur was taken on 23 September some 2,000 of Henry's force were dead or had been sent home through illness.

With winter closing in, Henry's war council advised returning to England. Henry had other plans. First he challenged Charles VI's son, Louis, to decide the matter in personal combat. When this offer was turned down Henry decided to ditch the idea of advancing into the heart of France and instead justify the huge cost of his invasion by at least making a show of intent. He would march his depleted force across enemy territory to Calais (which was already in English hands), from where they would return home. Henry's army, now numbering 9,000 and with just a week's rations, didn't leave Harfleur until 8 October.

Henry followed the line of the coast and at first made good progress. The French had chosen not to engage Henry in force at Harfleur but now their army shadowed the English. On 13 October Henry made for a crossing over the River Somme at Blanchetaque, but found it blocked by the French force. He took his army inland, trying to find another crossing that wasn't so well defended. Fighting skirmishes and running short of supplies, Henry was now in danger of being cornered. Though he could count on the loyalty of many of his men, who were veterans of old campaigns together, morale was running low. A chaplain with the English army worried that the French would, 'Weaken us by famine and overthrow us, who were so very few and wearied with much fatigue and weak from lack of food.' By chance, Henry found an unguarded crossing upriver and on 18 October managed to slip his army across. The French decided it was time to engage the English before they made their final escape. The site of the battlefield would be near a village called Agincourt, still some 35 miles from Calais.

As dawn broke on the morning of Friday 25th, St Crispin's Day, the English archers lined up their army on a slight rise 1,000yds above and to the south of the French. Henry could muster 1,600 men at arms, who formed up in the middle, and around 7,000 archers massed on either flank behind their long, sharpened wooden stakes. Agincourt was a narrow battlefield with woods on either side and the fighting would be done on newly ploughed fields sodden by overnight rain. Historians disagree as to how heavily outnumbered the English were. It was possibly as much as seven to one, but more probably as little as two to one. Certainly, the odds were heavily in favour of the French. Their army is thought to have had around 15,000 men, which included 10,000 men-at-arms, around 4,000 men with crossbows and a few hundred mounted knights. These were arranged on the battlefield in three lines, with the men-at-arms to the fore. The French nobles were keen to be in the vanguard of the victory they now felt sure would be theirs. The French crossbowmen seem to have been placed at the rear, and to have taken little part in the action that followed.

At 11 a.m. Henry, keen to capitalise on what was left of his army's resolve and impatient that the French still hadn't attacked, ordered his troops to advance. They then stopped and formed up again. Finally the French charged with their horsemen. The initial cavalry attack against the archers was met with a barrage of arrows from Henry's longbowmen, ranged on the flanks behind stakes, and the French were driven back. The mud meant that their horses couldn't gallop properly, and as they retreated, the sodden ground was churned up even more. Next, the French men-at-arms, perhaps 8,000 of them, began to march the few hundred yards towards the English on foot, aiming to engage in hand-to-hand combat. Dressed in armour and equipped with powerful short lances, maces and axes, they must have made a fearsome sight.

However, the mud badly held up the French advance. According to one chronicler, they 'sank up to their knees' in the quagmire in armour that weighed up to 60lb. With the French slowed up by the conditions, the English archers were able to pick them off with their arrows, which could pierce armour at close range. When the exhausted French eventually made it to the static English, a gruesome hand-to-hand contest ensued. Henry V himself was in the thick of the fighting and even had his crown dented by a blow. The narrowness of the battlefield also meant that it became congested – there were so many French knights pouring into the fray that they were barely able to wield their weapons. Soon a rout of the French had turned into a massacre and the dead lay piled several feet thick. The nimble English archers also saw their chance to attack the French at close quarters. As the French men-at-arms stumbled through the gloop the bowmen ran amok with their knives, stabbing through the eyeholes of the French knights' helmets.

Suffering huge losses, the French were soon melting away. The fighting had lasted less than three hours and by early afternoon there was no doubt that the English were the victors. The French had lost at least 5,000 men, including many of the nation's leading noblemen, while only a few hundred English had been killed. After the battle Henry also decided to kill a large number of the prisoners he had taken, contrary to the rules of chivalry. Perhaps he feared that his army could be attacked again and wanted to hurry on to Calais without having to worry about captives. Many French analysts later branded Henry a war criminal.

Even the cocksure Henry must have been amazed to arrive in Calais on 28 October with most of his army still with him. Back home he was hailed a hero and the battle was celebrated with a parade in London on 23 November. It was a turning point for Henry. Now he was not only safe on his own throne but able to push home his advantage in France too. In fact, it would take several years before he did so, eventually marrying Charles VI's daughter, Catherine of Valois, in 1420 and making a treaty that agreed he would succeed Charles as King of France when he died. In the end, though, it was Henry who died first, by two months, and his infant son, Henry VI, was unable to close the deal when it came to securing the French throne. The Hundred Years War still had more than three decades to go.

In the centuries that followed the Battle of Agincourt it was the English archers who got the credit for the victory. Their skills were, indeed, formidable. Each archer was able to fire six arrows a minute with precise accuracy. At the end of the action they supposedly flicked 'V' signs at the retreating French to show that they still had their bow-firing fingers. But the English men-at-arms had been just as important in delivering the knockout blow. Disorganisation in the French ranks had also proved a factor; King Charles VI wasn't there to lead his army and the noblemen in charge appear to have let confusion take hold in their ranks. Perhaps they had been too blasé about winning. They'd even prepared a special painted cart before the battle in which to parade the captured Henry. But it was the mud that may well have been the key factor in the outcome at Agincourt. Had it not been for the boggy ground, the French would have been able to advance on the English much faster and with, perhaps, devastating effect. Henry had gambled and won. And his victory was down to a very English factor – the weather.

21

THE OAK TREE THAT SAVED A MONARCHY

'The crown being put upon his head, a great shout begun, and he came forth to the throne, and there passed more ceremonies.' This was how the diarist Samuel Pepys described the Coronation of Charles II on 23 April 1661. Pepys had squeezed himself into Westminster Abbey to enjoy the occasion and then, after the lavish ceremony was over, got royally drunk celebrating the return of the monarchy.

The Restoration had come after some ten years during which Britain had been a Protectorate, ruled for the most part by Oliver Cromwell. But it was Charles' arrival in London nearly a year before his Coronation that was perhaps most resonant of how close the nation had come to being a republic for good. In May 1660 Charles had returned to England after being invited back to take up the throne. He landed at Dover before marching triumphantly through the capital's streets on 29 May, his birthday. The magnificent procession took some seven hours to pass and thousands of residents and soldiers, many with sprigs of oak in their hats, lined the route. The gesture was fitting, for in 1651 the branches of such a tree had been all that saved the 21-year-old Prince Charles from being captured by Cromwell's forces. Had he been captured he would no doubt have met a similar fate to his father, Charles I, who was executed in 1649 following Parliament's victory in the Civil War.

Interestingly, the Coronation which Pepys had witnessed was actually Prince Charles' second. Following his father's death the young Charles had been living in exile in France but in 1650 he decided to return to the fray, landing in Scotland. In January 1651, he had been crowned that nation's king. A few months later Charles had marched south with an army, hoping the English would also rally to his side in an audacious bid to reclaim the English throne too. But as he arrived in the Midlands it was clear that Charles' call for all men between the ages of 16 and 60 to join his quest had fallen on deaf ears. The country had been wearied by war and Charles' forces, mostly Scottish, were no match for Cromwell's New Model Army. On the 3 September 1651, at the Battle of Worcester, the Roundheads, numbering some 28,000, easily defeated Charles' Royalist force of just 16,000. When it was clear that the battle was lost Charles managed to escape the besieged city with a small band of retainers and fled north.

Over the next six weeks Charles would miraculously evade capture, criss-crossing the country while avoiding Cromwell's men at every turn. He successfully managed to pull off a string of disguises, all the more surprising since he was hard to miss at 6ft tall with the unmistakable gait of an aristocrat. What is more, there was soon a £1,000 bounty on his head with posters around the shires warning the country to be on the alert for any suspicious men who happened to be 'two yards high'.

In the aftermath of the battle at Worcester, Charles and his group had galloped towards the Shropshire/Staffordshire borders, a region with many Catholic families known to be loyal to the Stuart kings, whose own ties to the old religion were only thinly disguised. Charles and his party decided to make for the Boscobel Estate, owned by the Giffard family, arriving in the middle of the night on 4 September with the Parliamentarians in hot pursuit. Charles' group of worthies broke up – it was felt the prince would have a better chance of escape by travelling light. He was left in the care of five brothers called the Pendrells, who were tenants on the estate. That night they hurriedly helped the king change out of his finery and into the clothes of a woodsman. Charles' beard was shaved off, his locks were chopped back and he was eventually found some ill-fitting shoes. Fearful that those hunting him would arrive at any moment, Charles spent the next day hiding in a wood along with one of the brothers, Richard Pendrell, in the rain. At some point Charles decided that he would try and make for the relative safety of Wales, where he had friends. Accompanied by Pendrell he set out to cross the River Severn but was forced back by a suspicious miller and Parliamentarian posts which were guarding the river's bridges. The pair returned to Boscobel House on the morning of 6 September, where they discovered a Colonel Carlis also sheltering. Carlis had been one of those fighting a rearguard action for the Royalists at Worcester. With patrols still hunting the area, Charles and Carlis decide to take to the nearby trees once again. They chose a pollarded oak, which stood on its own, giving them a good view of the surrounding countryside so they could spot any foes approaching.

In 1680 Charles himself described the events of that day to Samuel Pepys:

> We went and carried with us some victuals for the whole day ... bread, cheese, small beer, and nothing else, and got up into a great oak that had been lopped three or four years before, and being grown out again very bushy and thick, could not be seen through, and here we stayed all day. While we were in this tree we saw soldiers going up and down in the thicket of the wood, searching for persons escaped, we seeing them, now and then, peeping out of the wood.

The soldiers eventually moved on and the pair remained undiscovered. But they spent the rest of the day in the tree before deciding to risk taking refuge in the house at nightfall, eating a meal of mutton. Charles then slept in one of the house's cramped priest holes – more used to harbouring those who said illicit masses.

In the coming weeks there were many more narrow escapes. Charles first moved on to Moseley Old Hall where, at one point during his stay, troops arrived to accuse its owner of fighting at the Battle of Worcester, but left without searching the house. Moving on to another great house, Charles then took on the disguise of a servant called William Jackson, accompanying a lady on a visit to her friend in Somerset. The plan was to escape to France via Bristol but, failing to find a boat in the city to take him, Charles and his small party headed towards the south coast.

In the ensuing days Charles found himself in a whole host of bizarre situations, at one point pretending to be half of a runaway couple as he aimed to make a rendezvous in Dorset with a boat bound for France. He was thwarted when the captain of the boat failed to turn up and was subsequently forced to spend the night at an inn full of Roundheads.

Finally, on 15 October, Charles arrived at Shoreham, Sussex, where another boat had been found that would take him across the Channel. The next day, aboard *The Surprise*, Charles landed safely in Fecamp in France, where he was reunited with his mother. Yet in the years that followed, Charles' dream of avenging his father and becoming King of England looked lost forever. The words that had been daubed on Charles I's statue in London's Royal Exchange seemed to sum up his fate: 'The last tyrant of kings died in the first year of liberty of England restored.'

However, when Oliver Cromwell died in 1658, his son Richard proved too weak a character to hold the country together and England soon descended into chaos as Parliament and the army wrestled for power. Samuel Pepys conveyed the contempt in which Parliament was held by this time when he wrote, 'Boys do now cry "Kiss my Parliament!" instead of "Kiss my arse!"'

With the aim of restoring stability, Parliament eventually decided to offer Charles the Crown. The Declaration of Breda would see him agree to a general pardon and, in practice, Charles was also forced to acknowledge the primacy of Parliament in matters of legislation. The pardon was not entirely observed – nine of those responsible for his father's death were eventually hanged. Those that had helped the king escape, including the Pendrells, were given titles and pensions for their efforts.

The story of the oak tree at Boscobel and its part in making the Restoration possible became known even before Charles had set foot back in Kent in 1660. Medallions struck abroad bearing Charles' image often had an oak tree on the reverse side. And, after the Restoration, the oak tree that had enveloped the king became a celebrity in its own right, henceforth known as the Royal Oak. It has long gone, but another, grown from one if its acorns, still stands on the spot. Meanwhile, from 1664, 29 May became known as Oak Apple Day, remaining a public holiday until 1859. Hundreds of pubs around the country also took on the name of the Royal Oak, where no doubt many toasted the king's health and told the astonishing tale of Charles II's arboreal adventure and daring escape to freedom.

22

THE TORTURED LIFE OF THE CROWN JEWELS AND AN UNLIKELY SURVIVOR

In folklore 'bad' King John was the arch-villain in the legend of Robin Hood, the outlaw who stole from the rich to feed the poor. The real King John was certainly bad at holding on to things: in 1215 he was forced to sign away some of his powers by the country's barons in Magna Carta and managed to lose many of his kingdom's overseas territories during his reign. The hapless sovereign, who by some accounts died from a 'surfeit of peaches', also managed to mislay his own Crown Jewels. They were swept away while he and his retinue attempted to cross the Wash in Lincolnshire during a period of civil war. No one is quite sure exactly what treasures were lost that day, but miraculously one piece of the regalia used in the Coronation of English kings and queens appears to have survived. And, in the tortured life history of the Crown Jewels over the next 800 years, this tiny but exquisite treasure would continue to avoid destruction. Today, it is the oldest item in the existing collection.

 During the Coronation of any British monarch there is a part of the ceremony which is considered particularly sacred. In an order of service that dates back to Edward the Confessor, the new sovereign takes the oath before sitting in the ancient King Edward's Chair. Holy oil is then poured from the beak of a golden, eagle-shaped vessel known as the ampulla onto a beautiful spoon. It is with this spoon that the Archbishop of Canterbury anoints the king or queen on the head, hands and heart.

The unique silver-gilt anointing spoon is a wonderful work of art thought to have been made by a London goldsmith. It is beautifully engraved and has a double-lobed oval bowl, perhaps originally designed for the archbishop to dip two fingers into during the anointing. It is believed to have been commissioned for King John's Coronation at Westminster Abbey, as its design is similar to that of a chalice found in the tomb of Archbishop Hubert Walter, who crowned John in 1199. The anointing spoon is listed in a 1349 inventory of the regalia as: 'Item one spoon, ancient form'. Though it is first described in use at the Coronation of James I, it had undoubtedly by then been used many times.

It was the fate of James' son, Charles I, that would pose the first great threat to the Crown Jewels since King John's baggage train mishap in the thirteenth century. By the mid-seventeenth century some of the regalia was kept at the Tower of London while other pieces were housed in Westminster Abbey. When Charles I was executed in 1649 the monks at Westminster Abbey were made to hand over the jewels – many of them part of the Coronation ceremony – which they had been keeping under lock and key during the upheavals of the English Civil War.

As a symbol of a tyrant king, and in a bid to ensure the death of the monarchy was permanent, the victorious Cromwell and the Parliamentarians sought to dispose of all the Crown Jewels as quickly as possible. The new republic also needed cash. A directive of August 1649 ordered that the trustees ensure the jewels were 'totally broken and that they melt down the gold and silver there and to sell the jewels to the best advantage of the Commonwealth'. The king's crowns, orb and sceptre were duly broken up with much of the gold and silver melted down for coinage.

Some items were indeed sold. Almost all of the regalia disappeared, never to be heard of again, except for one small piece. Documents from the time show that the anointing spoon was sold to one of Charles I's staff, Clement Kynnersley, a man who came with the fabulous title of the Yeoman of the Removing Wardrobe to Charles I. This meant that he looked after the sovereign's furnishings. Himself an incredible survivor of the political machinations of the time, Kynnersley paid a paltry 16 shillings for the spoon, reckoned to be the value of its weight, three ounces, on 27 December 1649. With Parliament now in possession of a huge array of the former monarch's belongings, and soon being required to furnish Oliver Cromwell, the Lord Protector, with a wardrobe, it seems that Kynnersley's services in organising the myriad list of goods were retained.

He was clearly a canny sort, for when, in 1660, King Charles II was restored to the throne, Kynnersley kept his job again. What is more, he claimed a reward for being able to return the spoon, the only complete item of the Crown Jewels, apart from three swords, handed back. Charles had the rest of his father's former Crown Jewels – including the gold St Edward's Crown set with 444 gems – remade at the cost of £32,000, then an enormous sum. But the original spoon duly played its part in Charles' 1661 Coronation, and thanks to Kynnersley must have provided a satisfying link to the Coronation of his father in 1626. The spoon was subsequently adorned with four pearls.

It wasn't the last time the Crown Jewels were to suffer ignominy. Even though they were all now kept in the Tower of London for safety, guarded by the famous yeoman warders, there was a bizarre attempt to steal them in 1671. Masterminding the plan was the infamous Irish-born 'Colonel' Thomas Blood, a mysterious figure who was a Parliamentarian and fell out of favour after the Restoration.

As they are today, in those days, as now, visitors were able to view the jewels for a fee. And in the spring of 1671, Blood, dressed as a priest and accompanied by an actress called Jenny Blaine posing as his wife, was able to get the confidence of the official keeper of the jewels, Talbot Edwards. Blaine faked a fainting fit, and Edwards helped 'revive' her. Blood returned a few days later to deliver a thank you gift of some gloves to Edwards' wife, and then established a friendship with the keeper, gaining an extensive tour of the Tower and even convincing Edwards to sell him his pistols. Blood also said he would introduce his nephew to Edwards' daughter with the prospect of marriage.

On 6 May 1671, Blood, the 'nephew' and two other accomplices arrived for the proposed meeting. Blood suggested that his party be shown the jewels first and, when Edwards' back was turned to open the Jewel House lock, the keeper was clubbed over the head then gagged. Blood grabbed St Edward's Crown and started hitting it with a mallet until it was flat enough to go under his clergyman's cassock. Another of Blood's gang shoved the Royal Orb down his trousers while the 'nephew' started sawing the sceptre in half in order to conceal it. But the robbers were thwarted when Edwards' son, a soldier, suddenly turned up and, along with others, pursued the fleeing Blood and his accomplices. Weighed down with his treasure Blood was soon apprehended.

Curiously, Blood was only kept in the Tower for a few weeks and then, after being questioned by the king himself, released. In fact Blood was not only pardoned for the crime, but also given a pension, which has led to a number of conspiracy theories surrounding the plot. Blood's escape from a harsher sentence may simply have been down to his 'gift of the gab' or, just possibly, because a cash-strapped Charles II had conspired to use him as his own agent to steal and sell the jewels for funds. At his cross-examination Charles is said to have asked Blood, tellingly, 'What if I should give you your life?' with the Colonel replying, 'I would endeavour to deserve it, Sire!' It is believed that from then on Blood carried out some of the Crown's less wholesome work. Meanwhile, the Crown Jewels were repaired and placed back in the Tower.

In 1841 a huge fire, which could be seen from miles around, nearly destroyed the entire collection of jewels. At this time the regalia were housed in the Martin Tower, part of the Tower of London complex, next to a huge armoury containing a vast array of firearms, cannons and gunpowder. It appears that the blaze began because of an overheated stove near the Bowyer Tower and quickly spread to the armoury where it began to rage out of control, threatening the jewels. Their survival was down to a quick-thinking policeman. With no one able to find the key to the case holding the jewels, he ran in and wrenched the bars apart with a crowbar. Though the fire was bearing down on the building, he then began bundling out the jewels to soldiers and warders who had come to his aid. *The Times* reported: 'A most extraordinary scene presented itself, the warders carrying crowns, sceptres and other valuables of royalty, between groups of soldiers, police, firemen ... to the Governor's residence.' Even though the Tower of London had its own fire engines, the armoury and several other parts of the site were left in ruins. Yet, when the Crown Jewels were inspected, they were found to be totally undamaged.

When the Second World War broke out a new threat emerged; German bombs falling dangerously close to Wakefield Tower, another part of the Tower of London complex, where the jewels were now kept. They were taken out, placed in padded boxes and moved from the Tower of London to a secret location, probably Windsor Castle.

Eight years after the war ended, they were on show again, this time at the Coronation of Elizabeth II. And at the appropriate part of the ceremony in Westminster Abbey, just as in King John's time, that same twelfth-century spoon was used to anoint the queen. The oil itself, made from oils of orange, rose, cinnamon, musk and ambergris, had to be recreated using an old recipe – a bomb had hit the Deanery containing the original phial of oil in May 1941. And if you were watching on television, you wouldn't have seen the anointing, as that part of the ceremony was considered so sacred that it took part under a canopy, away from the cameras.

23

THE LETTER THAT FOILED THE GUNPOWDER PLOT

The prosecutor described it as the 'Powder Treason', an audacious attempt by religious zealots to kill the Protestant king, wipe out Parliament and restore England to Catholicism. Celebrated in the UK every 5 November, the story of how Guy Fawkes failed to blow up the government is well known. But were it not for the help of Catholic-turned-Protestant Baron Monteagle, King James may not have had his narrow escape.

Had the 1605 plot succeeded, a return to popery would have been a real possibility in a country where many still hankered for the rule of Rome. The seed had been sown with Queen Elizabeth's death. When James, the Scottish king with the Catholic ancestry, ascended to the English throne on 24 March 1603, Catholics rejoiced. Sir Thomas Tresham, a Catholic who had spent twenty years in prison for not recognising Protestantism, made the proclamation in Northampton, an excellent opportunity, he believed, to show papist loyalty to the king. Around the country came renewed hope for religious tolerance.

However, two years after James' accession, Catholics remained dissatisfied. After all, James' own wife, the queen, Anne of Denmark, was a Catholic, assuring Pope Clement VIII that she was committed to Rome, even though she had married Protestant James. Catholics expected more from James. Yet his very first act when travelling from Scotland to London to take his new crown promised little: releasing prisoners in celebration along the way, James drew the line at murderers, traitors and papists. But he was a pragmatic politician too, aware that his future success, not least in the marital home, depended on a degree of religious toleration. Many recusant fines were rescinded or reduced. And, in general, people celebrating Mass in private were no longer hunted down.

Such minor advancements were insufficient for Catholic funda-mentalists, some of whom now spoke of tyrannicide – the killing of a tyrant for the greater good. When a Jesuit pamphlet called upon, 'anyone who is inclined to heed the prayers of the people' to kill the sovereign, Robert Catesby, a crusader willing to use the sword to protect the spiritual values he held dear, took note. But care was needed. Treason, even in the Catholic cause, didn't go down well with the Pope, who believed diplomacy was necessary if the faith was to be restored to England. Father George Blackwell, the Roman Catholic archpriest in England, forbade plots against the Crown.

Guy Fawkes, fresh from fighting as a mercenary for Spain in Flanders, knew little of Blackwell's edicts or the Pope's disapproval and joined the regicidal plan with Catesby and friends such as Thomas Percy and Francis Tresham, and brothers Thomas and Robert Wintour. After plotting for more than a year, Catesby drew more people into the circle, so it was not altogether surprising that it came to the attention of William Parker, the Fourth Baron Monteagle. In a complex web of family connections, Monteagle was married to Sir Thomas Tresham's daughter, Elizabeth, who was Catesby's cousin. Tresham, the man who had proclaimed James as king in Northampton, was in turn father to Robert and Francis Tresham, one of whom was much loved by Tom Wintour, a fellow conspirator. And that was the simple bit. Everyone knew everyone else. People talked.

The plan gathered steam when the plotters agreed to lease the cellars of a house in Westminster on the first day of 1605 (which at that time was 25 March), so they could execute their plan early in the new year – although Parliament was then delayed by plague. The owner of the house, John Whynniard, Keeper of the King's Wardrobe, had used the cellar as a storeroom, making it the perfect hiding place for material that no one would bother looking for. Acquiring sufficient gunpowder to take out Parliament and all within, the conspirators hid thirty-six barrels of explosives. When the government assembled on 5 November 1605, the king would die.

With the family connections, the fact that Lord Monteagle, as a peer, would be killed too troubled Catesby. But as his relationship with Monteagle was somewhat distant, he reconciled himself to murdering him anyway. Besides, Monteagle's ambivalent attitude to his faith – he had switched between Protestantism and Catholicism as the need suited – rendered him untrustworthy. In order to progress in the Jacobean court, Monteagle, Catholic at the time, wrote to the king announcing his conversion to Protestantism. This paved the way for him to become a baron through his mother's line and, even though his father, Lord Morley, was still alive, giving him a seat in Parliament. After previously being imprisoned for taking part in an uprising against Queen Elizabeth, this was the culmination of a marvelous reversal of fortune. So when, on Saturday 26 October, Monteagle received a disturbing letter, he knew what he must do.

William Parker, the Fourth Baron Monteagle, received a tip-off about the Powder Plot. (Portrait by John de Critz c. 1615. Courtesy of The Berger Collection at the Denver Art Museum)

The authorship of this letter remains in doubt (some think it was penned by Monteagle himself). Badly written and vague, the writer clearly knew something was afoot but either did not know, or chose not to reveal, exactly what. Delivered under the cover of darkness to Lord Monteagle's servant, Thomas Ward, who was accosted in the street, the contents were explosive:

> My Lord, out of the love I bear to some of your friends, I have a care of your preservation. Therefore I would advise you, as you tender your life, to devise some excuse to shift your attendance at this Parliament; for God and man hath concurred to punish the wickedness of this time. And think not slightly of this advertisement, but retire yourself into the country where you may expect the event in safety.

Despite the late hour, the young, ambitious peer, finding himself with something that could propel his prospects in the Jacobean court, headed to the home of Lord Salisbury. Salisbury, who had played a key role in the smooth transition that brought James to the English throne, had been warning of the duplicity of papists for most of his life and had no doubt about the letter's implications. With the king hunting in Royston, Salisbury would give the plot sufficient time to ripen.

Word about the tip-off quickly leaked. Monteagle's servant, the aforementioned Thomas Ward, with strong Catholic connections of his own, sent a message to Catesby who, preferring sport over politics, had been trying to engineer a trip to Royston to go hunting with the king. But the news that there was a traitor among the traitors was more important than an afternoon spent with the monarch he planned to murder. It was not, however, sufficiently alarming to call off the plot. The letter, thought Catesby, was too vague to pose a threat. Planning continued regardless, so that by the Wednesday, four days after the letter fell into Monteagle's hands, Guy Fawkes was in the cellar under the House of Lords, walking through the plans for the bombing.

On Friday 1 November, the king at last gained sight of the anonymous letter, absorbing its contents twice and pondering on one phrase: 'the danger is passed as soon as you have burnt the letter.' The famously cerebral monarch, experienced in the arts of conspiracy, concluded that something to do with powder was set to kill him. The Lord Chamberlain was ordered to search 'both above and below' Parliament although, showing no great urgency, he did not commence his checks until Monday

4 November, accompanied by Lord Monteagle. There, in the leased cellar, they came across an implausible amount of firewood.

This was the property of John Whynniard's new tenant, Thomas Percy, a Catholic who was known not to live in Westminster and who would therefore need little firewood. This was inadequate evidence for the king. Vowing to attend Parliament on 5 November unless something more substantial turned up, he ordered a second search. Towards midnight that same evening, Guy Fawkes was found in the cellar, getting ready to time his deadly fuse. He was, he told his captors, just a servant to Thomas Percy. A spot of torture, 'starting with the gentlest' at the king's behest, was required before the plot unravelled. It didn't take long.

Learning of Fawkes' capture, the plotters fled to their respective counties, delusional Catesby heading for the Midlands to encourage a Catholic uprising. In London people celebrated the narrow escape by lighting bonfires. Once the rack loosened Fawkes' tongue, it took just days for the plotters to be rounded up with some, including Fawkes, executed and Catesby shot by pursuers, although his body was later exhumed to be decapitated.

Lord Monteagle did well out of the Powder Treason. An affectionate letter he had written to Catesby just weeks before, containing words such as 'warmth, heat and fire' – suggesting that perhaps he understood the themes important in his friend's life at that time – was deemed insufficient to implicate him. Distancing himself from the plotters to whom he was related or counted among his friends, he received land worth £200 and £500 a year in cash. Playwright Ben Jonson called him 'saviour of my country'. Today Monteagle is forgotten. But as he mounted the scaffold to be hanged, drawn and quartered, Guy Fawkes' place in history was assured.

24

THE BRITISH REVOLUTION OF 1832

As the British Prime Minister Lord Liverpool and his Cabinet sat down to dinner on 23 February 1820, at the home of Lord Harrowby in London's Grosvenor Square, a gang armed with swords and pistols burst in and killed those attending. One of the gang, a former butcher called James Ings, then cut off the heads of two of the most prominent Cabinet members, put them on spikes and paraded them on Westminster Bridge for all to see.

This was, at least, the scenario envisaged by those involved in the Cato Street Conspiracy, an attempt to overthrow the government just as real as the Gunpowder Plot of 1605. Led by a disgruntled former farmer and soldier, Arthur Thistlewood, the conspirators were a group who advocated common ownership of land and had already taken part in an assault on the Tower of London in 1816. Now they intended to do away with the government in one dramatic act, hoping to ignite a popular revolution akin to that which had swept the ruling classes from power in France thirty years before. The plot was foiled by a double agent working in their midst, and on 1 May 1820, Thistlewood and four others were hanged for treason.

Though the conspirators were extremists with little wider support, the episode was symptomatic of an unease gripping the country. After the Napoleonic Wars ended in 1815 there was a rise in agitation against the status quo. Reform movements mushroomed, radical literature proliferated and the people, be they textile workers in Huddersfield or weavers in Glasgow, showed that they were prepared to rise up – violently if need be – to protest against bad conditions, just as the government showed that it was prepared to put down unrest with force. The most dramatic example of this repression was the so-called Peterloo Massacre. On 16 August 1819, at a meeting of 60,000 people in Manchester demanding parliamentary reform, cavalry were ordered to disperse the crowd. Fifteen people died and hundreds were injured.

However, it wasn't until there was a severe economic downturn in the early 1830s and another revolution in France that growing demands for political reform were transformed into a massive upheaval across Britain that threatened to turn ugly. It's often said that the English are not a revolutionary people. Yet by the time of the crisis which gripped the nation between 1830–32, the country had already fought at least one bloody civil war and executed a king. And many of those that lived through the ferment of the early nineteenth century, on all sides of opinion, believed that a British revolution, even a bloody one, could be on the cards.

By the 1830s the problem of political representation had become acute. The make-up of the House of Commons had failed to move with the times. Only a few people had the vote and the new industrialised cities and burgeoning middle class lacked a voice. Meanwhile, an increasingly radical working class sought representation in a bid to improve their lot. Importantly, adept political unions between the middle and working classes had emerged, giving organisation and leadership to the discontent.

The inadequacies of the old system were embodied by the famous rotten boroughs, places like Old Sarum, ancient constituencies where there were few electors and members were largely returned unopposed. Elections were held without a secret ballot and bribery, patronage and coercion were rife. Most Members of Parliament belonged to either the conservative Tory grouping or the more liberal Whig party, but both essentially represented the gentry. If this small elite did not give ground, events were bound to boil over.

The clamour for reform was focussed by the July 1830 revolution in France, which had swept away the new monarchy with little bloodshed. A failed harvest had made Britain restless too and agricultural riots sprang up across southern England. The Duke of Wellington, prime minister from 1828, might have been a national hero for his victory over Napoleon at Waterloo, but he was no man for the fevered atmosphere which now threatened to engulf the country. Already bamboozled by events that had seen him give Catholics the right to sit in Parliament in 1829 he was equally perplexed by the need to make any political reform, saying, 'The people of England are very quiet if left alone,' and if they weren't, 'there is a way to make them'. Then, in the autumn, Wellington shocked even other Tories with his *naïveté* by declaring that the existing parliamentary system had the 'full and entire confidence of the country'. In November 1830 he was forced to step aside.

The task of avoiding revolution by offering the country a degree of parliamentary reform now fell to the new prime minister, Lord Grey. Grey believed in the superiority of the aristocracy but understood that reform was now necessary if a revolution was to be avoided. He had to act quickly – a month after he came to power 10,000 skilled workmen marched on London's St James's Palace holding the French Tricolor. A limited reform bill was duly introduced in early 1831 but ran aground in the Commons. Grey called an election and with an increased majority got a new reform bill through. But then, in October, it was blocked by the Lords.

Over the next six months the country was in danger of sliding into chaos. In Bristol rioters seized the city, burning down buildings. The uprising was put down by soldiers and twelve people died, with five executed. Nottingham Castle was attacked and there was bad violence in Derby, Worcester and Bath. Elsewhere, angry demonstrations were held with some of the political unions put on a war footing. Contemporary observers were convinced that the country was about to go the way of France. Princess Lieven, wife of the Russian ambassador, wrote home, 'We too in England, are just on the brink of a revolution.' Without a proper police force outside London, or an army mobile or strong enough to quell widespread resistance, mass revolt might, indeed, be unstoppable.

Grey and the Whigs hurriedly brought forward a third, slightly amended reform bill and the question of creating new peers arose if the Lords did not agree this time. But when, in the spring of 1832, the Lords again rejected the bill Grey resigned. The country was now on a knife edge. There were huge demonstrations across the country; a 'Gathering of the Unions' in Birmingham attracted 100,000 people. The period became known as 'The Days of May', and one MP, Edward Littleton, thought Britain 'in a state little short of insurrection'.

After Grey's departure, the king, William IV, who had been obstructive throughout, asked Wellington to form a government, hoping the duke could pass a more limited bill. There was outrage. Leading London activist Francis Place called for a run on the banks. The Iron Duke, as he was nicknamed, was now a symbol of the old guard and was forced to put up iron shutters on the windows of his home when it was attacked by an angry mob. Thankfully, for the sake of peace, Wellington couldn't form an administration and Grey was recalled. The king was now forced to give Grey what he wanted: the threat to create a raft of new pro-reform Whig peers in the Lords if the bill were not now passed. Finally, seeing that the writing was on the wall, the Lords passed the bill on 4 June 1832. The king grudgingly gave his assent three days later, though pointedly refused to do so in person at Parliament as requested.

The actual terms of the Great Reform Act, as it became known, were modest. The rotten boroughs were abolished, new cities had more representation and the franchise was widened. But a property test meant that it was only the middle class who got the vote, with just one in seven adult males able to cast a ballot. It didn't stop a sulky Wellington, on seeing a wave of new MPs elected under the changed rules, saying, 'I never saw so many shocking bad hats in my life.'

The crisis had passed, but it had been a close shave. Reform Act historian E.P. Thompson wrote, 'In the autumn of 1831 and in the "Days of May" Britain was within an ace of revolution.' In fact, by the end of the crisis in 1832, given the sea change which had occurred in public life, a revolution of sorts had indeed happened. It wasn't so much what the act said, as the example it had set. While Grey had hoped that a reform bill would be the final word on constitutional change, it definitely wasn't. And the establishment had been badly shaken. Even two years after the bill had passed, Queen Adelaide, husband of William IV, was still under the fixed impression that, 'an English revolution is rapidly approaching, and that her own fate is to be that of Marie Antoinette'.

The 'revolutionary' baton was soon picked up by others. Chief among them was the more working-class Chartist movement. Their demands, published in 1838, seemed, at the time, outlandish. They included the vote for all men over 21, a secret ballot and payment for MPs. The movement reached a peak in 1848 when perhaps 150,000 people assembled on London's Kennington Common on 10 April with the aim of marching on Parliament armed with a petition containing millions of signatures demanding change. This was a year when revolutions again swept much of Europe and, despite the Chartists' leaders promise that the meeting would be peaceful, the British Government took no chances. Cavalry, with an 80-year-old Wellington in charge, were readied to prevent the Chartists crossing the River Thames. Cannons were brought up outside Buckingham Palace. The authorities needn't have bothered. By 2 p.m. heavy rain meant most of the crowds had drifted away. Yet the Chartists had made an impact – today most of their demands have become political reality.

25

HOW QUEEN VICTORIA WAS ALMOST POTTY KING ERNEST

When insane teenager Edward Oxford fired on the monarch's carriage as she travelled along Constitution Hill on 10 June, 1840, becoming the first of eight would-be assassins of Queen Victoria, he made the critical mistake of missing and then not escaping. Had he succeeded with his attempt – in the eyes of the court – to 'maliciously and traitorously ... shoot, assassinate and put to death our said Lady the Queen', the pregnant Victoria would probably have died childless. Into her place would have stepped the Duke of Cumberland, Prince Ernest, and the future course of history would have been very different, with the constitutional monarchy in Britain perhaps unlikely to survive for long.

Ernest, the scheming, philandering, probably incestuous and, it was widely assumed, murderous son of the much missed mad King George III, had long held designs on the throne. With two previous hiccups in the accession process – both George IV and William IV having failed to sire the requisite legitimate children – and teenage Princess Victoria seriously ill, possibly dying, of typhoid fever in 1835, Ernest had believed he could see his way to becoming monarch. But he was to be disappointed. Unlike her future husband, who was to die of the same disease, Victoria recovered and looked forward to a long life ahead of her. Not for the last time, Ernest was not to get his own way.

Even though at birth he was just fifth in line to the throne, Ernest's elder brothers died one by one, leaving him a step-but-one away from the Crown. Dropsical and drunken, William IV had fathered ten children by comic actress Dorethea Jordan, all of them illegitimate and therefore unable to inherit. So when the sole legitimate child of George IV, Princess Charlotte, died in 1817, only Victoria, the legitimate daughter of his dead brother, Edward, blocked Ernest's path to the throne.

Tall, sporty, but with bad eyesight, Ernest had spent much of his life in a manner befitting a gentleman with little to do but fornicate, gamble and interfere in politics. His strong opinions on the Irish 'problem', Catholics, immigration and the place of women in society bordered on the boorish. Ernest was subject to wagging tongues about whatever he did.

For instance, there was the child, possibly incestuously conceived at Weymouth after he had become a little too intimate with his sister, Princess Sophia. Escaping to the Continent to pursue his military career and forget about the whole business enabled him to strut about in 2ft-high white plume feathers as a colonel of the 15th Hussars. This, he found, was as British as one could get; the perfect opportunity to enforce his standards on others. Everyone, he decreed, should henceforth wear a moustache; dissenters would be flogged. For more serious misdeeds, he had men 'picketed', a form of torture used in the Spanish Inquisition.

If that was insufficient to define his character, back in London he was then caught in his bedroom with a naked, dead Sardinian servant, an incident that was to lead to exile. The dead man, Ernest's valet Joseph Sellis, had, according to Ernest at least, attempted to assassinate him as he slept. Woken by blows about the head, the duke fortuitously managed to turn Sellis' weapon upon himself, cutting his throat. Bearing six knife wounds himself – one serious enough for him to travel by sedan chair to a physician – Ernest found himself embroiled in another scandal. Although the duke had enjoyed 'a most providential escape', according to the surgeon, the royals were baffled, Princess Elizabeth writing: 'After a servant has lived with one fourteen years, how would one suppose him such a premeditated villain?' A jury returned a verdict of suicide. Whilst, at first the London newspapers had been sympathetic towards Ernest, the satirical press was more sceptical, running reports of midnight orgies and sodomy at the palace. Ernest decided the commotion was best watched from the Continent, where he remained for years.

During this self-imposed exile, love intervened when he met the married Frederica, Princess of Solms; but only once a respectable year had passed after the unexpected death of her prince, in 1814, could Ernest wed. With a royal bride, he returned to London, not least to claim his increased married prince allowance. However, his reputation went before him. The queen, declaring Frederica a wanton woman, refused to receive her at court. Parliament rubbed salt in the wounds, declining to increase the duke's allowance. Yet for all his faults, Ernest's marriage lasted.

Away from his family and career, Ernest's ultra-Protestant excesses began to occupy him all the more. Furious about concessions to the Irish, and determined to push the Protestant cause and stop the revolutionary Reform Bill going through Parliament, Ernest secretly campaigned to establish Orange lodges, of which he was Imperial Grand Master, throughout Ireland, Britain and the colonies. Although later claiming to have no knowledge of any lodge in any regiment, privately his beliefs were clear: Orangemen must save the Empire from Catholicism. Sending his friend, Lieutenant-Colonel William Blennerhassett Fairman, to 'strike the foe with awe', the campaign was angry, blinkered and incendiary. In 1832 a pamphlet, 'The Orange Exposure', called openly for members to 'depose the present monarch', William IV. Ernest, not the king, was becoming the figurehead for Anglicanism in England. The very thought bordered on treason. Yet 'If any row took place,' Fairman said, members 'would rally round the Duke of Cumberland'. *The Sunday News*, on 16 August 1835, suggested that Lodges were 'armed, organised and presided over by a Prince of the Blood ... near the Throne'.

Although his card was marked, Ernest began a whispering campaign. William, he suggested, was unfit to continue as king. The family affliction, madness, had taken hold. There was some justification for Ernest's intimations. The Duke of Wellington reportedly suggested that William had been confined to a straitjacket and his speeches had become incoherent rants. 'Some people think already about who will be Regent if this sad state continues,' the Duchess de Dino, companion to the French ambassador, reflected. As Victoria was still a child, Ernest was the only contender. Then came the news that Victoria was ill with typhoid fever. For five weeks she slipped in and out of consciousness, her long hair cut to the scalp to allow heat to escape.

Wellington worried. If Ernest gained the Crown, the country could be forced into civil war. With Victoria still ill, he confided his fears to his niece, Lady Burghersh: 'Among other evils with which this country is threatened is the loss of Princess Victoria.' Soon enough people in positions of power were so disquieted by the thought of a country headed by King Ernest, a man not showing the 'brotherly or filial' support befitting of a prince, that he was accused in the House of Commons of promoting treason. The Orange lodges that Ernest had encouraged may not be quite 'a conspiracy to alter the succession', Joseph Hume MP told the House, but Ernest was a 'dangerous man' with 'the power of assembling a body of 300,000 men'. What else could this be if not treason?

In the Lords, where Ernest, sat as a peer, had the privilege of speaking, he complained of being, 'abused, accused and treated in the most cruel manners that ever a human being was treated'. Some people believed that if the allegations of a plot against Victoria were true, he ought to be tried in the House of Lords for high treason. He would shed his last drop of blood for his niece, he claimed, unconvincingly.

Ernest survived the inquiry, and no uprising in his name emerged. There wasn't much of his reputation left to tarnish, but he remained next in line to the throne after Princess Victoria. She survived her illness to become queen in 1837, reigning for sixty-three years and giving her name to a whole era. In the same year Ernest became a king, but not of England: he succeeded as Ernest Augustus I of Hanover. His first act as sovereign was to abolish the constitution.

26

HOW THE FIRST VICTORIA CROSS WAS WON

For most people the abiding image of the Crimean War is the romantic, though disastrous, Charge of the Light Brigade, captured in the popular poem by Alfred Lord Tennyson. The action was part of the conflict between Russia and the allied armies of Britain and France, along with Sardinia and Turkey, which was fought out between 1853 and 1856 largely in the theatre of the Crimean Peninsula which protrudes into the Black Sea.

At the time the conflagration was not known as the the Crimean War, but more widely as the Russian War, and with good reason; one of the very first campaigns of the war – an important one – was fought not in Crimea, but more than 1,000 miles away in the Baltic Sea. And it was here that an act of incredible bravery during one of the campaign's naval battles helped create Britain's highest military decoration for valour in the face of the enemy. Charles Davis Lucas may not, today, be one of the household names associated with the war, like the nurse Florence Nightingale for example, but this forgotten hero's quick thinking not only narrowly saved his ship and its crew from disaster but also helped forge the Victoria Cross. His courage on a bright June evening in 1854 played a big part in the growing clamour for such a medal. A few months later, when Parliament was considering a new medal for bravery, it was Lucas' tremendous act of courage that was chosen as the first to be recognised. The Victoria Cross, officially instituted in January 1856, has since been awarded to 1,354 recipients throughout a string of conflicts across the world. But the story of the first man to win a VC remains one of the most remarkable tales linked to the honour.

Lucas was born in 1834 near Poyntzpass, County Armagh, in Ireland, into a wealthy landowning family with a military heritage. Aged just 13 he joined the Royal Navy, serving first aboard the HMS *Vengeance* and then HMS *Fox*, seeing action in the Second Anglo-Burmese War of 1852–53, winning the Indian Medal and rising to become a midshipman.

By early 1854 the great powers were limbering up for war, as they tussled over the fate of the fading Ottoman Empire. On 19 February Lucas was aboard the HMS *Hecla*, a six-gun steam paddle sloop, as it left Hull for the Baltic, to reconnoitre anchorages for an Anglo-French fleet. The British force was the largest assembled since Napoleonic times. Led by Sir Charles Napier, it embarked on 11 March, tasked with either defeating or blockading the Russian Baltic fleet, stationed near St Petersburg. This would have the added benefit of diverting resources away from the southern theatres of war, including the Crimea.

By June 21, as part of the naval campaign, the *Hecla*, along with the larger sixteen-gun *Odin* and *Valorous*, was attacking the large and important fortress of Bomarsund in the Åland Islands, which guarded the Gulf of Bothnia. The Russian fortress was heavily defended with around eighty guns and for some four hours the battle raged as the ships, and the fort's batteries exchanged fire. Bravely, some later said recklessly, the *Hecla*'s captain, William Hutcheon Hall, closed in on the fortress, manoeuvring his wooden ship within just 500yds of the fort. Then, in the thick of the fight, one of the shells raining down around the ship landed on the upper deck with the fuse still alight.The crew were immediately ordered to throw themselves flat on the deck. But, ignoring orders and to the astonishment of his crewmates, Lucas got up and swiftly ran towards the shell, grabbing it with his bare hands. Rushing to the side of the ship he tossed it as far as he could towards the frothing sea below where, moments later, it exploded before even having time to hit the water. No one was badly hurt and the ship suffered only minor damage.

Lucas had saved the ship and countless lives in the bargain. A grateful captain, who himself had been injured by a musket ball in an earlier Baltic skirmish, promoted Lucas to the rank of acting lieutenant on the spot. Before the Victoria Cross this was the only way acts of supreme valour from those of the lower ranks like Lucas' could be recognised. The very next day Captain Hall wrote to Sir Charles Napier:

> With regard to Mr. Lucas, I have the pleasure to report a remarkable instance of coolness and presence of mind in action, he having taken up, and thrown overboard, a live shell thrown on board the 'Hecla' by the enemy, while the fuse was burning.

Hall was convinced that Lucas had 'saved dozens of lives if not the entire ship's company'. Napier forwarded the request to the Admiralty and the promotion was duly confirmed.

Though ultimately indecisive, the action at Bomarsund in which the *Hecla* took part was useful in preparing a second attack in August

Charles Lucas, the first person to win a Victoria Cross.
(Courtesy of The Victoria Cross Society)

of the same year, which saw the fort finally surrender. Just months later, in December 1854, Lucas' bravery and similar acts led Captain Thomas Scobell MP to put a motion in front of the House of Commons to create 'an order of merit to persons serving in the army or navy for distinguished and prominent personal gallantry to which every grade should be admissible'. Backed by Prince Albert, who suggested the name of the subsequent medal, the Victoria Cross was officially instituted in 1856. The medals would be made out of bronze taken from Russian cannons captured in the Crimea.

Though Lucas was the first to be awarded the Victoria Cross he wasn't the first to physically receive his honour. In fact, he had to wait three years. At a ceremony held in Hyde Park on 26 June 1857, Queen Victoria pinned the medal, with its blue ribbon, on his chest. Some sixty-two VCs were handed out that day, and because they were done so in order of rank, Lucas was the fourth to be presented with his medal. Chronologically, however, his had been the first act of bravery awarded. The official citation read:

> At the height of the action a live shell landed on Hecla's upper deck, with its fuse still hissing. All hands were ordered to fling themselves flat on the deck, but Mr. Lucas with great presence of mind ran forward and hurled the shell into the sea, where it exploded with a tremendous roar before it hit the water. Thanks to Mr. Lucas's action no one was killed or seriously wounded.

Four other Victoria Crosses were eventually awarded for bravery in the Baltic theatre during the Crimean War. While the lack of a decisive sea battle was criticised domestically during the war, historians have since regarded Napier's fleet as having helped the allied forces win. The threat it posed to Russia's 'back door' meant thousands of troops and ships were tied down in the north while Russia's imports were strangled by the blockade.

Lucas himself would go on to serve on a string of ships and was promoted first to commander in 1862, captain in 1867 and, finally, after retiring in 1873, rear admiral. Sadly, Lucas later lost his VC on a train and it was never recovered. In 1878, his old captain, William Hall, summoned him to his deathbed where he had a special request for Lucas – to look after his wife, Hilare, and his only daughter, Frances. In 1879 Lucas married Frances and the pair went on to have three daughters together. Lucas lived out his days in leafy Kent, near Tunbridge Wells, dying in 1914 at the grand old age of 80 – just days after the First World War broke out.

27

THE LAST MAN OUT OF KABUL

Just after noon on 13 January 1842 a sentry gazed out from the mud walls of the fortress at Jalalabad when he suddenly spotted a dishevelled figure bent double over a pony making painfully slow progress towards the gate. As the rider gradually came closer, it was clear to Private Edward Teer that this was a fellow British soldier, though one barely able to cling on to the wounded nag beneath him. He was sporting just one boot and a uniform that had been torn to shreds.

Jalalabad was, at this time, a remote British outpost on the western side of the famous Khyber Pass, along the famous route between India's North-West Frontier and Afghanistan. But a British army, known to be marching the 90 miles back to the city from Kabul over the snowbound mountains, was overdue. Perhaps this horseman was an advance messenger, with news of its progress.

Teer raised the alarm and soldiers rushed to watch as a group of officers rode out to meet this apparition. Brought inside the gate the man announced himself as Dr William Brydon, assistant surgeon in the Bengal Army. He was suffering from frostbite and covered in wounds, yet Brydon was immediately peppered with questions from a garrison eager to know the fate of his comrades. Asked, 'Where is the rest of the army?' legend has it that Brydon replied simply, 'I am the army.'

Over the coming hours fires were lit along the fortress walls and bugles sounded every fifteen minutes in order to guide other British survivors to safety. None came. Brydon was apparently the only survivor of a 16,500-strong force made up of 4,500 British and Indian soldiers, along with 12,000 camp followers, which had vanished.

For centuries foreign powers have sent armies into Afghanistan only to have their fingers badly burned. And none failed more spectacularly than the British during the First Afghan War of 1838–42. In December 1838, the British, already ruling India, had sent a 21,000-strong army to Kabul in order to offset the perceived threat of a Russian invasion of Afghanistan to the north. The plan was to impose a pro-British regime in Afghanistan, with a former ruler, Shah Shuja, as their puppet.

By August 1839 this mission was completed, but the foundations of Shuja's rule remained shaky, and he could only be maintained in power with an occupying force consisting of several thousand British-led troops complete with their families and supporting staff. To many Afghans, who had believed the British promise that they would leave once their work was done, this looked like a conquering army. Its base in Kabul soon came under regular attack from an increasingly hostile native population. The main protagonist was Akhbar Khan, the son of Dost Muhammad, the ruler that the British had initially forced out for Shah Shuja. By January 1842, after the killing of several senior British officers, the British commander in Kabul, Major General William Elphinstone, became convinced that his army's position there was now untenable and began to negotiate with Afghan leaders for a safe passage out of the country. On 6 January a huge, unwieldy column complete with women and children left Kabul aiming to retreat back to India with the promise that they would not be attacked. Brydon, a Scottish medical officer posted in Kabul, left with them.

The subsequent seven-day march to Jalalabad would become one of the most distressing retreats in British military history, one which was seen at the time as an embarrassing and unmitigated disaster. A sickly Elphinstone, once described as 'the most incompetent solider who ever became general', appears to have dithered from the start and quickly lost control of the situation. In the negotiations with Afghan leader Akhbar Khan, the hapless general had agreed that his troops give up much of their artillery and other supplies before leaving. Despite whatever assurances he felt he had been given, the vast and shambolic column was then harried by the Afghans from the outset, with Elphinstone's soldiers forced to fight a fierce rearguard action. On the first day the British column travelled just 6 miles in freezing conditions as tribesmen made repeated raids on the baggage trains. Brydon later recalled how, that night, he had been forced to sleep in the snow clutching the bridle of his horse having already lost most of his possessions in an Afghan raid. He awoke to find that many of his comrades had frozen to death overnight.

The next day the column struggled on. Akhbar Khan had promised to escort it with his own men but was either unable or unprepared to stop the local Afghan tribesmen attacking the column, which they now did on horseback with swords or by firing muskets at it from the slopes of the narrow mountain passes that formed the only route back to Jalalabad. Encumbered with all manner of servants, equipment and family members, Elphinstone's men were slowly picked off along the icy route. By the end of the third day two-thirds were already dead. Brydon and the other medics had their work cut out tending to the wounded and dying, though these were increasingly left behind to fend for themselves as the column became strung out and the situation more desperate. Soon Brydon himself was suffering from snow blindness and starvation – resorting to eating wild liquorice plants.

Akhbar then made Elphinstone give up hostages in the form of the British wives, children and some husbands in return for calling off the tribesmen (he hoped to ransom the hostages later). But the deal didn't halt the slaughter. In the end Elphinstone was taken hostage too and the rest of the column marched on in the direction of Jalalabad without him. Discipline began to break down and more and more of the British were slain, with the Afghan attacks all the more terrifying after nightfall.

Amid the continuing melee Brydon was pulled from his horse by an assailant who lunged at his head with a knife, drawing blood as it sliced into his skull. Fortunately, the wily surgeon had put a copy of a popular journal called *Blackwood's Magazine* inside the forage cap he wore to keep out the bitter cold. It saved his life. Brydon then managed to use his own sword to slash at his attacker, who fled. At another point Brydon's horse was wounded but he was given a substitute pony by a wounded Indian solider who could not go on.

On the morning of 13 January, only a few hours from the relative safety of Jalalabad, there was a final stand of the remaining core of British soldiers, mostly from the 44th Regiment of Foot, against the Afghans on a hill at a place called Gandamack. But the British could only muster forty rounds of ammunition between them and were soon cut down. Six men, on horseback, had escaped the carnage and Brydon was among them. But they continued to be attacked and soon the other five had succumbed to musket balls or swords, leaving only Brydon fleeing for his life. When twenty enemy horsemen barred his way, this time armed only with stones, the doctor put his head down and galloped through the hail of rocks. After his sword became broken in another encounter he managed to get away by throwing the hilt of it in the face of a tribesman. In his own words, Brydon was now, 'Quite unarmed and on a poor animal I feared could not carry me to Jalalabad.' However, riding on, he suddenly found himself alone. The tribesmen had faded away into the hills. Then, through the haze, Brydon made out the walls of Jalalabad. For a moment he hesitated, not knowing whether it too had been taken by the Afghans. Then he glimpsed British uniforms on the walls and knew that he was saved.

It would later turn out that Brydon wasn't quite the only survivor. Two days later a Greek trader from the column, a Mr Baness, stumbled into Jalalabad only to die a day later. In the following weeks a number of straggling Indian Sepoys arrived. Brydon was the only European to make the journey in one piece, although some of the hostages taken by Akhbar, around 120 in all, had been spared death too.

After hearing Brydon's account, the garrison commander at Jalalabad, Major General Sir Robert Sale, was a worried man. His wife, Lady Florentia Sale, and daughter had been on the march. The son-in-law had been killed, but Lady Sale and her daughter were now among Akhbar's hostages. Were they still alive? General Sale also knew that an isolated Jalalabad was now itself under threat, and in the spring of 1842 Akhbar Khan duly laid siege to the city. But Sale's force of 2,000, including Brydon, held out until they were eventually relieved by a force under General Pollock from India in April 1842.

By this time Brydon's own story had spread not only across India but back home to Britain, causing shock and much criticism of a war which was seen as a costly folly. Even so, as revenge for the massacre of Elphinstone's column, the British launched a massive offensive in the autumn of 1842, with Brydon again among the troops, fighting their way back to Kabul and burning down its famous bazaar before swiftly leaving the country again. Akhbar's surviving hostages were released, with Lady Sale and her daughter among them. Elphinstone had, however, died in captivity. Shah Shuja, having been left in Kabul by the British to his fate, had been assassinated in April 1842. Dost Muhammad was eventually restored to the Afghan throne.

It wasn't the end of William Brydon's adventures. He stayed in India and in 1857 found himself at Lucknow, during the Indian Mutiny. This time he was shot, with shrapnel lodging in his spine, though the bulk of the bullet passed through his body. The British lost 2,500 people during the siege, but Brydon, along with his wife and children, survived and he was made a companion of the Order of the Bath for his efforts. Brydon died aged 61 in 1873, back at home in Scotland.

28

HOW PRINCE ALBERT AVERTED WAR BETWEEN BRITAIN AND THE UNITED STATES

In October 1860, whilst on a visit to Coburg in Germany, Prince Albert was in a carriage when the horses pulling it suddenly bolted. He managed to jump free moments before a collision with a waggon at a railway crossing. Albert sustained only bruises but was left badly shaken and a little later confided in his brother Ernest that he felt his 'time' would soon come. Queen Victoria's consort had been suffering with chronic stomach pain and by December 1861 he was, indeed, on his deathbed. However, just days before Albert passed away – plunging Queen Victoria into mourning and a depression from which she never recovered – his last act in public life helped Britain avoid a full-scale war with the United States.

There had been an uneasy peace between the two nations for nearly half a century, following the indecisive war of 1812 during which the most noteworthy event was the burning down of the White House in Washington DC by British forces. Then, in 1859, relations had become strained during what was known as the Pig War, a confrontation over the border between Canada and the United States. The sovereignty of the San Juan Islands in the north-west corner of what is now Washington State was in dispute and the row threatened to boil over after an American settler shot a pig belonging to an Irishman working for Britain's Hudson Bay Company. The situation escalated and soon both sides dispatched warships and soldiers to the region. Diplomacy eventually won the day and the only casualty remained the pig.

In late 1861 there was a much greater threat to relations between Britain and the United States during what has become known as the Trent Affair. The American Civil War had broken out in April 1861 and the Confederacy knew that securing official recognition of their statehood from either Britain or France could be critical in a victory over the Union. Yet, while Britain relied heavily on cotton from the secessionist Confederate states, it had strong trade links with the North too and decided to remain neutral. However, in November of that year

The last moments of HRH the Prince Consort, by an artist known only as Le Port or Oakley. Prince Albert died in December 1861. (The Wellcome Library, The Wellcome Trust, www.wellcomecollection.org)

there was an episode that challenged this situation and brought Britain and Abraham Lincoln's United States to the brink of conflict.

It began when the Confederate President, Jefferson Davis, decided to send more diplomats to Europe in a bid to persuade Britain to go to war with the Union. The men chosen were John Slidell and James Mason, but to get across the Atlantic they would first have to run the Union naval blockade of Confederate territory. In the dead of night, on 12 October 1861, they boarded a ship called the *Theodora* in Charleston, South Carolina, which managed to evade the Union ships in the darkness. Two days later the ship was in the Bahamas, and then sailed on to Cuba where Slidell and Mason discovered that they could link up with a British mail packet called the RMS *Trent*, which was leaving Havana, bound for Britain.

Union intelligence operatives knew about the mission, but thought the pair were aboard a different ship. Then, by chance, a Captain Charles Wilkes, in charge of a frigate called the USS *San Jacinto*, which had called into Cuba, learned of Slidell and Mason's departure and decided to intercept the *Trent*. His view was that the diplomats were effectively contraband and that he had the legal right to stop any ship carrying enemy dispatches.

On 8 November, off the Bahamas, the *San Jacinto* intercepted the *Trent*, which was flying the Union Jack, firing two shots across its bow, and sent a party on board. After a brief altercation with the *Trent's* captain, Slidell and Mason were seized and taken back to Boston, in the Union, and imprisoned. When news got out Wilkes was lauded as a hero in the North, even though he had acted without orders. Abraham Lincoln and his Cabinet were largely on Wilkes' side and antipathy towards the British was stoked in the press. The Philadelphia *Sunday Transcript* crowed, 'While the British government has been playing the villain, we have been playing the fool. Let her now do something beyond drivelling – let her fight.'

News of the capture of the pair did not arrive in Britain until 27 November, where there was outrage that a Union ship could stop a British vessel, forcibly removing passengers. Many saw the action as violating the nation's neutrality. It was felt that Lincoln's secretary of state, William H. Seward, had long been spoiling for a war with the old foe, and now reaction boiled over, with politicians and many of the public alike feeling that the *Trent* incident was an intentional provocation. *The London Chronicle* summed up the mood, stating:

> Mr. Seward ... is exerting himself to provoke a quarrel with all Europe, in that spirit of senseless egotism which induces the Americans, with their dwarf fleet and shapeless mass of incoherent squads which they call an army, to fancy themselves the equal of France by land and Great Britain by sea.

The bullish British Prime Minister, Lord Palmerston, was equally outraged, and in an emergency Cabinet meeting convened to address the crisis is said to have thrown his hat on the table vowing, 'I don't know whether you are going to stand this, but I'll be damned if I do.'

Communication across the Atlantic still took more than two weeks and when the initial reaction from Britain arrived in mid December, tensions were ratcheted up further. When he heard the news that Britain seemed intent upon war over the issue, Senator Orville Browning urged Lincoln to fight 'to the death'. An outraged Seward told the famous news correspondent William H. Russell that if Britain forced war on the United States, they would, 'wrap the whole world in flames'. However, the Union Government was still to discover the official response of the British Government.

On 30 November the British foreign secretary, Lord Russell, had sent Queen Victoria, at Windsor Castle, drafts of strongly worded letters for

Seward, which included an ultimatum that the Union should hand over the prisoners and apologise because they had contravened international law. The message was clear: if the Union did not reply positively within seven days Britain was prepared to go to war. As she had often done with matters of state, the queen sought Prince Albert's advice. Despite being so ill that he could barely hold a pen, Prince Albert read through the letters, striking out passages he felt too bellicose and recommending that the language be softened. On 1 December the letter was returned with a memo noting that the queen:

> ... should have liked to have seen the expression of a hope that the American captain did not act under instructions, or, if he did that he misapprehended them – that the United States government must be fully aware that the British Government could not allow its flag to be insulted ... and Her Majesty's Government are unwilling to believe that the United States Government intended wantonly to put an insult upon this country and to add to their many distressing complications by forcing a question of dispute upon us, and that we are therefore glad to believe ... that they would spontaneously offer such redress as alone could satisfy this country, viz: the restoration of the unfortunate passengers and a suitable apology.

The Cabinet accepted the amendments and a toned down letter was duly sent. It effectively gave the Union the chance of graceful exit if it acknowledged Wilkes had not been acting under orders and made some form of apology. Aggressive demands were replaced by 'expectations'. Across the Atlantic the tactful British envoy, Lord Lyons, had been smoothing the way for a positive reaction with Seward, presenting the formal British demands on 23 December.

Palmerston was convinced that, however the letter was worded, there would be a war anyway. The country made hurried preparations with 11,000 extra troops immediately sent to Canada, then under British rule, with a contingency for another 30,000 to be sent later if required. The navy was readied and plans to invade Union territory including Maine and New York drawn up.

Lincoln's Cabinet met on Christmas Day to discuss the situation. For all his bluster, Seward realised that war with both the South and Britain could actually end in disaster and urged restraint. Though much of his Cabinet resisted, Lincoln was eventually won over. In a carefully worded note to the British, the US admitted that Wilkes had acted without

Rear Admiral Charles Wilkes photographed in retirement. His interception of the RMS *Trent* and apprehension of two Confederate diplomats nearly sparked war between the United States and Britain. (Library of Congress)

authorisation and agreed to release the prisoners, though made no explicit apology. Fortunately it was just enough to take the heat out of the situation. Both sides stepped back from a war that would surely have been long and bloody.

By the time Slidell and Mason were set free, sailing for England on 1 January, Prince Albert was already dead. He passed away at 11 p.m. on the evening of 14 December surrounded by Queen Victoria and his children, the official cause being typhoid fever.

Partly thanks to Albert's moderating advice, war had been narrowly avoided. Ultimately, the biggest loser of the whole affair was the Confederacy, which now realised that it would be harder than ever to get official British recognition and that the nation was unlikely to come into the war on their side. If anything, it was the beginning of improved relations between the Union and Britain, with the two nations signing a landmark agreement in 1862 to work together on ending the Atlantic slave trade.

Wilkes, the hot-headed captain who had started the whole march to arms, soon went from hero to public humiliation. In 1864, after a dispute with his seniors, he was court-martialled for disobedience, disrespect, insubordination and conduct unbecoming an officer.

29

HOW ABRAHAM LINCOLN CHEATED DEATH AND WENT ON TO FREE THE SLAVES

By the time President Abraham Lincoln was shot in a theatre on 14 April 1865, by John Wilkes Booth, his place in history was already secure. Lincoln had successfully seen his nation through a bloody Civil War – the Confederate States surrendering a few days before his assassination. During the conflict Lincoln had also announced the emancipation of the slaves, leading to the Thirteenth Amendment of the US constitution. Thanks to his efforts, by the end of 1865, all slaves throughout the United States would be freed. After his death Lincoln achieved a kind of martyrdom and today ranks as one of the country's most revered past presidents, only rivalled, perhaps, by George Washington. The huge Lincoln Memorial, built in his honour in the 1920s, is still one of Washington DC's most impressive monuments. Yet Lincoln nearly never made it to the presidency, or indeed, adulthood. As a child and teenager he narrowly cheated death three times.

Lincoln was born in 1809 in a one-room log cabin on Sinking Spring Farm, near Hodgenville in the state of Kentucky. Despite this seemingly tough start, his father, Thomas, was a reasonably successful farmer. But Thomas became embroiled in a series of land disputes and when Lincoln was aged 2 the family moved to the nearby Knob Creek Farm, the first home the future president could remember in adulthood. It was also, incidentally, the first place he later recalled seeing slaves – as they were taken along a nearby road to be sold.

At Knob Creek Lincoln spent hours playing outside with his sister, Sarah, and also with a boy called Austin Gollaher, who was four years his senior. One Sunday afternoon, in 1816, the pair were playfully hunting partridges near the creek that gave the farm its name. The stream had become swollen by recent rains but they decided to try and cross it over a fallen log. Gollaher crossed safely but as the 6-year-old Lincoln attempted to negotiate the log too, he hesitated, wobbled and fell in. The young Lincoln couldn't swim. Neither could his pal, but a quick-thinking Gollaher quickly found a branch and held it out for a screaming Lincoln to grab, managing to haul the future president from the raging water.

Gollaher later remembered:

> He was almost dead, and I was badly scared. I rolled and pounded him in good earnest. Then I got him by the arms and shook him, the water meanwhile pouring out of his mouth. By this means, I succeeded in bringing him to, and soon he was all right.

Later in the same year Lincoln's family were forced to move again. Still plagued by legal issues over land ownership, Thomas Lincoln relocated to Spencer County, Indiana, which his son 'Abe' would remember as 'a wild region with many bears'. Not long afterwards, tragedy struck when Lincoln's mother, Nancy, died from consuming contaminated milk. Around the same time, the young Lincoln was to get into another scrape that would almost end in his own death. As Lincoln later wrote, in an 1860 pen portrait of himself, 'In his tenth year he was kicked by a horse and apparently killed for a time.'

The accident occurred when Lincoln, helping his father with farm work, had to take corn to be ground at a mill, 2 miles away, on horseback. It was getting late in the evening and Lincoln was getting impatient as he waited for his turn to convert the grist into flour. Finally hooking up the 'old mare' to the gristmill arm, he began whipping the animal, urging it to go faster while shouting, 'Git up, you ole hussy.' The horse didn't take kindly to this and kicked out at Lincoln with one of its hind legs. The 10-year-old was knocked unconscious and the local miller, Noah Gordon, seeing the boy bleeding from his forehead, thought he was dead. Lincoln's father was sent for and the still unconscious Lincoln put in his waggon. Once home, Lincoln was put to bed where he lay all night, still without moving. The next day his body apparently jerked to life and he awoke shouting, 'You ole hussy', as if finishing a sentence from the evening before.

With the nearest doctor miles away, the youngster received no proper medical attention but, afterwards, seemed completely recovered. However, his skull was almost certainly fractured and some experts have since speculated on whether this could have been a contributory factor in the mood swings and seizures from which Lincoln was known to have suffered in later life.

The theories are compounded by the fact that Lincoln's head would suffer another trauma nine years later. Now 19 years old and 6ft tall with a strong physique, Lincoln had begun to do some odd jobs and was taken on by a landowner called James Gentry to help his son, Allen, take a cargo of meat, corn and flour in a flatbed boat all the way down the Mississippi to the city of New Orleans. They were to trade with the local sugar plantations of Louisiana as they went.

One night during the journey, as Lincoln would later recall, 'they were attacked by seven negroes with intent to kill and rob them.' During the affray Lincoln was hit on the head with a club which would leave a permanent scar. But both Allen and Lincoln were tough and evidently managed to drive off their assailants. Or, as Lincoln put it, 'They were hurt some in the melee, but succeeded in driving the Negroes from the boat, and then "cut cable", "weighed anchor" and left.'

Somehow Lincoln had survived his early years and, despite a bout of malaria in 1830, was soon making his way in the world. He had been a studious child and, after a string of jobs including postmaster and surveyor, eventually became a lawyer. He was first elected to the state legislature of Illinois in 1834, and then Congress in 1846. On 6 November 1860, as the Republican candidate, he was elected President of the United States on less than 40 per cent of the popular vote. Two years earlier he had said, 'Government cannot endure permanently half slave, half free ...'

Many southern states could not accept his leadership and some had seceded even before Lincoln's inauguration. In fact, the new Confederacy selected its own president, Jefferson Davis, on 9 February 1861. As the country plunged towards a civil war which would ultimately determine the future of the Union and the fate of the slaves too, another, now half-forgotten, threat to Lincoln's life arrived. For Booth's later successful assassination was preceded by another, earlier plot.

As Lincoln prepared to leave his home in Springfield, Illinois, for his inauguration, there were those determined to oppose his presidency at all costs. He was saved from assassination in the city of Baltimore, Maryland, in February 1861, at this pivotal point in the country's history, thanks to a man called Allan Pinkerton. He was a former Chicago detective who had set up his own private detective agency and had been hired by the local railroad to ensure Lincoln's safety during his journey towards the capital.

Lincoln planned to visit some seventy towns en route to Washington, but it was at Baltimore that Pinkerton identified a critical threat. Maryland, though it actually remained in the Union during the Civil

President Abraham Lincoln photographed in 1864. But he nearly never made it into the White House. (Library of Congress)

War, was a slave state and many locals were certainly not well disposed to Lincoln. Pinkerton had information that the president elect was to be targeted on 23 February when he was due to arrive in Baltimore from Harrisburg. Working undercover, Pinkerton and his agents claimed to have met a barber called Cipriano Ferrandini, a captain in the Maryland militia and an avowed secessionist, with other conspirators. At one meeting Ferrandini swore that Lincoln 'must die' whilst wielding a dagger. Pinkerton later concluded that the plot would see a handful of assassins, armed with knives, attack Lincoln when he met crowds in Baltimore after arriving at the city's station.

When Pinkerton warned Lincoln to avoid Baltimore he was rebuffed. But Lincoln did agree to don the disguise of a cloth cap, rather than his usual stovepipe hat, and hurry through the city at night without stopping to meet the residents as planned. Pinkerton also arranged for the telegraph to the city to be cut to thwart communications between any would-be killers.

Pinkerton's plan was carried out successfully with Lincoln changing trains in Baltimore, as was necessary, in the early hours of the morning, arriving in Washington at 6 a.m. without incident. The detective then sent a coded telegram to the president of the Philadelphia, Wilmington & Baltimore Railroad which read: 'Plums delivered nuts safely.' The plots to kill Lincoln may not have been well organised and no one was ever convicted, but avoiding a stop in Baltimore may well have been a sensible precaution to prevent an attempt on Lincoln's life.

It certainly wasn't, however, a good public relations move for Lincoln at the time. Once safely in Washington he was lampooned for skulking into the city under the cover of darkness. Criticism came from all quarters of political opinion and both *Harpers Weekly* and *Vanity Fair* ran scathing cartoons in which a cowardly Lincoln was depicted slipping through Baltimore wearing a Scotch bonnet. The *Baltimore Sun* wrote, 'We do not believe the Presidency can ever be more degraded by any of his successors than it has by him, even before his inauguration,' and *The New York Tribune* lamented, 'It is the only instance recorded in our history in which the recognised head of a nation ... has been compelled, for fear of his life, to enter the capital in disguise.' Lincoln himself later regretted arriving in Washington, 'like a thief in the night'. With such an inauspicious start to his presidency and with war in the offing, few would have imagined that Lincoln would go on to be considered one of the greatest leaders in history.

AN ESCAPEE SLAVE AND THE UNDERGROUND RAILROAD TO FREEDOM

As a 12-year-old girl Harriet Tubman had an experience which would shape the rest of her life and mark her out as someone destined for greatness. She had been born into slavery as Araminta Ross and grew up on a plantation in Dorchester County, in the southern US state of Maryland, working as a house servant and in the fields. One day, whilst at a store buying some food for the plantation's cook, 'Minty' was ordered to help tie up another slave who had tried to escape. Realising the slave was about to be whipped by his overseer, the young Minty refused. As the slave ran away the angry overseer hurled a 2lb metal weight at him, but hit Minty instead, causing an injury which gave her headaches for the rest of her days.

By the autumn of 1849 Minty had changed her name to Harriet Tubman, after her marriage to a free black man called John. Even though John was free, she remained in slavery. After a death in the family, her owners, the Brodess family, tried to sell Tubman and eventually hired her out with her brothers, Ben and Henry, to another plantation owner. Fearing what might lie ahead, the diminutive Tubman, standing 5ft 2in tall, now vowed to escape to the slave-free North.

One night she and her brothers stole away. A reward notice was soon put in a local paper, offering a bounty of $100 each for their capture. However, lost in the countryside, Tubman's brothers got cold feet and decided to return of their own accord. Reluctantly, Tubman returned with them, but was soon determined to try and escape again. Whilst working in the fields one day Tubman had been approached by a Quaker woman, who told her to visit if she ever needed help. A few nights later, leaving her husband asleep and gathering up some food, Tubman fled to the Quaker woman's home. There she was given details of friendly safe houses where she could stay during what would be a 90-mile journey to the nearest non-slave territory.

Setting out on foot and following the light of the North Star, she walked through fields and woods, heeding the advice of the woman who had told

Escapee slave Harriet Tubman, who would help scores of others flee servitude. (Library of Congress)

her to wade through rivers in order to throw pursuers and their dogs off the scent. Helped by two more Quaker families, who hid her in waggons, Tubman eventually made it across the Mason–Dixon Line, which marked the border of the North and the state line of Pennsylvania.

Tubman later recalled, 'When I found I had crossed that line, I looked at my hands to see if I was the same person. There was such a glory over everything; the sun came like gold through the trees, and over the fields, and I felt like I was in Heaven.' She carried on to the city of Philadelphia, finding lodgings and, before long, odd jobs working in kitchens.

Shortly afterwards, in 1850, the Fugitive Slave Act was passed by Congress which stated that runaway slaves should be returned to their masters upon capture, even in the North, making Tubman vulnerable. Yet she was determined not to flee further north as caution demanded, but to return to the South in order to rescue the rest of her family.

During her own escape she had used what had become known as the Underground Railroad. It was not a railway but a network of escape routes leading to free states as well as Canada, used by around 1,000 of those held in bondage to flee to safety each year. Essential to the routes were sympathisers, abolitionists and free African Americans who often accommodated the slaves in safe houses. Those who helped run the Railroad were dubbed 'conductors'.

Over the next ten years Tubman would become one of the most successful conductors of all, given the nickname of 'Moses', in recognition of her brilliance in leading scores of slaves to safety. But her first priority was to start getting her own family out. In December 1850, Tubman learned that her niece, Kessiah, was to be sold along with her two children at the courthouse in Cambridge, Maryland. Kessiah was also married to a free black ship's carpenter called John Bowley. Harriet came up with a plan where Bowley would himself put in the highest bid at the auction, pretending to have enough money to complete the sale. When the day came, Bowley duly placed the highest bid and then, as arrangements were being made at the side of the courthouse for payment, he and his family simply slipped away unnoticed. Bowley rowed them in a canoe to Baltimore, where he linked up with Tubman who had been staying there in a safe house. She then brought them safely out of Maryland to Philadelphia. Months later Tubman was soon back rescuing her brother, Moses, and two other men.

In the autumn of 1851 Tubman returned again to Maryland, this time for her 'free' husband, even saving up for a suit that he could wear. He was, though, to all intents and purposes already able to do as he pleased. On arrival she discovered, to her shock, that in her absence, John had taken another wife. Tubman instead found some other slaves on a nearby plantation, gave one the suit and helped them escape. In the same year, mindful that they were still at risk from the Fugitive Act even in the North, Tubman shepherded eleven escaped slaves, including the members of her own family, north to Canada using the Railroad network.

For the next nine years she went back to repeatedly engineer the escape of more and more slaves, making thirteen trips back to the South and helping at least 120 slaves escape. She was the 'conductor' who, in her own words, 'never lost a passenger' despite the ever watchful, professional slave catchers roaming the land.

Tubman came up with many ruses to make sure she and her escapees weren't captured. She favoured leading the slaves on foot through the countryside in winter darkness – often on Saturday nights, as newspaper announcements about the absconders would not be published until Monday. As she got bolder, and began to form contacts with well-known abolitionists and to speak at anti-slavery meetings, Tubman's methods to get the slaves out got even more elaborate.

She took to wearing disguises and even, on one occasion, carried live chickens to make it look like she was still a slave running errands. Another time, to avoid the slave catchers, she dressed a group of male slaves as women. One day, knowing she had aroused some suspicion at a railway station, Tubman cleverly took to buying a train ticket South, instead of North, something an escapee was unlikely to do. She even carried a gun. During one escape she was forced to hide a group in a swamp for some time with no food, and when one of the slaves threatened to go back she pointed the gun at his head warning him to 'go on or die', so that he didn't endanger the rest of the mission. He and the rest of the group went on to make a successful escape. The authorities in Maryland were at a loss to explain the escape of so many slaves and thought a white abolitionist must be behind the scheme.

Tubman was still determined that as many of her own family as possible would escape the South. In December 1854 she went back to rescue three of her brothers, Robert, Ben and Henry, who were for sale, having made further unsuccessful attempts to escape. She wrote a letter to a friend to warn that she was coming. The escape was set for Christmas Eve, when the slave owner Eliza Brodess traditionally gave her slaves permission to visit their families. Harriet told her brother to make for her parents, Ben and Rit's, house. Then she conducted them to Wilmington, Delaware (still a slave state), on foot where a merchant called Thomas Garrett, a well-known operative in the Underground Railroad, found that Tubman's shoes had worn through on the journey. He found her new ones and helped the party on to Pennsylvania.

In the summer of 1857 Tubman returned again, this time for her elderly parents. Her father, Ben, had been freed in the 1840s and was able to buy the freedom of his wife, Rit, in 1855. The pair had continued to live in Maryland, themselves helping slaves to escape. But when Tubman learned that Ben was at risk of arrest, after harbouring eight escaped slaves, she made yet another journey to bring them, in secret, to safety, finally finding them a home in a community of former slaves in Canada.

When the American Civil War broke out in 1861, Tubman took her efforts to a different level. Not content with having helped so many slaves escape, she now threw herself into the work of a nurse and then spy, travelling back to the South in disguise to get information on troop movements from slaves and Confederate defences. She earned the nickname 'General Tubman' after leading raiding parties with black regiments, including one at Combahee Ferry in South Carolina which freed 700 slaves. After the war Tubman settled in Auburn, in New York State, and when she died in 1913, by now a national heroine, she was buried with full military honours.

31

THE TAXIDERMIST WHO SAVED THE AMERICAN BUFFALO

In the 1870s a man called Brewster M. Higley wrote the words to a poem which subsequently became the lyrics of a popular song, *Home on the Range*. The ditty was a loving homage to life in the American West and is, today, the state song of Kansas. Its familiar opening line, 'Oh, give me a home where the Buffalo roam', is still known to millions all over the world. Yet, by the time Higley penned the words, the buffalo was well on its way to becoming extinct.

The American buffalo, or American bison, is an impressive animal. An adult male, with its famous shaggy coat, stands at some 6ft tall and up to 9ft in length, weighing in at as much as 2,000lb. Buffalo can run at 35mph and, despite their cumbersome appearance, are able to jump 6ft in the air. For 12,000 years they had ranged across the North American grasslands in huge herds. In fact, just a hundred years before Higley's poetic tribute, it's estimated that there had been as many as 60 million buffalo roaming across North America, mainly in the Great Plains area of the United States, west of the Mississippi and east of the Rocky Mountains. Buffalo herds, which could be found numbering in the tens of thousands and stretching up to 25 miles in length, were a magnificent sight.

Native Americans had long hunted the buffalo, mainly for food, and would themselves sometimes kill large numbers. However, in the nineteenth century a much bigger threat to the buffalo's survival emerged as white settlers moved west. In 1832 the artist George Catlin, who specialised in painting Native Americans, predicted, 'The buffalo's doom is sealed.' And in the ensuing decades buffalo began to be hunted on an industrial scale. The hides were prized for their use as rugs and coats and fetched hefty sums. Huge numbers were exported to Europe. Hides were also used for machine belts in factories while buffalo tongues were considered a culinary delicacy. Often, once a buffalo had been killed, the rest of the carcass was simply left to rot.

Adding to the buffalo's demise were the new railways cutting through the plains, dividing up herds. The US Army was also a foe. It knew that depriving the Native Americans of their vital food source would help force them on to reservations. In fact, in 1875, General Philip Sheridan told Congress that buffalo hunters had done more than the army to solve the 'vexed Indian question' adding, 'let them kill, skin and sell until the buffaloes are exterminated'. The hunters didn't let him down. Thousands of buffalo were being killed every day. In 1874 the editor of a newspaper in Dodge City, Kansas, reckoned that on any given day 60,000–80,000 buffalo robes and hides could be found in the city's train yards, and in the same year President Ulysses S. Grant vetoed a bill aimed at giving the buffalo some protection. Professional hunters found buffalo easy to pick off and the best could kill up to a hundred at a time; the famous 'Buffalo Bill' Cody killed more than 4,000 in just eighteen months.

There were early efforts to halt the carnage. Buffalo Bill himself was one of those who repented, calling for the animal to be protected, and a handful of enthusiasts began to collect them in small, private herds. The buffalo was eventually saved from extinction, largely because of a man called William Temple Hornaday. Hornaday was an unlikely and rather flawed hero. Born on a farm in Indiana in 1854, he had started his working life as a taxidermist – more used to stuffing animals than conserving them. Hornaday also loved hunting. As a young man he had travelled widely across the globe, skinning elephants, shooting tigers and tracking crocodiles. In 1882, aged just 28, he landed the post of Chief Taxidermist for the United States National Museum at the Smithsonian in Washington DC. By now it was clear to anyone who cared to study the subject that the buffalo was soon to be extinct. Hornaday and his colleagues at the museum felt it was unfortunate, but unavoidable. At least, if they acted quickly, they could get some samples to stuff for the record.

In 1886 Hornaday headed the grandly titled 'Smithsonian Institution Buffalo Outfit' and travelled to Montana with the aim of collecting some prime buffalo specimens – by tracking and shooting them. He and his team of cowboys found it difficult to find any buffalo, but finally managed to bag twenty-five animals, which Hornaday described as 'the finest and

The buffalo display at the Museum of the Northern Great Plains. The animals were collected in 1886 by William T. Hornaday, who later went on to help save the species. (Courtesy of Overholser Historical Research Center, Fort Benton, Montana, USA)

most complete series of buffalo skins ever collected for a museum'. The best were stuffed, with six soon on display at the Smithsonian in a large glass and mahogany case.

Hornaday had described the trip as 'great sport', but he, like others, felt a growing sense of ill ease. As he had gazed over the plains of Montana and seen them strewn with the scattered skeletons of thousands of dead buffalo, bleached white by the sun, he had been touched by the animal's demise, describing the bones as 'ghastly monuments of slaughter'.

The hunter was to turn conservationist and, in 1889, he published *The Extermination of the American Bison*. In it Hornaday revealed the findings of a survey he had conducted of ranchers and soldiers, which found that only 1,091 buffalo were left in the whole of the United States. This was down from some 15 million in the 1860s. The USA's first national park had been established at Yellowstone in 1872 but Hornaday found that even here there were just a handful of bison left, thanks to poachers. In the book he railed against what man had done to the buffalo, describing,

'Man's reckless greed, his wanton destructiveness, and improvidence in not husbanding such resources as come to him from the hand of nature.' Hornaday added that there was no reason to hope that a single wild and unprotected buffalo 'will remain alive in ten years hence'. The book did much to rouse wider public awareness of the buffalo's plight. Yet his prediction that the bison would be extinct in the wild was realised within just five years when hunters finished off the last four wild buffalo in Colorado.

By 1887 Hornaday had realised that the best way to save the buffalo from total extinction was to save examples of live, pure breed animals. In that year he wrote to his superior at the museum with a sense of urgency saying:

> In view of the fact that thus far this government has done nothing to preserve alive any specimens of the American Bison, the most striking and conspicuous species on this continent, I have the honor to propose that the Smithsonian Institution ... take immediate steps to procure either by gift or purchase, as may be necessary, the nucleus of a herd of live buffaloes ... it now seems necessary for us to assume the responsibility of forming and preserving a herd of live buffaloes which may, in a small measure, atone for the national disgrace that attaches to the heartless and senseless extermination of the species in a wild state.

Hornaday had already brought back a live calf called Sandy, and soon acquired other buffalo for a new Department of Living Animals at the Smithsonian. A year later Hornaday was successful in getting the government to turn this into the National Zoological Park with himself as its director. The buffalo became one of the attraction's biggest draws. Hornaday later fell out with the director of the Smithsonian and ended up as director at the New York Zoological Park, later known as the Bronx Zoo. Here, in 1899, Hornaday established another buffalo herd and set up a captive breeding programme – essential if the animal where ever to be reintroduced to its natural habitat.

By the dawn of the twentieth century there were still only around 1,000 buffalo anywhere in the United States, virtually all in private collections, but Hornaday's work had helped spark a new interest in conservation, with efforts being made to restore the bison herd at Yellowstone National Park. He had secured an influential ally too; Theodore Roosevelt had long shared some of Hornaday's misgivings about the buffalo. On an 1889 hunting trip to Idaho he had admitted to 'a certain half melancholy feeling as I gazed on these bison, themselves part of the last remnant of a doomed and nearly vanished race'.

Roosevelt was the man who gave the teddy bear its name after refusing to shoot a tied up bear on another hunting trip. And by the time he became president in 1901 he was, like Hornaday, a concerned conservationist. While not being against hunting, he wanted to redress the balance between man and beast. In 1905 Hornaday and Roosevelt were instrumental in creating the American Bison Society, which lobbied for new reserves in which to protect the buffalo. In 1907 the government backed the creation of the Wichita Bison Range in southern Oklahoma with fifteen bison donated by the Bronx Zoo where Hornaday was still in charge. It was the first reintroduction of animals anywhere in North America. Then, in 1908, Roosevelt signed a law creating an 18,500 acre National Bison Range in Montana. Other herds were subsequently successfully established, with the Bronx Zoo also supplying buffalo for parks in South Dakota and Nebraska. By as early as 1911 Hornaday found himself able to declare that the buffalo was no longer endangered.

Hornaday himself remains a controversial figure. In 1906 he was involved in a scandal in which an African pygmy called Ota Benga was displayed as an exhibit at the Bronx Zoo. It caused public outrage. But Hornaday's role in one of the first animal conservation projects in history is secure. And while the buffalo will probably never be back to their eighteenth-century levels, conservation has continued to the point where there are, today, some half a million buffalo alive throughout North America.

32

THE GERMAN WHO HELPED WELLINGTON WIN AT WATERLOO

The death of a single warhorse nearly robbed the Duke of Wellington of his victory at Waterloo, an engagement which the British general described as 'The nearest run thing you ever saw in your life' to English politician Thomas Creevey. Wellington's triumph over Napoleon on 18 June 1815 effectively ended the latter's rule as Emperor of France and brought to a close more than two decades of wars that had ravaged Europe since the French Revolution. But, as the duke acknowledged, he had defeated Napoleon by a narrow margin and, for much of the battle, the outcome had hung in the balance. As it would turn out, the chance survival of another general, who had his steed shot away from under him just forty-eight hours before Waterloo, would prove vital in hammering home the nail in Napoleon's military and political coffin.

To most, the Battle of Waterloo is famous as a British victory over the French, one in which the genius of the old campaigner Wellington finally outwitted his long-time foe, Napoleon. Yet the reality was much more muddied, just like the terrain on the day the battle was fought. Waterloo shouldn't have happened at all. Napoleon had already been defeated by the allied armies of Russia, Prussia and Britain (among others) and deposed in France in 1814. Exiled on the Mediterranean island of Elba, he had escaped and returned to Paris, where he had quickly managed to resume his throne as emperor in a last audacious bid for glory that would become known as The Hundred Days.

The combined allied armies of the Seventh Coalition duly began to reassemble, hoping to crush Napoleon for good by marching in unison on Paris. Napoleon decided to strike first. In a lightning move he marched a hurriedly reformed, 128,000-strong army to the border of what is modern day Belgium, hoping to drive a wedge between the first two opposing armies that had gathered against him: Wellington's, made up of mainly British, Belgian and Dutch troops, and a nearby Prussian force.

Wellington knew he had to stop Napoleon taking Brussels at all costs if a new, protracted war was to be avoided. On the morning of the Battle of Waterloo, just south of the city, some 68,000 men under Wellington, with 160 big guns, faced off against 74,000 French with 250 guns. By the end of the day Napoleon had been soundly thrashed. Absolutely pivotal in this outcome was the role of Field Marshal Gebhard Leberecht von Blücher, the commander of the Prussians. The arrival of his men in support of Wellington, towards the end of the battle, was *the* decisive moment in an epic struggle.

By 1815 the charismatic Blücher was already 72 years old with a military career dating back to the 1760s. He was a veteran at fighting the French and while he and the Prussians had often come off second best, Blücher had victories over Napoleon under his belt too, most importantly at the Battle of Leipzig in 1813, which had forced Napoleon's armies back towards France, bringing to an end the Emperor's hopes of continental domination.

Blücher was a shrewd commander who was also extremely popular with his troops. However, two days before the Battle of Waterloo he was on the end of what would turn out to be Napoleon's last victory in the field. Napoleon had decided to deal with the Prussian army first, hoping to knock them out of the contest before taking on Wellington. The Battle of Ligny, fought on 16 June, just 15 miles from Waterloo, saw Blücher lose a fifth of his army, as the slightly smaller but better equipped French proved too strong for the Prussians.

Blücher was always ready to throw himself into the action, and in the middle of the battle, despite his age, he decided to lead a cavalry charge himself. He rode a magnificent grey stallion – a horse which had been given to him by Britain's Prince Regent. As he galloped towards the advancing French his horse was shot in the left flank. The horse fell and Blücher, knocked unconscious, became trapped underneath the dead animal. Meanwhile, cavalry charges raged back and forth over him. A quick-thinking aide, seeing what had happened, leapt from his horse and covered the old general with a cloak, disguising his medals from the French, who had no idea that the Prussian commander was at their mercy. Blücher was later 'dragged out ... bruised and half conscious' by some of his own men and taken to a field hospital.

That day the Prussians suffered 20,000 casualties and were forced to retreat a few miles north to a town called Wavre to lick their wounds. Napoleon had won an initial victory, but had lost 12,000 men himself. And while Blücher had survived by the skin of his teeth, so had most of his army. These facts would prove fundamental in the battle that ensued at Waterloo. As the historian Andrew Uffindell stated in *The Eagle's Last Triumph*, 'After Blücher joined Wellington in force at Waterloo, the French never stood a chance.'

In the aftermath of Ligny, Blücher's wounds were bathed in brandy. He had wanted to drink some too, but his doctor would only allow him a swig of champagne. Within hours Blücher was back on another horse, going among his soldiers, laughing and joking. A fierce debate then ensued between himself and von Gneisenau, his second in command. Gneisenau was angry that Wellington had failed to come to the aid of the Prussians at Ligny and felt that they should therefore retreat towards the Rhine where the army might survive to fight another day. But Blücher wanted to stay and support Wellington with the forces he had left. Thankfully for the Iron Duke, it was Blücher who won the argument. With Napoleon now limbering up to take on Wellington's army at Waterloo, Blücher wrote to Wellington promising to send 50,000 men to help.

On 18 June Wellington lined up his forces along a ridge and prepared for Napoleon to attack. The French duly opened up proceedings at around 11.30 a.m. An initial battle for the farm buildings at Hougoumont, a stronghold of the allied forces in front of Wellington's main line, would continue for most of the day and seriously hold up the French attack. Over the coming hours the battle ebbed and flowed. As waves of infantry and cavalry – supported by fearsome guns – pounded Wellington's forces his own soldiers held steady, helped by the decision to form his infantry into squares. But, by the late afternoon, Wellington had lost the crucial farm of La Haye Sainte and suffered heavy casualties. The French still had more reserves to throw at Wellington's remaining troops, and it's no surprise that, surveying the scene, Wellington is reported to have prayed, 'Give me night, or give me Blücher.'

The Prussians were indeed on their way, albeit slowly. Wavre was only about 10 miles away, but the rain and narrow roads had made the journey to Waterloo, dragging heavy artillery, interminable. Finally, in the late afternoon, an advance Prussian corps under General Bülow, consisting of around 20,000 men, arrived. It immediately engaged the right flank of the French army. Also making his way to Waterloo was the white-haired Blücher, urging on his tired troops, 'I have promised my brother Wellington and surely you don't want me to break my word.'

For several hours the Prussians pinned down around 13,000 of Napoleon's men. By 8 p.m. there were 40,000 Prussians in the field and Wellington, who had withstood Napoleon's last throw of the dice – a frontal attack by his crack Imperial Guard – now saw his chance. He ordered a general advance. It was too much for Napoleon's army, which was forced to retreat towards Paris. The victorious commanders met on the battlefield at 9 p.m. with Blücher greeting Wellington as 'My dear comrade!' The cost of victory had been heavy: the French had lost 25,000 men, Wellington 15,000 and Blücher 7,000.

After Waterloo, Blücher helped cement the French defeat at Paris, which the allied troops occupied on 7 July. He celebrated by spending his time in the city gambling, and even took part in a horse race – where he was thrown off his mount once again. At least he was still able to ride. Some blamed Napoleon's defeat at Waterloo on his haemorrhoids, which left the Emperor unable to spend much time in the saddle, meaning he could not survey the battlefield properly.

There were, however, much more important reasons for Napoleon's defeat than his piles. There was the bravery and resolve of Wellington's men. Then there was the poor weather which had forced Napoleon to delay his attack, allowing the Prussians time to arrive. And there was Napoleon's decision to send Marshal de Grouchy, with 33,000 of his men, to hold the Prussians at Wavre. As we have seen, Blücher's army had been able to escape to relieve Wellington while Grouchy was left conducting a sideshow against the rest of his men. Napoleon's message to Grouchy to get back to Waterloo with all haste, sent halfway through the battle, arrived too late to be of any use.

Crucially, in all this, it was Blücher who had personally committed to making sure help for Wellington did arrive. Wellington might not have been totally routed had the Prussians not come, but the allied troops certainly wouldn't have been able to deliver the sucker punch to Napoleon. Indeed, Wellington had indicated in a letter to Blücher just before Waterloo that if he did not get Prussian support his army would probably retreat towards Brussels. And for all Wellington's skill on the day, one of his own senior commanders, the Prince of Orange, was in no doubt about the day's turning point saying, 'The affair was entirely decided by the attack which the Prussians made on the enemy's right.' The duke himself, immediately after the battle, wrote, 'I should not do justice to my own feelings or to Marshal Blücher and the Prussian army, if I did not attribute the successful result of this arduous day to the cordial and timely assistance I received from them.' But it was left to Napoleon, captured and exiled on the remote island of St Helena in the Atlantic, to sum up the determined character of Marshal Blücher that had helped seal his fate, 'That old devil ... I had hardly finished beating him, when he again confronted me, ready to fight all over again.'

33

CHARLES DICKENS' CLOSE SHAVE

He was the famous novelist who captivated Victorian society with his powerful narratives and dramatic plots, but Charles Dickens, author of such great works as *Oliver Twist* and *Great Expectations*, was himself almost the victim of a tragedy worthy of one of his books – and he nearly lost a vital manuscript for one of his most intriguing novels in the process.

By 1865 Dickens was already seriously famous. His first hit had been *The Pickwick Papers*, which appeared in monthly serial form in 1836, and a string of other novels followed, including *A Christmas Carol, Nicholas Nickleby* and a *Tale of Two Cities*. He was feted around the world and his public readings of his own works were a sell out.

Dickens' personal life had seen a big transformation too. In 1858 the writer had left his wife, Catherine. Since the age of 45 he had been conducting a secret affair with the actress Ellen Ternan, and when Catherine found a packet containing a gold bracelet from her husband to Ternan, the 22-year-old marriage swiftly came to an end. It was on a trip back from Paris with Ternan that the 53-year-old author almost perished and with him the manuscript from his latest book, *Our Mutual Friend*, a spellbinding tale exploring the effect of money on the human psyche. The holiday was supposed to be restorative; before he left he wrote, 'Work and worry ... would soon make an end of me.'

On 9 June 1865, after crossing the Channel from Boulogne to Folkestone, he had boarded the front first-class carriage of the 2.38 p.m. boat train bound for Charing Cross along with Ellen, known as Nelly, and her mother. Dickens took off his coat, putting it up on a rack above the seats. Stuffed into one of its pockets was the manuscript for the latest instalment of *Our Mutual Friend*. During the trip he had managed to make good progress with work on the sixteenth out of nineteen instalments. The story was coming to its climax.

It was a bright sunny day and a group of gangers were busy carrying out repair work on the line to London where it crossed an iron viaduct over the River Beult, near Staplehurst in Kent. Crucially, the foreman in charge of the works, John Benge, had misread the timetable, believing he had time to replace two rails that had been lifted in order to remove some timbers before the next train arrived. He was expecting the 'Tidal Express', as it was known, at 5.20 p.m.

In fact Dickens' train was already hurtling towards the crossing and its driver had no idea that there was a 40ft section of track missing ahead of him. Just after 3 p.m. the train was just 500ft from the bridge when he spotted a workman frantically waving a red flag and hit the brakes. But the train was travelling at 50mph on a downward gradient and there was not enough time to stop short of the viaduct. The crash investigator later estimated that the train had been going at 30mph when it hit the gap in the track, with disastrous consequences. Somehow the momentum carried the engine over, but five of the train's carriages plunged into the river below as the supports buckled. One carriage, at the front, was left dangling at an angle over the precipice, held back only by its coupling. Inside were Dickens and his two companions, thrust into one corner by the impact.

In a letter written to his friend Thomas Mitton a few days later, Dickens recalled, 'I was in the carriage that did not go over into the stream. It was caught upon the turn by some of the ruin of the bridge and hung suspended and balanced in an apparently impossible manner ... suddenly we were off the rail.'

Getting out of a window and onto the bridge, Dickens hailed two train guards who were running up and down a remaining portion of the bridge. He shouted at them, 'Do stop an instant and look at me, and tell me whether you don't know me.' One of them replied, 'We know you very well, Mr Dickens.' Dickens then demanded, 'My good fellow for God's sake give me your key, and send one of those labourers here, and I'll empty this carriage.'

Using some planks of wood they got Ellen and her mother out. Retrieving a flask of brandy and his hat at the same time Dickens then rushed to tend to the injured and dying lying scattered about the crash scene. Dickens spent three hours helping, even using his hat as a vessel to bring drinking water and wash wounds.

In his letter to Mitton, Dickens recalled:

Suddenly I came upon a staggering man covered with blood (I think he must have been flung clean out of his carriage) with such a frightful cut across the skull that I couldn't bear to look at him. I poured some water over his face, and gave him some to drink, and gave him some brandy, and laid him down on the grass, and he said, 'I am gone', and died afterwards.

Then I stumbled over a lady lying on her back against a little pollard tree, with the blood streaming over her face (which was lead colour) in a number of distinct little streams from the head. I asked her if she could swallow a little brandy, and she just nodded, and I gave her some and left her for somebody else. The next time I passed her, she was dead.

Dickens added, 'No imagination can conceive the ruin of the carriages, or the extraordinary weights under which the people were lying, or the complications into which they were twisted up among iron and wood, and mud and water.' Ten people lost their lives in the disaster, with another fifty injured. One of them, who had been trapped under some wreckage, reckoned they owed their life to Dickens' aid at the crash scene.

It was only some time later at the crash site that Dickens remembered he had left the manuscript for *Our Mutual Friend* behind in his perilously poised carriage. In the letter to Mitton he recalled, 'I instantly remembered that I had the MS of a novel with me and clambered back into the carriage for it.'

Dickens went on to complete *Our Mutual Friend* and, in the postscript, alluded to how the book's characters had survived the Staplehurst rail crash along with the author:

> On Friday the Ninth of June in the present year, Mr and Mrs Boffin (in their manuscript dress of receiving Mr and Mrs Lammle at breakfast) were on the South Eastern Railway with me, in a terribly destructive accident. When I had done what I could to help others, I climbed back into my carriage—turned over a viaduct, and caught aslant upon the turn—to extricate the worthy couple. They were much soiled, but otherwise unhurt. The same happy result attended Miss Bella Wilfer on her wedding day, and Mr Riderhood inspecting Bradley Headstone's red neckerchief as he lay asleep. I remember with devout thankfulness that I can never be much nearer parting company with my readers for ever, than I was then, until there shall be written against my life, the two words with which I have this day closed this book:—THE END

Dickens insisted that in the immediate aftermath of the Staplehurst crash he was not 'in the least flustered' but admitted to being shaky afterwards. And, though he survived, the crash had taken its toll on his nerves. The writer tried to avoid train travel from then on and lived only five more years, dying on 9 June 1870, the exact anniversary of the disaster. He would never finish his next novel, *The Mystery of Edwin Drood*. Yet the incident – and Dickens' survival – left us with one of his most gripping yarns, for the great author drew on his experiences in the disaster, as well as from the Clayton Tunnel crash of 1861, to write a thrilling, if chilling, short story, *The Signal-Man*, in which the central character has a premonition of his own death in a railway accident.

34

HOW ST PANCRAS WAS SAVED FROM THE BULLDOZER

On a cold morning in December 1961 the sound of pneumatic drills pierced the North London air. A demolition firm had begun the painstaking work of dismantling the historic Doric portico that had been standing at the entrance to Euston station since 1837. Despite a campaign by some of the leading politicians, writers and architectural experts of the day, it had been deemed that the 70ft Euston Arch stood in the way of plans for a new, more practical station. Richard Seifert's subsequent airport-style terminus at Euston, now much derided, was designed to cater for the electrification of Britain's West Coast Main Line and in the process capture the spirit of the post-war age.

One of those who had bitterly opposed the destruction of Philip Hardwick's grand Grecian gateway at Euston was the poet John Betjeman. And when the threat to another of the capital's great railway landmarks came five years later he, together with a small band of passionate supporters, was determined that this time the wrecking ball would not win.

The gothic extravagance that is St Pancras Station was constructed in the late nineteenth century, a time of great railway barons and competing train companies keen to show off their commercial and industrial muscle. London already had some grand termini. Brunel's Paddington served the west, King's Cross served the north, while Euston served the north-west. But one of the nation's most successful companies, the Midland Railway, still lacked its own station in the city. In a bid to outdo its rivals, construction of St Pancras began in 1867, coinciding with the building of a new line from Bedford to London, connecting up the rest of the company's network. Completed in 1868, St Pancras' 100ft single-span train shed, designed by William Barlow, was then the largest enclosed space in the world. But it was Sir Gilbert Scott's red-brick Midland Grand Hotel, which fronted the station and was opened by Queen Victoria in 1873, that was the real showpiece. No expense had been spared in the construction of what one commentator called a 'veritable railway palace' with its soaring spires, pointed arch windows and iconic 240ft clock tower. Inside, the hotel boasted luxurious

The concourse of St Pancras station after its £800 million restoration and redevelopment. (© Peter Spurgeon, www.peterspurgeon.net)

fittings and facilities to match its brash exterior. Granite and limestone, combined with gold leaf and murals, abounded along with comfortable coffee lounges and bars. There was a billiard room, a hairdresser and even a smoking room specifically for ladies. The wrought-iron staircase with its ornate, sweeping balustrades was a modern wonder and The Midland Grand was soon full of technological innovations too: toilets that flushed, a revolving door, clever chutes for dirty laundry. The final bill for St Pancras had come in at a then eye-watering £500,000.

However, by the early twentieth century the Midland Grand was lagging behind. The plumbing was inadequate – there were only twenty rooms with en-suite bathrooms, out of 300 bedrooms. Guests were beginning to expect more; and the demands of running the place (each room had its own fireplace) were punishing. At a dinner in 1933 the company's own chairman, Sir Josiah Stamp, called the hotel 'completely obsolete'. It closed in 1935, becoming known as St Pancras Chambers and being used to house railway offices. Changes in the wider railway world had been affecting St Pancras too. In the early 1920s, as part of the reorganisation of the railway firms into 'the big four', the Midland Railway became part of the new London, Midland and Scottish, with Euston as its premier London station. Then came the infamous Beeching cuts of the early 1960s, which saw 5,000 miles of the nation's railway tracks ripped up. In 1966, with the railways now nationalised under British Rail, came a new proposal for St Pancras too. Services would be run into a new station combining St Pancras and King's Cross,

The facade of the Midland Grand Hotel, now the St Pancras Renaissance London Hotel, which originally opened in 1873. (© James Moore)

its neighbour to the east. The plan might even mean the demolition of both stations.

Five years before, in the run up to the loss of the Euston Arch, personal appeals to the likes of Harold Macmillan, then prime minister, had fallen on deaf ears. Even the idea of moving the arch to another spot where it could be preserved was dismissed as too expensive. Betjeman, vice chairman of the Victorian Society, along with the body's chair, the renowned architectural historian, Nikolaus Pevsner, were determined that St Pancras should not suffer the same fate. Betjeman wrote lovingly of the station: 'that cluster of towers and pinnacles seen from Pentonville Hill and outlined against a foggy sunset, and the great arc of Barlow's train shed gaping to devour incoming engines, and the sudden burst of exuberant Gothic of the hotel seen from gloomy Judd Street.'

This time, thanks to a leak of the proposed idea from a contact at British Rail, Betjeman and his allies had a head start. They acted quickly to stoke up opposition, but recruiting influential names to their cause proved difficult. By the 1960s Victorian architecture had fallen out of favour. Those that saw a new age of clean lines and minimalist buildings, efficiently designed to perform their function, felt little love for Scott's neo-Gothic facade. Even many of those who could see its artistic merits were prepared to see it go as the march of the 'white heat of technology' went on. And, after all, hadn't the Midland's designer Gilbert Scott himself called it a building 'too good for its purpose'.

On 14 June 1966 Betjeman wrote to Sir John Summerson, then curator of Sir John Soane's Museum, hoping for his backing, saying that the station is 'to be pulled down'. 'Would you be prepared to write an appreciative article on it?' he asked, adding, 'You count and I don't.' Summerson, a big fan of Georgian architecture, wrote back saying that he had taken a recently detailed look at the building but concluded that its architecture was, in essence, 'nauseating'. He replied that he couldn't bring himself to write anything in its favour. Betjeman bewailed that St Pancras seemed destined to be 'too beautiful and too romantic to survive'.

Then the pro-St Pancras movement received a stroke of luck. Lord Kennet, then the Labour parliamentary secretary to the Ministry of Housing and Local Government, became a supporter. Questioned in Parliament, he assured that every step would be taken 'to avoid a repetition' of what had happened at Euston. He was pivotal in the government's decision, on 2 November 1967, to promote St Pancras to Grade 1 listed status, putting it on a par with buildings like Windsor

A statue of Sir John Betjeman, who helped save St Pancras from the wrecking ball. (© James Moore)

Castle and Canterbury Cathedral. It thwarted British Rail's plan. The structure seemed to have been saved for the nation.

However, the listing did little to halt St Pancras' decline as a railway terminus. In the 1970s a cash-strapped British Rail took out advertisements detailing how it was committed to preserving the heritage of buildings like St Pancras, but the facts seemed to reveal otherwise. This was exemplified by the selling of the station's great clock in 1978 to an American collector for £250,000. Unfortunately, during its removal the clock fell to the floor, smashing into pieces, and the bits were sold off instead, for £25, to an interested train driver who was retiring. In the same era the booking office only survived thanks to a public inquiry, while the beer industry, which had stored its barrels in the vaults under the concourse, moved its transport to the roads. In 1984, when Betjeman died, St Pancras was still standing. However, by 1988 most of the suburban services were directed away from the terminus thanks to the new Thameslink line and even the railway offices departed to leave a largely shut up, soot-covered ghost of a place with few trains.

Then, in the mid-1990s came St Pancras' ultimate salvation as a railway hub. The station emerged as a prime candidate for a new terminus for the Channel Tunnel Rail Link. In an £800 million restoration project lasting six years, the station was completely overhauled and returned to its former splendour. In November 2007 the queen opened the re-christened St Pancras International, and in 2011 the Midland Grand Hotel, now renamed the St Pancras Renaissance London Hotel, welcomed in guests once more.

Ironically, as all this was going on, the 1960s Euston station narrowly escaped being knocked down, with an order that it be revamped instead. Latterly there is even a movement to have the Euston Arch rebuilt using the existing stone, much of which has been miraculously salvaged from the River Lea in East London.

The original Saint Pancras, the Roman martyr who gave his name to the parish was a 14-year-old boy who had been beheaded by the Emperor Diocletian for refusing to renounce his Christian beliefs in the fourth century. Fortunately, the railway station that bears his name lives on. And today there is a statue of Betjeman, as well as a plaque in tribute to Lord Kennet, inside the terminus recalling their contribution in saving it from a similar, untimely end.

35

WHEN THE EIFFEL TOWER
WAS NEARLY TOPPLED

A 'gigantic black smokestack'; a 'dishonour to Paris'; a 'hulking metal beast crouched on all fours'; a 'truly tragic street lamp'. These were just some of the vitriolic broadsides fired at the proposal to erect a huge iron lattice tower at the entrance to Paris' World Fair of 1889. The structure, which became known as the Eiffel Tower, was intended as a bold statement of French pride, the focal point of an exhibition being organised to mark a century since the French Revolution. But scores of famous artists and writers angrily decried the project's architectural merits. In February 1887, with foundations already being dug for the tower on the city's Champ de Mars, they clubbed together to send a letter to construction director Charles Alphand, which read:

> We the undersigned writers, painters, sculptors, architects passionate devotes of Paris' beauty intact until now have come to protest with all the power and vehemence at our command, in the face of faltering French good taste and of the threat now posed to the very art and history of France, against the construction of the useless and monstrous Eiffel Tower at the heart of our city which the public habitually the benchmark of good sense and fairness, has already mischievously christened the tower of Babel ...

Among the French luminaries who signed the letter were the writers Alexandre Dumas and Guy de Maupassant. Maupassant hated the tower so much that when it was eventually built, in spite of the protests, he took to eating lunch in its second-floor restaurant. His argument was that this was the only place in his beloved city where he didn't have to look at the 'tall skinny pyramid of iron ladders'. The opponents of the tower called themselves the 'Committee of Three Hundred', one for each metre of the projected height of the tower, which would become the tallest building in the world.

It wasn't just aesthetic misgivings that had plagued the tower's engineer Gustave Eiffel in his bid to construct something unique. Some Parisians feared for their safety, believing that the tower would fall over

The Eiffel Tower during its controversial construction. It was only meant to be temporary and was due to be taken down in 1909. (Collection Tour Eiffel)

and destroy their homes, with one citizen taking to the courts to try and get construction halted. There were even fears that if lightning hit the tower the force would kill all the fish in the Seine.

That the tower had attracted such spite was somewhat surprising, given that the city's authorities had already decreed that it would only be there for twenty years. Of course, when the Eiffel Tower eventually opened in May 1889, in record time and under budget, it was a massive success. By October, 6 million people had visited. The tower paid for itself within two years. To their credit some of those who had originally hated the idea changed their minds, and others celebrated the tower with gusto. The artist Paul Gauguin called it part of 'a new decorative art', while the inventor Thomas Edison visited in September 1889, saluting it as a 'gigantic and original specimen of modern engineering'.

Despite attracting millions more visitors over the coming years, the Eiffel Tower was still due to be dismantled after 1909. Its continued existence wasn't helped by the dent which Eiffel himself took to his reputation over the Panama Canal. Eiffel had been involved in the design and building of the canal's locks, but the project was soon mired in financial disaster and Eiffel became embroiled in the scandal. He was sentenced to two years in jail before being acquitted on appeal.

Following the 1900 World Fair, in which the Eiffel Tower was again the star attraction, complete with new lifts, voices were again raised against its continued existence. Many influential figures within the city council believed that it simply had no useful purpose. Eiffel himself knew that tourism alone would not be enough to save it beyond 1909. Science, he realised, could be the key. In the nick of time the French army began using the tower for telegraphic experiments, and in 1905 a radio aerial was erected. Two years later messages were successfully sent to ships as far away as Casablanca and, by 1913, an antenna at the top of the Eiffel Tower was used to send signals to the United States. When the First World War broke out the tower's value as a technological asset would

The engineer Gustave Eiffel. He persuaded the authorities that his tower could be of more use than a mere tourist attraction. (Collection Tour Eiffel)

crush any remaining opposition to it becoming a permanent fixture. In 1914, German forces were closing in on Paris with advance units even able to see the tower. The Allies were eventually able to hold them back, in what became known as the First Battle of the Marne, partly due the fact that the transmitter on top of the tower was able to jam German communications. As the war went on the Eiffel Tower was also used to intercept the German army's radio messages, which even helped snare the infamous spy Mata Hari.

When the war ended in 1918 the Eiffel Tower became an established more than of the skyline once and for all. In 1920 visitor numbers rose to over 400,000 a year and the tower began transmitting the first public radio programmes. There were, though, some gullible folk who obviously believed Parisians were still prepared to part with it. In 1925 con artist Victor Lusting managed to convince a businessman, Andre Poisson, that it was to be sold for scrap and duly collected the cash. When the fraud was exposed Poisson was so embarrassed he didn't even press charges.

The next threat to the tower was very real and came not from city bureaucrats but from Adolf Hitler during the Second World War. This time the Germans were able to conquer Paris within weeks. And in June 1940, Adolf Hitler was famously photographed beside the structure, revelling in France's surrender. However, tower officials had cut the lift cables, meaning Hitler was denied the chance to go to the top. In 1944, as Allied troops came close to liberating the city, the Nazi leader aimed to get his revenge by giving orders for its destruction along with the rest of the city, rather than surrender his prize.

The man given the task was General Dietrich von Cholitz, hand-picked by Hitler for his ruthlessness. Cholitz was no stranger to the scorched earth philosophy of warfare and had already overseen the brutal bombing of Rotterdam in 1940. At the siege of the Soviet city of Sevastopol in 1942 he had made Russian prisoners of war load guns against their own comrades.

On 7 August 1944, Cholitz was made military governor of Paris and, as the military situation worsened, was told by Hitler, 'The city must not fall into the enemy's hand except lying in complete debris.' Explosives were to be placed around prominent landmarks like the Eiffel Tower, while the bridges across the Seine and other strategic locations were also mined. Raging at the bombs raining down on German cities Hitler asked, 'Why should we care if Paris is destroyed?'

On 17 August, Cholitz received Pierre Charles Tattinger, Mayor of Paris, in his headquarters and informed him what was to be done.

Tattinger took him onto a balcony overlooking the city and asked him to imagine himself as a tourist of the future thinking, 'One day I could have destroyed this, and I preserved it as a gift to humanity.'

Two days later French Resistance units rose up in earnest against the occupation, prompting the Allied commanders to consider liberating Paris rather than bypassing it, which had been their original plan. Meanwhile, Cholitz began to realise he did not have the forces to defend the city in a prolonged siege while taking on the Resistance as well. On 23 August German engineers began inspecting the Eiffel Tower looking for a good place to lay charges. And the next day, with fierce battles against the Resistance still raging and Allied forces closing in on the city, Cholitz vowed to personally shoot anyone who suggested abandoning Paris without a fight. Crucially, however, Cholitz still hesitated to blow the city sky high, even lying to his superiors by telling them that the destruction had already begun.

On 25 August the 17,000-strong German garrison surrendered to the French general Philippe Leclerc de Hauteclocque, part of the advance liberating forces converging on the city. Thanks to some brave Parisians the French Tricolor was already flying from the top of the Eiffel Tower.

Whether or not Cholitz really had intended to save Paris is still not clear to this day. In his memoirs he certainly claimed to have done so and later said that, 'If for the first time I had disobeyed, it was because I knew that Hitler was insane.' Whatever the truth the orders to blow up the city, including the Eiffel Tower, were never carried out, while back in Germany Hitler was still angrily asking Colonel General Jodl, his chief of staff, 'Is Paris burning?'

36

HOW ISAMBARD KINGDOM BRUNEL NEARLY ENGINEERED HIS OWN DOWNFALL

In a 2002 television poll conducted by the BBC to find the 'Greatest Briton', the engineer Isambard Kingdom Brunel came second only to Winston Churchill. It seems that Brunel's famous achievements, which include the construction of the Great Western Railway and the pioneering ocean liner SS *Great Britain*, as well as many other famous projects, have made him a national, perhaps international, treasure. But Brunel, who admitted to enjoying the frisson of danger, might never have actually got to build any of the famous landmarks associated with him, for, as a young man, he was nearly killed in a horrific accident deep below ground.

Isambard was born in 1806, the son of another great engineer, Marc Isambard Brunel. Having learned to draw at the age of 4 and, it was said, geometry by the age of 8, he was sent to school in France, before returning, in 1822, to work for his father. Though much admired in his time, Marc experienced a roller-coaster career and even spent time in a debtor's prison in 1821. Realising his worth, the government had paid for his release and, in 1825, he started on a new scheme, the building of a tunnel under the River Thames between Rotherhithe on the south bank and Wapping on the north.

The tunnel was initially intended for transporting goods, via horse-drawn carriage, from the docks either side of the river. And it would involve revolutionary engineering, using a new tunnel shield designed by Marc. The shield worked as a series of frames placed against the excavation face, with sections that could be dug out individually, allowing the shield to advance in the cavity beyond and, in theory, protecting workers from collapses into the bargain. The retaining walls of the tunnel would be bricked behind them as they pushed through.

A shaft was sunk at the Rotherhithe end and work on the tunnel began to progress, with some 600 miners employed on site. The day-to-day digging through the soft clay, just 75ft below the river's surface, was brutal, as those who had attempted to build earlier tunnels had discovered. Flooding was a constant problem. In fact they were working so close to the river bed that old boots and bottles would be found in the mud that was excavated. There was also a serious lack of ventilation down below and the fumes given off by sewage in the water caused many who worked on the tunnel to fall ill. With Marc already in poor health, his resident engineer, William Armstrong, soon fell ill too. In April 1826 the decision was taken to replace him with the younger Brunel.

Isambard was just 20 years old but he threw himself into the job, thinking nothing of going several nights without sleep as he oversaw the excavations. This was a man who believed in getting his hands dirty, but Isambard's fierce drive worried his father. On 16 January 1827, Marc noted in his journal, 'I am very much concerned at his being so unmindful of his health. He may pay dear for it.'

By 18 May in the same year, some 549ft of the Thames Tunnel had been dug out when, suddenly, a portion of the roof collapsed. Isambard not only saved a man from drowning but also showed further bravery by descending to the bottom of the Thames in a diving bell to inspect the damage. There the hole was found and subsequently plugged with thousands of bags full of clay and gravel. The excited Isambard noted in his journal that he enjoyed 'the occasional risk attending our subaquatic adventure'. It took until November to pump out the water and repair the tunnel. To mark the moment, a banquet was held inside for dignitaries, with 120 miners treated to steak and beer and entertained by the band of the Coldstream Guards.

The festivities proved to be somewhat premature. Water was still trickling in. But Isambard was determined to push on; they were now some 605ft through. But at six o'clock on the morning of 12 January 1828, disaster struck again. Brunel had been down inside the tunnel since 10 p.m. the previous evening and was overseeing work on the shield with two of the senior miners when one of the segments of the frame burst open and water spewed in. Isambard immediately ordered the miners to the surface, but now a torrent poured forth, with the water quickly up to their waists as they tried to make their way back down the tunnel to the exit stairs. Then the lights went out, plunging the tunnel into darkness, and a large piece of timber frame collapsed hitting Isambard on the leg, momentarily forcing him under water. Managing to move the lump of wood, he surfaced and clung to one of the tunnel's arches. But as he worked his way towards the shaft he was again caught in the rising water. Luckily for Isambard, assistant engineer Richard Beamish, who had been working aloft, had rushed to the scene. Finding his progress impeded on the main stairs by fleeing workmen he ran to the separate visitors stairs, forcing the locked door with a crowbar. Hurrying down, he saw Isambard floating towards him up the shaft and yanked him out just in time, seconds before the torrent would have drowned the young engineer or dragged him back on the recoiling wave of water. When he arrived back at the surface Isambard was barely conscious but still breathing. The others who had been working alongside Brunel were not so fortunate. They had been swept to their deaths; six killed in all, including the two senior miners who had been next to Isambard. Beamish later wrote that when Isambard came round all he could mutter was the names of his dead colleagues.

Within hours of the accident Isambard was back on his feet trying to assess the damage. But it was quickly clear that, along with a badly injured knee, he had suffered internal injuries. The medical attention on offer seems to have been scant with 'bleeding' and a concoction called 'sugar of lead' doing little to help. After a few days, the young engineer was sent to recuperate in Brighton, but it would take months for him to get back on his feet properly. A month after the accident Isambard attempted to ride a horse and wrote that he had suffered a 'violent haemorrhage'.

Back at the tunnel the efforts to plug the new hole continued, but in August the money dried up and work soon stopped completely. It wouldn't start again for seven years. It took six months for Isambard to fully recover and, now without work, he sunk into depression. But the spare time afforded to him by the accident might have been a blessing in disguise. A year later he heard that plans were needed for a new bridge at Clifton in Bristol. Eventually, in 1831, his design was chosen for the crossing. Thanks to delays in the project, Isambard would never actually see his suspension bridge completed, but it began an association with the city of Bristol which would spur him on to bigger things. He designed new docks for its harbour and in 1833 was appointed chief engineer for the new railway from London to the west. The breathtaking tunnels and bridges along the lines, later dubbed 'God's Wonderful Railway', made his name with the network. Isambard went on to design the SS *Great Britain*, the first screw-propelled ocean-going iron steam ship, launched in 1843 as part of his masterplan to forge a connection by rail and sea from London to America.

In the very same year, after new money had been found for its completion, the Thames Tunnel finally opened. It was soon being described as the eighth wonder of the world and helped to win Isambard's father a knighthood. Measuring 35ft across, 20ft high and 1,300ft long, it was the first tunnel under a navigable river. A million people walked through to marvel at it during the first ten weeks of operation. Though there was no money for the huge spiral ramps intended to take horse drawn goods through the underground passage, it would soon find new life as a railway tunnel.

By the time the Thames Tunnel was finished, Isambard was already gaining fame. But just a few days after its official opening on 25 March 1843, his life was threatened once more, though this time in a more bizarre way. On 3 April Isambard was resting at home, making his children laugh by showing them some magic tricks. During one trick he pretended to pass a half-sovereign from his ear into his mouth, but the coin accidentally slipped down his throat. In the following days he developed a bad cough and a doctor was called. It turned out that the coin had actually gone down Isambard's windpipe and become lodged in his trachea, threatening to choke him at any moment. The medical establishment seemed puzzled as to how to proceed.

Typically, the engineer came up with his own design of forceps to help dislodge the coin. The renowned surgeon Benjamin Brodie was called to perform a tracheotomy using them to fish out the coin, but to no avail. Eventually Isambard was placed upon a board and upended in the hope that gravity would do its work. Amazingly, after a few tries, the coin did indeed fall back into his mouth, much to the relief of Isambard, the doctors and the public, who had become captivated by his unusual plight during the fourteen days he was in danger. News quickly spread of the engineer's salvation, with the historian and politician Thomas Macaulay running through the Athenaeum Club proclaiming of the coin, 'It's out, it's out!'

37

THE UNSINKABLE ARTHUR JOHN PRIEST

The RMS *Titanic* was famously supposed to be unsinkable. Yet, on 15 April 1912, after hitting an iceberg, she sank to the bottom of the Atlantic with the loss of more than 1,500 lives. While it had proved that the *Titanic*, which foundered on its maiden voyage, was, in fact, very sinkable, one man on board would go on to earn the right to be called unsinkable himself. For Arthur John Priest survived not only the tragedy of the *Titanic* but, astonishingly, the sinking of three other ships too.

Born in Southampton in 1887, Priest, like thousands of others in the city, got work aboard the huge ships that plied the port. He became a stoker, and on 20 September 1911, at the age of 24, found himself working aboard the *Titanic*'s sister ship, RMS *Olympic*, captained by Captain Edward Smith, the man who would also skipper the fateful *Titanic*. On her fifth voyage the *Olympic*, which sported every Edwardian luxury imaginable, including Turkish baths and swimming pools, was leaving Southampton. The ship was travelling closely alongside the HMS *Hawke*, a cruiser, when the two collided. The *Hawke*'s bow was badly damaged, while the *Olympic* was holed below the waterline. Fortunately no one was killed and Priest, along with the 1,300 passengers, didn't even get their feet wet as the *Olympic* limped back to land under its own steam. While the *Olympic*'s owner, the White Star Line, was later found at fault for the accident, the fact that the liner had stayed afloat – partly thanks to the closure of its watertight compartments – gave added weight to the hype that both it and the *Titanic* were 'unsinkable'.

Less than a year later, Priest found himself aboard the equally opulent *Titanic* as it steamed across the Atlantic on route to New York. While first-class passengers above enjoyed fine dining and facilities like an on-board gymnasium, Priest, on £6 a month, was working alongside 175 others in the bowels of the vessel. His job was to help feed the ship's twenty-nine boilers with 600 tonnes of coal a day. It was hot work. Another stoker, George Kemish, spoke of being 'roasted by the heat'. But Priest, along with his fellow firemen, was soon to find himself plunged into the icy waters of the ocean when an iceberg tore a huge hole in the *Titanic*'s hull at 11.40 p.m.

Another fireman who also survived, James Crimmins, told later how:

> The bump threw us off our feet. We were told to stay at our posts. No-one seemed excited and it never occurred to anyone that the ship would sink ... We knew she had hit an iceberg and the situation took a more serious turn when we were ordered to draw the fires from the boilers.

In his account, Crimmins also tells of how a little later a shout went up, 'Every man for himself!' To escape, Priest would have had to climb several levels and wend his way through endless corridors to the deck. Somehow he managed to swim to lifeboat no. 15. Priest had suffered four frostbitten toes and an injured leg, but emerged alive from the rescue ship *Carpathia* three days later on the dock at New York. Back home his family must have feared the worst. It was assumed that none of the stokers could have survived as they would be too far down to have time to get into the boats. In fact, he was one of forty-four firemen to escape the *Titanic*, with many jumping into the freezing ocean wearing only the vest and short pants they worked in.

Two years later, when the First World War broke out, the undeterred Priest was among the first to volunteer for action. And his wartime experiences were to be as turbulent and terrifying as any faced by the soldiers engaged on the Western Front. Priest was again working as

Arthur John Priest, the remarkable stoker who survived the *Titanic* and several other sinkings. (Southampton City Archives, www. southampton.gov. uk/archives)

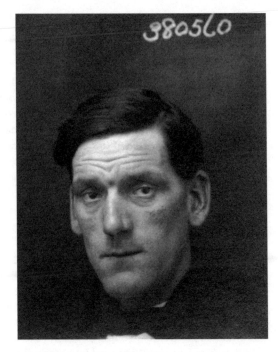

a stoker, this time on the HMS *Alcantara*, when the ship encountered the German raider *Grief* on 29 February 1916 in the North Sea. The German ship had been disguised as a Norwegian craft the *Rena*. It was attempting to run the Allied naval blockade that had been crippling Germany's economy. When the *Grief* failed to respond to attempts at communication, the captain of the *Alcantara*, Thomas Wardle, closed in and ordered her to stop so he could carry out an inspection. The *Grief*'s crew quickly lowered their Norwegian flag and opened fire. The *Alcantara* itself hurriedly returned fire. A vicious exchange at close range went on for twelve minutes, and by the time more British ships arrived to help, the *Alcantara* was sinking. The crippled *Grief* was soon finished off too, with the British ships HMS *Comus* and HMS *Munster* picking up survivors from both. Some seventy-four men had been killed aboard the *Alcantara*. But once again Priest had survived, albeit with shrapnel wounds to the leg and burns.

Quickly recovering and returning to work, Priest found himself aboard the *Britannic*, another of the *Titanic*'s sister ships. But the *Britannic*, completed in 1915, would never serve its intended purpose, carrying civilian passengers across the Atlantic. It was requisitioned in 1916 to carry the wounded from Gallipoli, during that disastrous campaign which cost 44,000 Allied lives, and began criss-crossing the Mediterranean, ferrying hundreds of casualties back to Britain. Priest must have shivered the first time he went aboard. Even though it was slightly larger than the *Titanic* and decked out with its hospital ship red crosses, the *Britannic* would have looked uncannily like the ship he had miraculously escaped from four years earlier. At least this time it had extra lifeboats. It would need them. At 8.12 a.m. on 21 November, the *Britannic* was returning to the Dardanelles, near Greece, when an explosion ripped through her hull. The captain knew the ship was in deep trouble. He ordered the watertight doors closed to buy time, sent out a distress signal and readied the lifeboats. Luckily for Priest, as the ship began taking on more water, the captain also ordered the boiler rooms evacuated. The *Britannic* had hit a mine and sank beneath the waves in just fifty-five minutes. A nurse on board, Violet Jessop, who, like Priest had survived the *Titanic*, later recalled:

> She dipped her head a little, then a little lower and still lower. All the deck machinery fell into the sea like a child's toys. Then she took a fearful plunge, her stern rearing hundreds of feet into the air until with a final roar, she disappeared into the depths, the noise of her going resounding through the water with undreamt of violence.

However, of the 1,066 passengers aboard, some 1,036 were picked up by rescue ships. Those extra lifeboats and the warmer temperatures in the water had been crucial. Again, Priest was one of the survivors, although, almost inevitably, within months he was back on board another hospital ship, the *Donegal*. Hospital ships were now being targeted by U-boats as the Germans believed the British were contravening the Hague Convention by using them to transport able-bodied troops. The tactic had caused outrage in Britain. The *Donegal* managed to out-run one attempted attack by a submarine on 1 March 1917. But on 17 April, as it was once more carrying wounded soldiers back across the Channel from the trenches in France, it was hit by a torpedo. Within sight of the English coast, the *Donegal* went down stern first half, an hour after it had been hit. One of those on board the *Donegal* was Archie Jewell, who had been the lookout on the *Titanic* and had survived. This time he wasn't so lucky, being among the forty-one soldiers and crew who perished. However, once again, Priest was plucked from the sea alive.

By now Priest's remarkable story of serial survival was coming to wider attention. On 23 April *The Times* reported:

> The remarkable adventures of a young fireman have been brought to light through the sinking of the Donegal. John Priest, who lives in Southampton, is only 29 years of age. He has been on the sea since his youth, and has served in many waters. He has seen four of the vessels in which he was serving sink, and three others have been damaged ... His last ship was the Donegal from which he escaped with a rather serious injury to his head.

Presumably because of his injuries, Priest was discharged. He won the General Service and Mercantile Marine War Medals for his dedicated service. After the war Priest is said to have felt that, such was his reputation, men would refuse to sail with him. He died of pneumonia on 11 February 1937 on dry land, in his home town. He was survived by his wife, Annie, and two sons, George and Fred.

38

THE MAN WHO OPERATED ON HIMSELF IN THE ANTARCTIC

In 2010 a popular film was made out of the true story of a man who had cut off his own arm. Aron Ralston had become trapped by a boulder in a Utah canyon and, after five days without the hope of rescue, had decided to amputate the limb with a rather blunt multi-tool. He survived to tell the tale and to see his story on the big screen in Danny Boyle's *127 Hours*.

Ralston is one of a small handful of people who have carried out such self-surgery successfully. But while the youngster is now rightly famous for his daring escape, another man, Leonid Rogozov, deserves to be just as well known. For he achieved a feat no less eye-watering than Ralston's: he saved his own life by operating on his abdomen while on an expedition to the freezing Antarctic.

Perhaps it was growing up in a remote part of Siberia that made Rogozov tough enough for the extraordinary drama that was to unfold when, on 5 November 1960, he boarded a ship called the *Ob* in Leningrad (now St Petersburg). Aged just 26, the recently graduated doctor was to be a member of the sixth Soviet Antarctic expedition. Along with a host of other powers, the Soviet Union had kept a presence on the Continent since the mid-1950s, and on this occasion the mission was intent on establishing a new polar research base, Novolazarevskaya Station. The *Ob* would carry Rogozov and a small team more than 10,000 miles south into the icy wilderness to begin their task.

After thirty-six days at sea the small party of scientists and support workers landed at the ice shelf on the Princess Astrid Coast and began work during the long days of the Antarctic summer. The base was finished in February 1961 and a team of twelve then steeled themselves to hunker down for the Antarctic winter. There was little hope of anyone getting in or out for months. Rogozov was the only doctor attached to the unit, but with a team chosen partly for their robust fitness levels it was felt Rogozov wouldn't have much to do. He spent his days working as a part-time meteorologist and driving an all-terrain vehicle. Ironically, while the rest of the team stayed well, Rogozov was the one who would fall dangerously ill.

Waking on the morning of 29 April 1961, Rogozov felt decidedly rough, noting the symptoms of weakness and nausea. As the day went on he started suffering from severe pain in the stomach. It quickly became focussed on the lower right-hand part of his abdomen. Rogozov took his own temperature and confirmed that, as suspected, he also had a fever.

With growing horror Rogozov realised that he had the symptoms of a life-threatening condition. He wrote in his journal, 'It seems that I have appendicitis. I am keeping quiet about it, even smiling. Why frighten my friends? Who could be of help? A polar explorer's only encounter with medicine is likely to have been in a dentist's chair.' Left untreated the appendix can burst, leading to life-threatening infections. The inflamed appendix must be removed as soon as possible to avoid death. Optimistically, Rogozov pumped himself with antibiotics, but by the next day his condition had deteriorated. His fever was worse, he was vomiting and there were signs that peritonitis was setting in, threatening his vital organs. He wrote in his diary of the pain, 'it hurts like the devil ... wailing like a hundred jackals.' The budding surgeon knew that without an operation he could be dead within hours. But, with a blizzard raging outside, there was no chance of being airlifted out. As it was, the nearest plane was more than 1,000 miles away. Slowly, the realisation dawned on Rogozov; if he wanted to live he would have to operate on himself. He noted, 'It's almost impossible ... but I can't just fold my arms and give up.' Rogozov broke the news to the rest of the team and, in a state of bewilderment, they started making preparations for surgery under direction from the doctor.

If he was to perform the unthinkable, Rogozov would need some help. He recruited one of the team's mechanics, Zinovy Teplinsky, to hold a mirror so that he could see what he was doing during the operation. A meteorologist, Alexandr Artemev, was chosen to pass Rogozov instruments and to hold retractors, having to kneel down throughout much of the surgery. The pair, turning white as sheets as they realised the magnitude of the task, were told how to administer drugs and artificial respiration in the event that their patient lost consciousness. As Rogozov put it, they 'were instructed in proper behaviour during the operation'. Two others in the base's team administered a local anaesthetic before the appendectomy was begun. Because the instruments Rogozov would use had been stored in plunging temperatures outside, they would at least be suitably sterile.

At 10 p.m. on the evening of 30 April Rogozov, propped himself up on some pillows on his own bed, turned slightly to his side and made the first incision. He cut through 10–12cm of the abdominal wall to expose the appendix. It was slow work. Rogozov felt nauseous and about forty minutes in to the operation, almost passed out. Somehow, each time he felt faint, he managed to continue, skilfully wielding his scalpel to remove the diseased and perforated appendix. Rogozov later wrote, 'Sometimes I had to work entirely by feel.'

Also on hand during the operation was the base chief, Vladislav Gerbovich, in case one of the other assistants fainted. He wrote:

When Rogozov had made the incision and was manipulating his own innards as he removed the appendix, his intestine gurgled, which was highly unpleasant for us; it made one want to turn away, flee, not look – but I kept my head and stayed. Artemev and Teplinsky also held their places, although it later turned out they had both gone quite dizzy and were close to fainting ... Rogozov himself was calm and focused on his work, but sweat was running down his face and he frequently asked Teplinsky to wipe his forehead.

After Rogozov had removed the appendix, antibiotics were pumped into the wound by one of the assistants and at midnight, after some stitches had been made to seal things up, the operation was finished. There was nothing for Rogozov to do but try and get some rest and hope for the best.

Rogozov later told how his 'postoperative condition was moderately poor'. But after four days the signs of peritonitis had gone, and after five days his temperature returned to normal. He added, 'after seven days the stitches were removed. The wound was completely healed.'

Had he left the surgery a day later Rogozov's appendix would have burst and he would have surely died. Amazingly, within two weeks, Rogozov returned to his usual duties at the base. But his story soon became the toast of the Soviet Union and he was awarded the Order of the Red Banner of Labour. In 1962 – a year after saving his own life – he returned to his homeland where he continued to work as a doctor until his death in 2000. Perhaps not wanting to tempt fate, Rogozov never went back to the Antarctic.

Though rare, Rogozov's tale is not quite unique. In 1921 a rather eccentric Dr Kaye in the United States had removed his own appendix to show how local anaesthetics could work. Unlike Rogozov, however, he didn't perform the act thousands of miles from any form of emergency medical back-up.

39

HOW A MOULDY MELON SAVED THOUSANDS OF ALLIED LIVES ON D-DAY

As the troops landed on the shores of Normandy on 6 June 1944, the medics who accompanied them carried a new weapon. It was not one that could be used against the enemy, but it was the ultimate defence for soldiers who had been wounded. During the first twenty-four hours of the Normandy landings, pivotal in the liberation of mainland Europe from German occupation during the Second World War, there were around 12,000 Allied casualties with more than 2,500 soldiers killed.

Yet some 3,000 lives were saved during Operation Overlord thanks to a new wonder drug, penicillin, able to fight the infections which often set in after servicemen had been injured in action.

British scientist Alexander Fleming has gone down in history as the man who discovered penicillin. In 1928, while studying influenza, the bacteriologist went on holiday from his job at St Mary's Hospital in London. Returning, he noticed some blue-green mould growing in one of the petri dishes he had been using which was contaminated with the *staphylococcus* bacterium. Interestingly, the fungus had a bacteria-free area around it. Fleming realised that something in the mould must be killing the bacteria. After further experiments he found that the mould was *penicillum notatum* and named the anti bacterial substance he had lighted upon penicillin.

But it wasn't Fleming who would develop penicillin into a workable antibiotic agent. That job was left to a small group of largely forgotten scientists who set off in a race against time to develop and mass produce enough penicillin for use on the battlefield and, ultimately, in civilian life too.

At first, Fleming had even been sceptical that the antibacterial properties of penicillin had a medical application. Isolating pure penicillin, in the kind of quantities necessary to make it a useful agent to use against serious infections, was difficult. But in 1939, with war clouds gathering over Europe, Howard Florey, an Australian scientist at Oxford University, took another look at Fleming's work. With the help of a team that included the biochemist Ernst Chain, a Jewish refugee from Germany, and a British-born scientist called Norman Heatley, he began work to see if penicillin could be developed into something that would save lives.

Over the next two years they discovered a way to purify small amounts of penicillin. Then, in May 1940, the month in which the British army had to be evacuated from Dunkirk, they injected it into four of eight mice who had been infected with fatal doses of bacteria. The ones that had not been injected died immediately but the others survived.

The scientific community now realised that antibiotics could make a massive difference in the war (which Britain was losing), curing both soldiers and civilians of deadly infections, as long as it could be harnessed in large enough quantities. This was their biggest headache. Heatley had even resorted to growing the mould in bedpans. But with bombs now raining down on Britain from German planes, the academics buried themselves away in the lab trying to produce enough penicillin for clinical trials on humans. Knowing they were on to something big,

Florey and Heatley even smeared spores over their coats, to save their research, in case they had to suddenly close down the operation when the Germans invaded.

In early 1941 the team came across the case of Albert Alexander, a policeman who was dying in an Oxfordshire hospital after suffering a simple scratch while pruning roses. In those days, without the availability of antibiotics, an infected injury as slight as this could rapidly become life threatening and Alexander had already lost an eye. The team began administering Alexander with penicillin and his condition began to improve. Sadly, however, there still wasn't enough of the stuff to complete his treatment. Alexander died a few weeks later.

But penicillin's pioneers had proved that it could be used to cure infection and had the potential to radically transform the world of medicine. Now they needed a way to make lots of it. The resources to do so simply weren't available in Britain, so, in the summer of 1941, Florey and Heatley flew to America where enthusiasm for their work was growing. On the plane journey across the Atlantic, Florey carried a small briefcase with cotton-wrapped test tubes on his lap. Inside were small amounts of penicillin culture.

With the backing of the Rockefeller Foundation and the US Department of Agriculture, a research facility in Peoria, Illinois, was identified as the place where there was already expertise in the kind of fermentation that would be needed to produce industrial levels of penicillin. Heatley immediately headed to Peoria and, over the next few months, yields of penicillin had increased ten-fold by growing penicillin mould in something called corn steep liquor, a by-product in the manufacture of cornstarch. It still wasn't enough. Then, in December 1941, the Americans entered the war, and the race to produce penicillin on a massive scale hotted up. The US War Department made the creation of useable amounts of penicillin a research priority, second only to their planned development of an atomic bomb.

Progress was painfully slow. In early 1942, there was still only enough penicillin in the US to treat ten patients. But in that year the first life was saved, when a woman called Anne Miller, who had suffered a miscarriage, was cured of blood poisoning. Then, in 1943, came a breakthrough in the manufacturing process. A worldwide hunt had been launched for mould that would deliver the highest quantities of penicillin, with soil samples collected from as far afield as South Africa and India. But then, an enthusiastic worker in the Peoria lab itself, Mary Hunt, brought in a rotting cantaloupe melon from a local market. The mould on it, identified as *penicillin chrysogenum*, produced 3,000 times the amount of penicillin originally created by Fleming. It became the strain from which most of the world's penicillin would be made. Now mass production could begin in earnest.

In the same year, Florey flew to North Africa and showed that penicillin could help cure gangrene in the wounds of soldiers fighting there; he even flew to Russia, to help Britain and America's ally start manufacturing penicillin there too. That summer, pharmaceutical giants such as Pfizer were set to work making vast amounts of penicillin. By 1944 total US production was up to 130 billion units a month, with British factories chipping in too. In May 1944 *Time* magazine carried a front page picture of Fleming, who had actually had little to do with the wartime work, with the words, 'His penicillin will save more lives than war can spend.'

By June 1944, when General Eisenhower was ready to launch D-Day, there were 2.3 million doses – 180 tonnes – available to the million-plus men poised to pour across the English Channel and enough to treat all the casualties who needed it. US Army instructions said that penicillin was to be administered by powder in open wounds or by a drip as near the battlefield as possible. An advert for one US pharmaceutical lab showed an American GI being given penicillin on the battlefield, with the tagline: 'Thanks to penicillin he will come home'.

It's believed that penicillin improved the survival rate in American soldiers alone by up to 15 per cent. It was also particularly useful in tackling the many cases of sexually transmitted infection that beset the Allied forces. By the end of the war it was being produced on a vast scale across the world, and after the war penicillin was made widely available to civilian doctors. In 1945, in recognition of their work, the Nobel Prize in Medicine was awarded to Florey, Chain and Fleming. Strangely, Heatley did not get to share in the prize.

The development of penicillin in time for D-Day was one of the factors that gave the Allies the upper hand as they drove on into Germany. Few wounded German soldiers ever got it. Despite knowing of penicillin, the Germans never managed to achieve the necessary scientific breakthroughs that would allow them make it any significant quantities. This was partly down to Florey, who rumbled early attempts by the Germans to get some of his own cultures in a clandestine operation involving a Swiss company. He also warned Fleming to be on his guard when it came to handing out samples. Penicillin was only ever used on a handful of Germans. One of them was Adolf Hitler – treated for an injury to his hand after the failed July 1944 bomb plot. Less than a year later he was dead, having put an end to his own life, while thousands of victorious Allied soldiers were only alive to celebrate VE Day, thanks to the revolutionary medicine.

40

SAVING MILLIONS FROM DEADLY GAS IN THE FIRST WORLD WAR

In the early evening on 1 May 1915, near the town of Ypres in Belgium, at a low rise in the British line known as Hill 60, a deadly yellowish-green cloud drifted across no-man's-land. This was one of the first gas attacks of the First World War and the British soldiers, sitting in their trenches were equipped with little more than damp face cloths with which to defend themselves against the terrifying new weapon being deployed. The Germans had unleashed sixty canisters of chlorine which, carried by the wind, slowly engulfed the ranks of the first battalion of the Dorset Regiment, leaving them gasping for air and effectively drowning as liquid filled their lungs.

Somehow, the few soldiers who had not succumbed managed to fight off the German attack which ensued. But the toll was brutal. The official history of the war later recorded the effects thus, 'Ninety men died from gas poisoning in the trenches or before they could be got to a dressing station; of the 207 brought to the nearest dressing stations, 46 died almost immediately and 12 after long suffering.'

On the Dorsets' flank, a unit of the Bedfordshire Regiment also fell victim, with private Ted Warner single-handedly defending his trench against the German advance before reinforcements arrived. Ted, posthumously awarded the Victoria Cross for his bravery, died the next morning from gas inhalation.

The episode marked a new, gruesome chapter in the war for British troops, though it was not quite the first time gas had been used during the conflict. The Germans had already tested tear gas shells against the Russians on the Eastern Front, and by the spring of 1915 they began using gas in earnest on the Western Front, first on French colonial troops and Canadian forces in April, before the attack on the British at Hill 60 in early May.

Over the next three years both sides would launch themselves into a vicious period of unrestrained chemical warfare. Many different agents were used. Following chlorine, the deadlier phosgene was used, a more effective killer since it was both colourless and almost odourless. In 1917 both sides started deploying mustard gas, which caused horrendous blisters as well as external and internal bleeding.

More than a million men were ultimately injured or maimed by gas during the First World War, with 91,000 dying as a result of inhaling the toxins. In his poem *Dulce et Decorum Est*, Wilfred Owen vividly described the fear that gas induced among the soldiers on the Western Front:

> GAS! Gas! Quick, boys! – An ecstasy of fumbling,
> Fitting the clumsy helmets just in time;
> But someone still was yelling out and stumbling,
> And floundering like a man in fire or lime ...
> Dim, through the misty panes and thick green light,
> As under a green sea, I saw him drowning.

What is remarkable, however, is that, as a proportion of the overall casualties, relatively few British soldiers were actually killed by gas during the four years of the First World War. The figure is reckoned to be just over 8,000 dead. In fact, though they were often the victim of gas attacks, many of the troops escaped the deadly effects of inhalation thanks to the efforts of a forgotten hero of the conflict, a man who dedicated himself to inventing the first easily portable, mass-produced gas mask.

When war broke out, Edward Harrison, already a successful pharmaceutical chemist, rushed to enlist. But he was already in his mid-forties and was initially turned down. In 1915 he tried again, this time fibbing about his age, and was admitted as a private to the 1st Sportsman's Battalion of the Royal Fusiliers. Even before the war, Harrison had showed his commitment to using his skills to protect people. In 1909 he had published *Secret Remedies: What They Cost and What They Contain*, an investigation of 'miracle' cures on the market, which eventually led to better regulation of medicines.

Now his knowledge would be used to save millions from the threat of chemical weapons. During 1915 the only defence against gas, both among Allied and German troops, had been a variety of rudimentary masks and hoods impregnated with chemicals to counteract the gas,

An Australian chaplain wearing a box respirator to protect against gas attacks, Fleurbaix, France, in 1916.

with the Germans and French working on similar designs. None of these were particularly effective and the British Government began to work on box respirators, more elaborate masks with pipes and filters. In 1915 they brought together a team of scientists to experiment on a practical gas mask, with Harrison, then serving in France, among them.

Harrison, promoted to lieutenant in the Royal Engineers, began work in the Anti-Gas Department at the Royal Army Medical College in Millbank, London. He worked tirelessly, leading a group of enthusiastic young chemists as they tried to perfect a workable gas mask, able to protect against the potentially huge range of poisons that could be used by the enemy. Harrison would often test protective devices through a trial and error process; wearing them himself whilst sealed in a gas-filled room. He was motivated by a sense of urgency, aware that in a race to develop new weapons any delay in perfecting a defence could be critical.

The Large Box Respirator, often known as Harrison's Tower, was the result. A more practical-sized version, essential if it was to be carried into battle, called the Small Box Respirator, was also developed within months. The idea was to have a separate box, worn on a shoulder strap, containing a range of filters, including charcoal and other substances able to defend against a range of gases while allowing oxygen through. This canister was then attached via a rubber hosepipe to a tightly fitting rubber face piece. The soldier inhaled through the mouthpiece and was able to exhale this way too, with the addition of a flutter valve. Inside the mask there was also a clip to stop the wearer breathing through their nose. Each respirator was individually fitted to a soldier, who was exposed to tear gas for five minutes to make sure it was working.

By August 1916 the Small Box Respirator was being distributed to thousands of troops and became standard for the rest of the war. It was also used by other Allied armies, including the Americans when they joined the fray in 1917.

Sadly, just days before the respirator became regular issue, Harrison's eldest son was killed during the Battle of the Somme, which went on to cost the Allies half a million casualties that year. Harrison was soon made lieutenant colonel for his efforts and awarded the Legion d'Honneur by the French, the nation's highest military accolade. One General Hartley later remembered that Harrison wasn't only vital in the development of the respirator, but in its mass manufacture:

> Colonel Harrison was one of the great discoveries of the war ... he organised the manufacture of the respirator on a large scale and it is a great testimony to his foresight and energy that in spite of all the difficulties of production the supplies promised to France never failed.

One of his obituaries observed that, had Harrison's death occurred earlier, it would have been a 'calamity to the cause of the allies'. And in a recently discovered letter to his widow, the then Minister of Munitions, Winston Churchill, wrote, 'It is in large measure to him that our troops have been given effectual protection from the German poisonous gases.'

But Harrison would not live to see the end of the war. On 4 November 1918, just one week before Armistice Day, he died, aged 49, from pneumonia after contracting influenza. The effects of working in fume-filled rooms had taken their toll on his lungs. Harrison was buried with full military honours at Brompton Cemetery in West London.

The Royal Society of Chemistry credit Harrison's invention with saving hundreds of thousands of lives. And today, at the head of the war memorial at their offices, there is an image of a gas attack and this tribute to Harrison: 'To save our armies from poison gas he gave his last full measure of devotion.' It echoes a 1918 article in the *Journal of the Society of Chemical Industry*, which recorded that in life Harrison's motto had been, 'Give! Give self! Give service!'

41

THE SECOND WORLD WAR GAS ATTACKS THAT NEVER WERE

In May 1945 a church minister called Archie Mitchell was leading a church picnic at a beauty spot in the mountains of Oregon in the north-west of the United States with his wife Elsie and five local children. When Elsie and the kids went to investigate what appeared to be the remains of a deflated balloon there was an explosion. All six were killed. They were to be the only casualties of enemy action on American soil during the Second World War, the victims of a Japanese 'fire balloon'.

In the dying days of the war the Japanese released 9,000 of these balloons carrying incendiary bombs across the Pacific. They hadn't done much damage but the American authorities had hushed up their existence in case of panic; they were concerned that the balloons might be used to deliver chemical or biological weapons. There was foundation for the concerns – the Japanese were already known to have used mustard and tear gas during their war with the Chinese, which had begun in 1937. In one single Japanese gas attack on the Chinese lines during October 1941 there were 600 fatalities. They had experimented with biological weapons over Chinese cities too.

In the event, a Japanese gas or biological attack against the United States never came – in fact the country's chemical weapons programme was already being wound down. And, apart from the use of poisons by Japan in China, mass chemical warfare was one of the evils that did not rear its head in any of the major theatres of battle during the Second World War. In a global conflagration which saw the use of the atom bomb and the extermination of millions during the Holocaust, partly through the use of deadly gases, it was, at least, one thing to be thankful for. Yet, between 1939–45, the world had actually come within a hair's breadth of entering into chemical Armageddon several times.

The use of deadly gasses during the First World War had caused untold suffering, and under the terms of the Treaty of Versailles a defeated Germany was banned from making chemical or biological weapons. Then, in 1925, the United States, along with twenty-eight other nations, signed the Geneva Protocol banning a 'first use' of chemical weapons against an enemy. It didn't stop the big powers preparing for the possibility of chemical warfare in the 1920s and '30s, even if the weapons they manufactured were, ostensibly, only to be used defensively.

In 1935 Mussolini's Italy used mustard bombs against Abyssinian tribesmen, and when a global war broke out in 1939 there was no reason to think that this new conflict would be any different to the First World War. Gas might be just another weapon in the arsenals used by both sides.

After Hitler's rise to power during the interwar years, the Germans had discovered deadly nerve agents, including Tabun, which could cause death in minutes, and when war broke out the Nazis slowly built a stockpile of toxic gases. The British certainly expected the Germans to use gas in bombing attacks on cities. As early as the 1938 Munich crisis, 30 million gas masks had been manufactured in Britain, the number rising to 70 million by 1941. And throughout the war it was assumed by the Allies that chemical weapons could be used both upon civilians and troops at any moment. Their armies travelled with portable chemical weapons labs and decontamination equipment. Soldiers carried detector kits and many had uniforms impregnated against gas attacks and, of course, masks. But the Allies were building up their own stockpiles of chemical weapons too, prepared to retaliate in kind if necessary.

In the wake of the British defeat at Dunkirk in 1940 senior military officials even proposed using gas against the Germans first, in the event of an invasion of home soil. Winston Churchill ordered production of mustard gas to be speeded up, sanctioning a plan to shower Germans soldiers with the poison on British beaches if Hitler's army landed. By 1942 Britain had 20,000 tonnes of gas at its disposal and, in May that year, when there was a fear that Hitler might use his chemical weapons against Russia, Churchill vowed to retaliate in support using 'our great and growing air superiority in the west to carry gas warfare on the largest possible scale far and wide upon the towns and cities of Germany'.

By now the United States were in the war too and had launched their own massive programme of chemical weapons production, eventually stockpiling 146,000 tonnes of toxins. The Allies stationed the weapons at strategic points across the globe, and a measure of how ready they were to use them in the event of an offensive by the Axis powers was demonstrated by a tragic incident in 1943. By this time the Allies were occupying Southern Italy and on 2 December a German air raid on the port of Bari damaged the SS *John Harvey*, an American ship that was secretly carrying 100 tonnes of mustard gas. The attack led to a huge release of the chemical, with 600 soldiers and civilians succumbing and more than eighty dying from the effects.

After the Normandy landings of 1944 Churchill again showed that he had few qualms about being the first to unleash chemical warfare. Enraged about the hundreds of Britons being killed by Hitler's new V-1 rocket campaign against London, he proposed retaliating with a gas attack on German rocket facilities and industrial centres. In a minute to his chiefs of staff on 6 July 1944, he wrote, 'I want a cold blooded calculation made as to how it would pay us to use poison gas ... it may be several weeks or even months before I shall ask you to drench Germany with poison gas and if we do it, let us do it 100 per cent.' He was eventually persuaded that conventional bombing was more practical and that the danger of a German retaliation with its own gas could not be ruled out.

Fortunately, for most of the war, Hitler also ruled out using gas because the level of the inevitable retaliation by the Allies was an unknown quantity. Though the Nazis possessed lethal new nerve agents, his scientists wrongly imagined that the Allies had them too. It was a fair assumption. After all, went the thinking, his enemies' research teams had not been blocked for years by the Versailles Treaty as Germany's had.

There is a theory that Hitler simply despised gas warfare. As a foot soldier in the First World War he himself had been the victim of a gas attack at Ypres in October 1918. However, it seems unlikely, given that he was prepared to put Jews to death in gas chambers, that he thought gas warfare particularly distasteful. Indeed, in 1944, Hitler, now cornered, did consider using gas to halt the advance of the Soviet armies in the east. But by this time Allied air superiority meant German cities were likely to come off worse in an ensuing exchange of chemical agents. What's more, the German civilian population was short of gas masks. Albert Speer, Minister of Armaments, eventually convinced Hitler that the use of chemical weapons would be a costly diversion. Interestingly, had Hitler employed gas, Allied military experts believe it could have been effective, holding up the Normandy campaign by as much as six months.

In the Pacific theatre of the Second World War – and arguably beyond – the fact that chemical weapons were not used was largely down to the fervent moral objections of US President Franklin D. Roosevelt. In June 1943, he said vehemently, 'Use of such weapons has been outlawed by the general opinion of civilized mankind ... I state categorically that we shall under no circumstances resort to the use of such weapons unless they are first used by our enemies.' But as the war ground on, American forces began to take heavy casualties as they endeavoured to liberate Pacific islands from the Japanese. In early 1945, in the battle for Iwo Jima, the Americans lost 6,800 men, taking the island with 20,000 wounded. Yet an official Allied report for the Americans had shown that gas would be incredibly effective against the dug-in Japanese positions that were so difficult to dislodge. Polls in the US showed growing public support for the use of gas against the Japanese, with newspaper headlines screaming, 'We should gas Japan'. Roosevelt stood firm. The country's Chemical Warfare Service complained that any proposal they put up 'was immediately rejected due to personal bias'.

When Roosevelt died on 12 April 1945, and with casualties mounting in the slow progress of the army towards Japan, the US military began to look seriously at the 'first strike' chemical option again. The 82-day battle for Okinawa fought that summer cost 12,500 American lives and plans for chemical warfare were duly drawn up. Army chief George C. Marshall was for it, given the losses, but by this stage the government was already moving towards the atomic option for bringing about the swift end to the war with Japan. In August 1945 the new president, Harry S. Truman, halted the debate when he ordered an atomic bomb to be dropped over Hiroshima.

After the war much of the huge stockpile of US chemical bombs was dumped in the sea. But, in occupying Germany, the Allies had already discovered the Nazi nerve agent capacity. It was to usher in a new age of chemical weapons research – just as the Cold War took hold.

42

THE MAN WHO LOOKED
INTO THE ABYSS

The town of Chernobyl in Ukraine and, more recently, Fukushima in Japan are places whose names have become synonymous with nuclear accidents. In the early days of the atomic age, however, it was Britain that held its breath, narrowly avoiding its own nuclear catastrophe. The incident at Windscale in Cumbria saw radiation released across the UK. Yet if it had not been for the efforts of some of the brave workers at the site, the accident could have been much more serious, leaving part of Britain uninhabitable for decades and thousands suffering from cancer.

At 5 p.m. on the night of 10 October 1957, Tom Tuohy, deputy general manager at the plant, was at home attending to his family who were suffering with the flu, when the phone rang. The anxious voice at the other end was his boss who said simply, 'Come at once. Pile number one is on fire.'

The 'Pile' was one of two reactors, known as Windscale Pile no. 1 and Windscale Pile no. 2, built after the Second World War near the Cumbrian village of Seascale. Unlike the nearby Calder Hall, which had come on stream in 1956, they were not involved in generating power for the nation's electricity grid, but solely as part of Britain's top secret bid to build atomic bombs. After 1945 the United States had declined to share its nuclear arsenal with its wartime ally. A peeved British Government decided to go it alone, with Ernest Bevin famously saying in 1946, 'We've got to have this thing over here whatever it costs. We've got to have the bloody Union Jack on top of it.'

Operational since the early 1950s, the piles at Windscale, with their pair of 400ft chimneys, were designed to make plutonium for nuclear weapons – up to 200lb of the stuff a year. And material produced there was subsequently used in the UK's first nuclear weapon test in the Monte Bello Islands, off the coast of Western Australia, in 1952.

The design of the plant was key in the drama that would play out during the autumn of 1957. The reactor needed to be kept cool, because of the massive amounts of heat produced by nuclear fission. At Windscale uranium was encased in aluminium rods which were themselves placed in thousands of channels within around 2,000 tonnes of graphite. The spent fuel was then used to make plutonium. While reactors in the US used a water system to keep the rods cool, in Britain huge fans were used, sending 2 tonnes of air a second up the towering chimneys. Despite the installation of filters in the chimneys, known as Cockcroft Follies, there was a risk that any release of radiation could be sent up the chimneys and over the surrounding countryside. The nature of the Windscale piles also meant that they were at risk of a sudden build up in heat, which had to be managed by complicated processes called Wigner energy releases, which involved carefully raising and then lowering the power level.

As the 1950s went on Britain endeavoured to stay in the race to develop bigger and better nuclear weapons, but struggled to keep up with the Soviet Union and USA. It wasn't enough to have an atomic bomb, now Britain needed a hydrogen bomb. Modifications were made to the Windscale reactors in order to make tritium, needed for an H-bomb, and Britain duly tested its first H-bomb over Christmas Island in 1957 (though some believe it wasn't a true hydrogen bomb and that it was a bluff to convince the Americans). The nuclear weapons programme was hugely costly and British Prime Minister Harold Macmillan was already involved in delicate negotiations with the Americans to share nuclear secrets and forge a closer alliance against the Soviet threat. To be treated as an equal, the British needed to be able to demonstrate that they were keeping up technologically. Would the pressure tell at Windscale? It was in the midst of the Anglo-American negotiations that the accident struck.

On 8 October, according to the instruments read by the scientists on duty, one of the controlled Wigner energy releases appeared not to have happened properly. Unwittingly, too much heat was applied. Instead of the energy release happening as usual, and the reactor cooling down, the core gradually got hotter. Over the next few days developments were monitored with increasing alarm as the temperature inside the reactor kept rising. But it was only on 10 October that it became clear how bad the problem was. On taking out an inspection plug workers realised to their horror that the reactor was now glowing. A number of workers went in to push out the overheated fuel rods, to try and make a firebreak, using steel bars, but their efforts made little difference.

After receiving the shock call, Tuohy told his wife that she and the children should stay inside and close the windows, then quickly drove to the nearby works. Once there he took charge, donning full protective clothing and breathing apparatus, and climbed 80ft to the top of the reactor building to get a proper look at what was happening at the back of the pile via an inspection hole. He saw that the situation was now desperate.

By 8 p.m. there was no doubt that the reactor was on fire and that some radiation was already being released into the atmosphere. The chief constable of Cumberland was warned of the emergency and evacuation plans were readied. In the coming hours Tuohy climbed the reactor several more times, discarding his radiation monitor so that no one could haul him away telling him he'd had too much exposure.

Around midnight, with the help of the fire brigade, makeshift hoses started being positioned high up on the reactor. But, as yet, they weren't turned on. It was felt that cooling using water was too dangerous as it could lead to a reaction which might cause a major explosion, releasing a huge cloud of radiation. Next, carbon dioxide from the nearby Calder Hall was used, but it failed to put out the flames. The fire was simply too hot.

An estimated 11 tonnes of uranium in 120 fuel channels were now on fire, and temperatures were soaring to as much as $1,300°C$. The 7ft concrete shielding, which encased the reactor, had to be kept cool and was in danger of collapse.

At 8.55 a.m. on 11 October the decision was finally taken to use water. It had never been done before and was high risk. But if left to burn out itself the fire might shower radioactivity over much of northern Britain. By now the fire had been raging out of control for hours. Tuohy ordered everyone apart from himself and the fire chief out of the reactor building and the hoses were turned on.

At first the water didn't seem to be working. Then Tuohy decided to have the fans, which were supposed to be helping cool the pile, shut off, as they were also fanning the flames. By midday, Tuohy gazed down once more on the reactor and saw with relief that the fires finally seemed to be abating. More water was pumped through and the flames gradually died away. Tuohy later remembered, 'You've got this blazing inferno with these flames belting out; to know that you've licked it, that was a marvellous feeling.' He added, 'I went up to check several times until I was satisfied that the fire was out. I did stand to one side, sort of hopefully ... but if you're staring straight at the core of a shut-down reactor you're going to get quite a bit of radiation.'

And some radiation had got out. Following the accident, levels of iodine-131, short-lived but with its risk of thyroid cancer, was found in milk. All milk within a 200-mile radius of Windscale was poured away, with a ban continuing for a month. But the wider health risk was subsequently ruled to be tiny, with even the workers involved suffering few lasting health effects. Tom Tuohy himself emigrated to Australia and lived to the grand old age of 90. The piles at Windscale were shut down and encased in concrete.

It could all have been much worse. If Tuohy and his colleagues had not acted fast there might well have been a release of radiation similar to that at Chernobyl in 1986, which was 1,000 times worse than the leak at Windscale. As well as more than thirty direct deaths, the World Health Organisation estimates that a further 9,000 have died (or will die) from cancer as a result of the accident in Ukraine.

In the end the Windscale incident did not derail Macmillan's scheme to share nuclear secrets with the USA. The day before he heard news of the fire, Macmillan had written to President Eisenhower, 'Has not the time come when we could go further towards pooling our efforts and decide how to best to use them for our common good.' And on 23 October Eisenhower and Macmillan announced a Declaration of Common Purpose agreeing to share nuclear information. Windscale had done its job, but disaster had been narrowly avoided and vital lessons on nuclear safety had been learned.

43

AN ESCAPE FROM THE VOLCANO THAT BURIED POMPEII

On a hot summer's day in AD 79 a small earthquake shook the town of Misenum in the region of Campania, southern Italy, near what is now the city of Naples. It was one of many tremors that struck the area from time to time, and a Roman man called Gaius Plinius Caecilius Secundus, better known as Pliny the Younger, was barely disturbed from his studies. The 17-year-old Pliny was used to the earth occasionally moving beneath his feet, although he couldn't remember the infamous earthquake, some sixteen years before, that had badly damaged the nearby cities of Herculaneum and Pompeii. They had since recovered and no one seriously linked the mild earthquakes, which now seemed to be a regular occurrence, with the placid Mount Vesuvius nearby, its slopes covered with bountiful fields and vineyards. There were old legends of fiery eruptions once spouting forth from the great cone, but no one could remember it actually happening.

As a Roman from a high-ranking family, Pliny the Younger enjoyed the good life in Campania, a part of the empire that was booming economically; the region's fertile, volcanic soil served up delicious food and wine, and it was blessed with a climate that meant its coastline was peppered with luxurious villas. Since the death of his own father, Pliny had been living with his uncle, Pliny the Elder, who was already considered an important writer, celebrated for his epic, recently finished scientific work *Naturalis Historia*. He was also commander of the imperial navy's base at Misenum, located just 20 miles from Vesuvius along the Bay of Naples. The city of Pompeii, soon to go down in history, was a little further along the coast to the south-east.

It wasn't just Pliny the Younger who hadn't taken much notice of the recent tremors; neither had many others in the small town. But in the early afternoon of 24 August something unusual caught the eye of Pliny the Younger's mother. She noticed a large cloud rising from the direction of Mount Vesuvius, towering over the landscape, and pointed it out to her brother, Pliny the Elder. Having just taken a relaxing lunch and enjoyed a bath he climbed to a high point to investigate.

In the first of two letters to the great Roman historian Tacitus, describing the volcanic eruption at Vesuvius and the events surrounding it, the younger Pliny later reported what he and his uncle saw that day: 'Its general appearance can be best expressed as being like an umbrella pine, for it rose to a great height on a sort of trunk and then split off into branches ... sometimes it looked white, sometimes blotched and dirty.'

Unknown to Pliny and the other Romans living in the shadow of Mount Vesuvius, the seismic activity that they had been experiencing in the preceding years was actually a warning that the mountain was about to blow its top, as it had now done, suddenly and with brutal force. The cloud emanating from the volcano rose quickly to some 66,000ft and tonnes of ash and pumice began to rain down, carried south by the wind. The wealthy city of Pompeii, home to 20,000 people, was in the direct firing line, just 9 miles away. Roofs began to collapse, buried under the weight of the debris, which in places lay 8ft thick. Some residents began to flee the city, though debris already clogged the port and onshore winds made escape difficult.

Back at Misenum Pliny the Elder realised something of great magnitude was happening and ordered his boat to be readied so that he

A modern-day view of Mount Vesuvius across the Bay of Naples.
(© Attilio Lombardo)

could set off across the bay to investigate. Before he left, an exhausted messenger arrived from his friend Rectina whose home was at the foot of the mountain. She was evidently terrified by what was happening and begged Pliny the Elder to rescue her and her family. Pliny the Elder now ordered the whole fleet to sea. His nephew tells how he, 'hurried to the place which everyone else was hastily leaving, steering his course straight for the danger zone'. Once afloat, his boat was soon deluged with ash and pumice but Pliny the Elder ordered his helmsman to press on.

The young Pliny had been given some work to do by his uncle and stayed behind, still unaware of how serious the situation was. As night fell he bathed and had dinner, but he was now beginning to feel uneasy, dozing 'fitfully' before suddenly being jolted upright by a sudden wave of strong tremors. He recalled:

> That night the shocks were so violent that everything felt as if it were not only shaken but overturned. My mother hurried into my room and found me already getting up to wake her ... we sat down in the forecourt of the house, between the buildings and the sea close by.

Pliny the Younger tried to read a book and make notes to calm his nerves, even when he was berated for lingering by a friend of his uncle's. As a grey dawn light emerged the buildings around them were beginning to buckle, and Pliny and his mother took the decision to leave by land after all. They made for clear, open ground where at least they would not be crushed by falling masonry.

He recalled, 'The buildings round us were already tottering, and the open space we were in was too small for us not to be in real and imminent danger if the house collapsed. This finally decided us to leave the town. We were followed by a panic-stricken mob of people.'

At Vesuvius, more ash and pumice had poured forth, choking the towns of Herculaneum and Pompeii, just 6 miles south. By the early morning, pyroclastic flows, not lava but avalanches of super-heated gas and rock, were rolling down the mountain. These were followed by pyroclastic surges, clouds of ash and gasses able to move at 60mph. They crashed down onto both the towns, killing anyone who still remained alive. Fire and lightning rent the sky and deadly surges of ash and gas also surged towards Naples and Misenum.

As Pliny and his party fled, the ground was still swaying violently. Pliny wrote, 'The carriages we had ordered to be brought out began to run in different directions though the ground was quite level, and would not remain stationary even when wedged with stones.' And as he gazed out to sea he witnessed something extraordinary, what we now know was almost certainly a tsunami, 'We also saw the sea sucked away and apparently forced back by the earthquake: at any rate it receded from the shore so that quantities of sea creatures were left stranded on dry sand.'

Gazing back towards Vesuvius he recorded, 'a fearful black cloud was rent by forked and quivering bursts of flame.' Soon Misenum disappeared underneath a large black cloud. Pliny the Elder's friend, who had accompanied them, now pleaded with the younger Pliny to press on and save himself, saying, 'If your uncle is still alive, he will want you both to be saved; if he is dead, he would want you to survive him – why put off your escape?'

Pliny was still worried about what had happened to his uncle and hesitated. His mother begged him to leave her and to get to safety as quickly as he could. But Pliny later recalled, 'I refused to save myself without her, and grasping her hand forced her to quicken her pace ... ashes were already falling, not as yet very thickly. I looked round: a dense black cloud was coming up behind us, spreading over the earth like a flood.'

Pliny and his mother left the road to escape the throng of people. Trudging on through the gloom until it got so dark that they imagined it must be night, they sat down to rest:

> You could hear the shrieks of women, the wailing of infants, and the shouting of men; some were calling their parents, others their children or their wives, trying to recognise them by their voices ... Many besought the aid of the gods, but still more imagined there were no gods left, and that the universe was plunged into eternal darkness for evermore.

The ash was now falling thickly and the pair had to get up and shake it off several times in case it completely covered and suffocated them. Pliny says he was gripped by a belief 'that the whole world was dying with me and I with it'.

The next morning they were greeted by thinning clouds and a pale, sulphurous sunshine. Still worried about the fate of his uncle, Pliny and his mother took the decision to head back into Misenum, 'We were terrified to see everything changed, buried deep in ashes like snowdrifts ... Fear predominated, for the earthquakes went on.'

The ruins of Roman Pompeii. (© James Moore)

Fortunately for Pliny the Younger and those at Misenum, the killer surge never quite reached them. The youngster would later learn that his uncle had been forced to land a few miles down the coast from Pompeii, at Stabiae, and had tried to reassure the locals there, even taking another bath and dinner with his friend Pomponianus. However, with ash and pumice still raining down and more quakes he was soon awake again. He and his party tied pillows to their heads to protect them from the falling debris.

Pliny wrote to Tacitus that, 'the approaching fire drove the others to take flight', but his uncle stayed behind. A day later, when the danger had passed, his body was found intact but lifeless. Pliny the Younger speculated that the sulphurous fumes had killed him, but it's more likely that he simply had a heart attack.

No one knows exactly how many died as a result of the eruption at Vesuvius, or how many people escaped, but it's estimated that at least 16,000 died at Herculaneum and Pompeii in the violent surges of ash, gas and rock. The cities were buried and never reoccupied. Pliny the Younger went on to study law and became a prosecutor and Roman senator. He is reckoned to have written his vivid account of the eruption some twenty-five years after the event, but it was still so accurate that volcanologists later called the initial phase of an eruption like the one at Vesuvius 'Plinian', in his honour.

44

THE FIRST BRITISH 'HOME RUN' FROM COLDITZ

The Siege of Calais in May 1940 is a largely ignored chapter of the Battle of France, which ultimately ended in the famous rescue of 338,000 Allied troops from Dunkirk. The fierce resistance provided by a small British force at Calais was one of the factors that enabled the miraculous evacuation of so many troops back across the Channel from Dunkirk, known as Operation Dynamo.

When the invading Germans broke through the Allied line in May 1940 they made for the coast and cut the British Expeditionary Force off from their main supply ports further south. The British decided to land a small number of infantry and tanks to try and hold Calais in order to resupply the hundreds of thousands of troops still fighting in northern France. But they were ill equipped to tackle the German Panzer tanks bearing down on them and were soon outnumbered three to one. After three days of vicious fighting, and despite the bravery shown by the garrison, the port was lost and several thousand British soldiers were taken captive.

One of those captured at Calais was Airey Neave, then a 24-year-old gunner officer in the Royal Artillery. During the engagement he was wounded in the left side, a bullet missing his heart by half an inch. The injured Neave was taken prisoner as the British made a last stand near the Gare Maritime. In his book *They Have Their Exits*, Neave recalled, 'A field-grey figure appeared shouting and waving a revolver. Then a large man in German uniform and a Red Cross armband put me gently on a stretcher. I was a prisoner of war.' Taken at first to a French hospital, he was then moved to Oflag IX A/H, a castle in Spangenburg, deep inside

Airey Neave DSO, OBE, MC. He was the first British soldier to make a successful 'home run' from Colditz Castle. (Courtesy of Airey Neave's family and Airey Neave Trust, www.aireyneavetrust. org.uk)

Germany, and from February 1941, was housed at Stalag XX-A, a huge POW camp in a fortress at Thorn in Poland.

Neave pondered escape from the moment he was taken prisoner. After recovering from his injury, his first serious attempt to break out came in April 1941, teaming up with a fellow inmate, an RAF Hurricane pilot called Norman Forbes. Once out, the pair aimed to travel across Poland to the Soviet front line 200 miles away, or to steal a plane at an aerodrome they knew about north of Warsaw. On 19 April the duo managed to slip away from a working detail outside the camp and made off through the countryside disguised as Poles. However, a few days later they were captured by German soldiers and, when Neave's map of the aerodrome was discovered, briefly detained by the Gestapo as spies. Both were eventually returned to Thorn where they were locked away in a windowless storeroom by vengeful guards. Then, one morning in May, Neave was led away with some other officers. He soon learned that their destination was to be Oflag IV-C, more popularly known as Colditz Castle.

The forbidding ancient fortress in Saxony was used by the Germans to hold senior enemy officers who had already tried to escape from other camps. Dubbed the 'Bad Boys Camp', it was built on sheer cliffs with walls 7ft thick. Colditz was heavily garrisoned with seventy German soldiers overseeing some 500 assorted Allied prisoners including Poles, French, Dutch and Belgians, as well as the British. Those incarcerated included famous names from the war, such as the RAF fighter ace Douglas Bader. Despite the formidable challenges and dangers of escape, the nature of its inmates seemed to make them even more determined to break out than those at other camps.

By the time Neave arrived at Colditz, a French General, called Alain Le Ray, had already become the first successful escapee by evading his guards during an exercise outside the castle walls. In July 1941 Dutch officers arrived. Among them was Hans Larive, who had knowledge of the so-called Singen escape route. During a previous escape in 1940 he had been captured at the Swiss border; the Gestapo officer who had interrogated him was so cocky that he revealed a way that Larive could have safely crossed to safety without detection. This information would prove invaluable to future escapees, including Neave.

When two Dutch officers escaped in August by hiding under a manhole cover during a rugby game, Neave was determined to give his own escape plan a try. He had already worked in failed escape tunnels at the castle and now favoured a different approach. On 28 August, Neave, sanctioned by 'Escape Officer' Captain Pat Reid, tried to get out disguised as a German corporal, wearing a badly faked uniform consisting of an old Polish army tunic and hat that he had decorated with stage scenery paint. Neave could speak a smattering of German and, after roll call, marched towards the castle's main door, managing to talk his way past the first guard by handing him a stolen brass disc, one of those used as passes by his captors. But Neave was soon rumbled as he attempted to pilfer a bicycle. Thrown into solitary confinement, Neave was at first told he would be shot but was later simply mocked by the Kommandant who poured scorn on his shoddy approximation of a German uniform.

Neave was undeterred. On 5 January 1942 he tried again, this time along with a Dutch officer, Lieutenant Anthony Luteyn, a fluent German speaker. Pat Reid had discovered that a wooden stage used for performances by internees in the third floor camp theatre extended over a room in a part of a castle that wasn't being used. A hole was cut in the ceiling of this room from the area under the stage and, lowering himself down on bedsheets, Reid picked a lock and found that the room led to a passage over the inner courtyard gate, which itself led to an attic above the guardhouse. A false trapdoor was made to disguise the hole through which Reid had come, and Neave and Luteyn were chosen to try and escape through it. This time the pair would wear altered Dutch uniforms, which were similar to German ones. Authentic looking buttons and insignia were made from lead piping.

On the snowy night of the escape, Reid let Neave and Luteyn under the stage and then into the room below via the trapdoor where they discarded their British uniforms for 'German' ones, with civilian clothes underneath. Reid then led them to the guardhouse attic, from which they used a spiral staircase to make their way down into the courtyard, passing the German Mess on the way. The guards at the gate were unlikely to question two soldiers coming out of their own guardhouse, and as the pair passed by they exchanged platitudes in German in order to seem natural.

Knowing that they would need proper papers to pass the last, main entrance, Neave and Luteyn went through a wicket gate which led across a dry moat near the German guards' married quarters – a route Neave had spotted earlier. Encountering a soldier from the married quarters, Luteyn berated him in German for not saluting. Further on they shinned over the last, roughly built, 12ft stone wall before discarding their German uniforms. Travelling on foot and by train, Neave and Luteyn found their way to the city of Leipzig posing as Dutch electrical workers. At one point Neave nearly gave himself away when he got out some Red Cross chocolate to eat. The pair also had to share a train compartment with an SS officer as they continued to the town of Ulm. Here they were sent to have their papers checked, but managed to lose their guard before journeying via tram, and again on foot, to the forests near Singen, just miles from the Swiss frontier. In the dead of night, on 9 January, they evaded German border guards in the snow whilst wearing white beekeepers' coats, which they'd pinched, and made it into neutral Switzerland.

From there, with the help of the Resistance, Neave managed to return to Britain through France, Spain and Gibraltar, arriving three months after first escaping Colditz. Neave's was the first successful British 'home run' from the castle. While there were about 180 escape attempts made from Colditz, just thirty-two prisoners of all nationalities successfully absconded during the war.

Neave went on to work for the wartime secret service unit known as MI9, planning escapes for other Allied soldiers trapped in Europe and, when the war ended, worked as part of the International Military Tribunal in Nuremberg, serving indictments on former Nazi war leaders. He was also to have a distinguished career as a Member of Parliament.

However, having survived the horrors of the Second World War, Neave's life was to end tragically. By 1979, shortly before the general election that would bring Margaret Thatcher to power, Neave was shadow secretary for Northern Ireland and a man known for his tough stance on terrorism. Just before 3 p.m. on 30 March, Neave's car was blown up by a bomb as he drove it out of the car park at the Palace of Westminster. The explosion, believed to have been the work of a socialist Republican group called the Irish National Liberation Army, left Neave fighting for his life. He later died in hospital.

It was a sad end for a man whose thrilling escape from Colditz had provided other escapees with inspiration, though it was the part he and his comrades played at Calais – the unlikely extraction of the British army from the field of battle at Dunkirk – which perhaps helped most in the bigger picture of the war. In answer to critics who later sneered that the action at Calais was merely a useless sacrifice and that Adolf Hitler was to blame for missing his opportunity to bear down on Dunkirk, Neave wrote in his memoir, *Flames of Calais*, 'One thing is indisputable; the Tenth Panzer Division was delayed at Calais for four days and not by Hitler!'

THE NIGHT MARGARET THATCHER WAS BOMBED

On 15 September 1984, a single man, seemingly enjoying a weekend by the seaside, checked into Brighton's prestigious Grand Hotel. Roy Walsh was travelling light. Mid-thirties, good looking and with the nightlife of Brighton to occupy him over the next three nights, he cut an unremarkable figure as he checked in and was given the keys to a room on the sixth floor. But over the course of the weekend, Walsh's actions would result in the narrowest escape for the country's leaders since Guy Fawkes was caught under Parliament in 1605. Removing paneling from the bath, Walsh primed 20–30lb of explosives and set a timer several weeks hence. After checking out of the Grand, all he – and the Provisional IRA of which he was an agent – had to do was wait.

By the middle of October, the Conservative party conference was gearing itself up for the highlight of the week, the much-anticipated prime minister's speech. Margaret Thatcher's address to the party faithful that Friday would reflect on an eventful eighteen months. Riding high on a second election success, buoyed after battling the Argentinians to retain control of the Falkland Islands and locking horns with the miners, now six months into a national strike, Mrs Thatcher was at the height of her powers. So, when the Brighton bomb ripped through the middle of the Grand shortly before three o'clock in the morning on 12 October, the famously nocturnal leader was not yet thinking about retiring for the night.

All but two of the British Cabinet was staying at the Grand Hotel that night, most with rooms at the front so they could enjoy uninterrupted sea views. Only the leader of the House of Lords, Willie Whitelaw, and defence secretary Michael Heseltine, the man who was eventually to incite Margaret Thatcher's downfall, were absent: Heseltine was abroad and Whitelaw was residing at a country estate just outside Brighton.

This early autumn, the night was warm, the sea calm. At 2.54 a.m., with Mrs Thatcher's energy showing no sign of diminishing – she had added a final flourish to her keynote speech for the following morning in her first floor suite, before turning her attention to a paper about the Liverpool Garden Festival – the bomb exploded to devastating effect.

'A loud thud shook the room,' Mrs Thatcher recalled. 'There were a few seconds' silence and then there was a second, slightly different noise, in fact created by falling masonry. I knew immediately that it was a bomb.'

Through a fog of dust, the emergency services arrived to scenes of carnage. Slowly, methodically and over the noise of generators and chainsaws, they began a search and rescue operation, taking care as they extracted the dead, maimed and injured. The walking wounded headed for the esplanade where soon politicians, spouses and their retinue gathered in dressing gowns and slippers, caked in dust and debris. Many delegates decamped to the refuge of the neighbouring Metropole Hotel, only to find themselves evacuated for a second time when police warned of the possibility of another device. Among the last to be rescued – three hours after the blast – were Cabinet ministers Norman Tebbit and John Wakeman. Mr Tebbit's grimace formed a defining image of the night; his wife was left paralysed after the bombing. Acerbic diarist and Conservative MP Alan Clark confided to his best-selling journal that, 'The scene was one of total confusion, people scurrying hither and thither, barely a police officer to be seen.'

Mrs Thatcher and husband Dennis did not scurry hither and thither. Although it was evident to both prime minister and consort that there had been a bomb, they proceeded with fortitude and calm. On hearing the explosion, Mr Thatcher popped his head round the bedroom door to check the prime minister was safe, then returned to dress. Mrs Thatcher thought first of her conference speech, which was no longer in her room, having gone off for typing. The prime minister had been lucky, the location of her suite fortuitously cushioning her from the full impact of the blast. After being led away, initially to an office while firemen worked out the safest possible route, she spent what was left of the night at Lewes Police College, planning a response.

On one matter the prime minister was resolute: the show would go on, on schedule and with its leader firmly in place, on stage for the world to see. To a standing ovation, at 9.30 a.m. on Friday 12 October 1984, the prime minister walked onto the stage at the Brighton Conference Centre to listen to a debate about Northern Ireland. Delivering her own speech that afternoon, she kept to her original agenda. Only her opening remarks focussed on what she, and the delegates, had suffered the night before:

The bomb attack ... was an attempt not only to disrupt and terminate our conference; It was an attempt to cripple Her Majesty's democratically-elected government. That is the scale of the outrage in which we have all shared, and the fact that we are gathered here now – shocked, but composed and determined – is a sign not only that this attack has failed, but that all attempts to destroy democracy by terrorism will fail.

The Provisional IRA provided a chilling summary: 'Today we were unlucky,' they said. 'But remember we only have to be lucky once. You will have to be lucky always. Give Ireland peace and there will be no war.'

Five people died as a result of the Brighton bomb, thirty more were seriously injured and many lives changed irrevocably. It was quickly established that Roy Walsh, the man who had stayed on the sixth floor, in room 629. Walsh was really IRA agent Patrick Magee. Leaving Brighton immediately after planting the bomb and staying for some time in Holland, Magee remained undetected for a while. But having left partial fingerprints on his hotel registration form on check-in, he escaped justice for just nine months before being arrested in July 1985. Convicted of five counts of murder and a number of other charges, and receiving eight life sentences; Magee served fourteen years of the minimum thirty-five recommended. The judge told him, 'You intended to wipe out a large part of the government and you nearly did.'

Magee later said he regretted the loss of life, but not the bombing itself. 'All avenues were closed to us. Our only recourse was to engage in violent conflict,' he remarked. However, it eventually transpired that successive governments had indeed been exploring other avenues for peace. When eventually the IRA's legitimate political arm Sinn Fein and the British began to talk, at first secretly via British agents acting in Northern Ireland and the Republic – with the knowledge of the Conservative government – it proved a pathway to peace. Yet even as those tentative talks began – Mrs Thatcher continuing to propound her proposition that one never negotiates with terrorists – the Provisional IRA's campaign continued. In 1991, as John Major's new administration increased secret contact, another IRA attack came even closer to killing the prime minister, this time in the sanctity of Downing Street. Three mortar rounds fired from close range at Number 10 came within 15 metres of hitting the Cabinet room with the weekly session in full flow. One bomb slammed into the Downing Street garden. 'I think we'd better start again somewhere else,' said Major, collecting his papers. Two years later in Downing Street, the prime minister signed the Joint Declaration on Peace. The IRA declared its ceasefire within months. It wasn't quite peace, but the subsequent

Good Friday Agreement of 1998 paved the way for all sides to give up their weapons and bring a tentative end to the Troubles.

After his release under the terms of the Good Friday Agreement, Magee eventually formed an association with Jo Berry, daughter of Sir Anthony Berry, an MP murdered in the Brighton bombing. Together, Magee and Berry addressed the seemingly unsolvable conflict, their message being that only through mutual understanding could peace be achieved. On the twenty-fifth anniversary of the bombing, Ms Berry sat alongside her father's murderer in the House of Commons. 'It's like inviting Guy Fawkes!' she said of the man who had become her friend, 'I want to show the MPs what war is about, that they need to humanise the enemy. If you don't talk, then there's just going to be violence. No one is born a terrorist.'

46

ESCAPING HENRY VIII'S CHOPPING BLOCK BY A WHISKER

As a young man King Henry VIII is said to have taunted the Grim Reaper on a number of occasions. One tale has him nearly drowning during a hunting trip whilst attempting to vault a river; another has Henry escaping a fire which engulfed an inn in Hitchin, Hertfordshire, where he was lodging. But during his forties came an incident in which Henry's life really did hang in the balance. And, had he died at that particular moment in history, it would have had serious ramifications.

In popular culture Henry VIII is generally portrayed as a lumbering, bloated figure. Indeed, by some estimates he is reckoned to have weighed in at 28 stone by the time of his death. But in his earlier life Henry was agile and loved hunting and sport. He was an enthusiastic tennis player, enjoyed wrestling and regularly climbed on to a steed to enjoy a spot of jousting.

At the age of 44, he was still taking part in tournaments, but he was to joust for the last time on 24 January 1536 at Greenwich Palace, near London. Wearing full armour he was thrown from his horse, which then fell on top of him. At first the king was thought to be dead. Henry lay unconscious for two hours before he came round, and a pregnant Anne

Boleyn – the wife he would later have executed – was told he would probably die.

Some experts have linked the possibility that Henry suffered a brain injury during the accident with what seems to have been a change in temperament. The period following 1536 certainly saw England's notorious monarch carry out some of his most callous acts and conduct some of his most ruthless policies. Had Henry perished at the joust, so much would have been different. The Dissolution of the Monasteries would almost certainly never have been completed and, coming so soon after his break with Rome, England might well have become a Catholic country again. Many of those who later incurred Henry's ire would also have had their own lucky escapes from the scaffold, Anne Boleyn, executed in May 1536, and Catherine Howard, his fifth wife, among them.

Unlike Anne and Catherine, one of those who Henry condemned to death would survive by the narrowest of margins. And the lucky man who escaped the sovereign's axe was the very person who had warned Anne Boleyn of the king's imminent demise that January day at the Greenwich Palace joust.

Thomas Howard, Third Duke of Norfolk, was, at one time, one of King Henry's most trusted aides and part of a family that wielded huge power in England. He was also uncle to both Anne Boleyn and Catherine Howard. A man who could trace his own family tree to Edward I, Norfolk's rise within the Tudor hierarchy began on the battlefield, distinguishing himself at the Battle of Flodden Field in 1513. Inheriting the Duke of Norfolk title from his father in 1524, he became close to the young King Henry. According to the historian E.W. Ives, he would 'have helped his king to hell if Henry had wanted to go there'. Norfolk's star rose further when his niece, Anne Boleyn, caught Henry's eye. She became Henry's wife in 1533, with Norfolk having helped Henry elbow aside Cardinal Thomas Wolsey, who had failed to secure a papal annulment to the king's marriage to Catherine of Aragon.

By 1536 Henry was tiring of his union with Anne and began conducting an affair with Jane Seymour. In the meantime Norfolk's own relationship with Anne had taken a battering. Among other things, Anne blamed him for the shock she had suffered on learning of the king's jousting accident, which probably contributed to Anne miscarrying a male heir a week later. And, when Henry decided to do away with Anne, it seems that Norfolk had no problem in being the man picked to preside over her trial.

Anne's execution might have distanced Norfolk from the king but, in fact, Howard demonstrated his continuing loyalty to the Crown by helping to put down the serious uprising by Catholics in the north known as the Pilgrimage of Grace. It certainly helped him regain favour; but Norfolk was now at loggerheads with Thomas Cromwell, a man who had overtaken him in Henry's inner circle and with whom Norfolk disagreed over church reform. But following the death of Henry's third wife, Jane Seymour, and his subsequent disastrous match with his fourth, Anne of Cleves, which Cromwell had masterminded, Norfolk took full advantage.

During the marriage to Anne of Cleves, Norfolk had found his niece, Catherine Howard, a place at Court as a lady in waiting where, as he had hoped, she was soon noticed by the king. Henry married Catherine on 28 July 1540, the very day that the king had Norfolk's bitter foe, Cromwell, put to death. Norfolk was in the ascendant. Catherine, by contrast, was dead within two years, beheaded after her alleged infidelities were exposed.

Again it might have been the end for Norfolk, just as it was for Cromwell, but the great survivor hung on, partly helped by his keenness to once again help investigate his own niece's 'crimes'. In the ensuing years, Norfolk, awarded the title Earl Marshal, also led more military campaigns for Henry in Scotland and France. But Norfolk had been wounded by the collapse of the Howard marriage, and, as his court rivals jostled for power in the death throes of Henry's reign, they found a way to stick the knife in further.

It was a furore concerning Norfolk's eldest son which dislodged the duke's grasp of the greasy pole. In December 1546 Henry Howard, the Earl of Surrey, both a poet and himself one of Henry's military commanders, was arrested on a rather half-baked charge of conspiracy to usurp the throne – supposedly evidenced by the fact that he had added an ancient royal crest to his own coat of arms. Norfolk, accused of conniving in his son's plot, was also arrested, and both were imprisoned in the Tower of London.

Norfolk pleaded to King Henry, 'I am sure that some great enemy of mine hath informed your Majestie of some untrue matter against me.' But in his last years the paranoid king could become convinced in a trice that those around him had crossed the hazy line between loyalty and treason. Henry would show no sympathy, despite Norfolk's long years of dedicated service. Perhaps Norfolk should have spent more time with his family than on matters of state. Soon, his estranged wife, daughter and mistress were also lining up to give evidence against him.

Surrey was sentenced to death on 12 January 1547, after a short trial, and beheaded on 19 January. Norfolk fought to escape the same fate by confessing 'high treason, in keeping secret the false acts of my son', and offered his lands to the king, hoping for mercy. But even on his own deathbed, Henry's bloodlust was not assuaged. Thanks to his confession, Norfolk didn't even get a trial. On 27 January a bill was passed allowing his immediate execution, which was planned for the following day.

Then, at 2 a.m. on the morning of 28 January, Henry VIII died. Waking that same morning, Norfolk, still unaware of Henry's passing, must have expected to meet his maker too. Yet the duke remained alive in the Tower where, three days later, he was able to hear the canons being fired to announce that Henry's son, the 9-year-old Edward, was now king. Legally, Norfolk's sentence could still have been carried out, but seems to have lapsed as his rivals at court concentrated on jockeying for position and influence in the new regime. There may also have been a feeling that an execution would not be a good omen for a new reign, following one which had been so bathed in blood. After all, it is reckoned that King Henry VIII did away with more of the nation's elite than any other English ruler. By the skin of his teeth Norfolk would not be one of them.

However, Norfolk's enemies, such as the Earl of Hertford, now effectively running the country, didn't want the old duke on the loose. For six years Norfolk remained in the Tower while his lands were divided up among the nation's new heavyweights. Incredibly, despite already being in his early 70s at the time of his reprieve, Norfolk would outlive the sickly new king, too. Edward died, aged 15, in 1553. And, thanks to his Catholic sympathies, Norfolk was released upon the accession of the next monarch, Queen Mary, who, after ousting Lady Jane Grey, had returned the nation to the old religion. Norfolk was pardoned, restored to his dukedom and appointed to Mary's Privy Council. He was given compensation for the lands he had lost and went on to head military campaigns during Mary's reign.

Against all the odds, Norfolk died peacefully in his bed on 25 August 1554, aged 81. Yet his family was never far from trouble during the rest of the Tudor dynasty. In 1572 his grandson, also called Thomas Howard, was unable to cheat the axe, being executed for his alleged part in the Ridolfi plot, a botched attempt to assassinate Queen Elizabeth I.

47

THE MEN THEY COULDN'T HANG

Having been transported from England at the beginning of the nineteenth century, Joseph Samuels had expected to see out the rest of his days in a British penal colony in Australia. But found guilty of murdering a police officer after escaping into the wilderness and subsequently robbing a house in Sydney, the end had finally come. Sentenced to hang, and in front of an excitable crowd, Samuels prayed and waited for the cart to be pulled from under his feet. Around his neck, a rope made of hemp. At his side, another felon, convicted for a different crime.

The wheels of justice had taken just a matter of weeks to turn from the date of the robbery on 26 August 1803, to execution day on 26 September. Samuels could blame a mixture of stupidity and bad company for his predicament. Whilst £24 in guineas, silver dollars and change was a profitable day for this band of robbers, taking the desk containing the booty was, in retrospect, an act of idiocy. Even though the gang had quickly hidden the cash, conveying a piece of household furniture from one house to another aroused suspicion. Once their lodging house was identified – and that didn't take long – an officer called Constable Luker was on their tail, vowing, 'By daybreak I shall have taken up the scoundrels.' As a lone officer tackling outlaws with nothing to lose, this was recklessly ambitious. Luker's 'breathless corpse', a cutlass embedded in the head, was found the following morning. The hunt for the murderers was on.

Roads out of Sydney were blocked and dozens of known criminals rounded up. Soon two people, William Bladders and Isaac Simmonds, purporting to be a constable himself, were arrested and charged with murder. Three more, John Russel, Richard Jackson and the one eventually to hang, Joseph Samuels, were detained for questioning. John Russel said nothing; William Bladders claimed he had slaughtered a pig that very morning, hence the dried blood on his clothing; and Simmonds stated that his frequent nosebleeds were the cause of his blood-splatted handkerchiefs. Joseph Samuels and Richard Jackson both confessed to the robbery, but each pinned Luker's death on the other. Jackson revealed the whereabouts of the stolen desk but denied everything about killing the constable. Samuels said much the same, taking magistrates into the bush to locate the money. When it came to pleas, however, the desk trumped the cash. Jackson was accepted as a Crown witness against his friend.

So, on 26 September 1803, Joseph Samuels found himself alongside a robber called James Hardwicke debating which act had been the most stupid: stealing a desk or, as in Hardwicke's case, ransacking a room in a prison used to house debtors – which by definition was only going to provide sparse pickings. Now it was the end. Realising that his soul would be tormented for eternity if he didn't use his final moments with a clergyman to confess, Samuels, hesitant at first, admitted he was a robber but denied murder absolutely. In fact, he said, the killer was amongst them, in the crowd, come to watch an innocent man hang for his crime. Then, a frisson of excitement as Samuels named the culprit, Constable Simmonds.

This proclamation from the scaffold was dynamite, not least because Simmonds had been brought from prison to watch his associate hang. According to the *Sydney Gazette*, on 2 October 1803, Samuels' words quickly, 'gained credit among the spectators, in whose breasts a sentiment of abhorrence was universally awakened'. Were they about to witness the execution of an innocent man whilst the guilty looked on? The crowd certainly thought so. 'Odium and suspicion were attached to Simmonds from the very first,' the paper explained. 'Most of the spectators pronounced judgment against him in their hearts. The multitude burst forth into invective.'

This invective soon turned so violent that troopers had to intervene to protect Simmonds, and only once he was removed for his own safety could the hanging go ahead. The *Sydney Gazette* reported that with the noose now dangling at Samuels' side, a court representative arrived on horseback, flustered and clearly relieved that the executioner had not yet set to work.

A reprieve had indeed been granted. But it was Hardwicke, the ineffectual prison robber, who was to be set free. To the cheers of his friends, he was taken down from the cart. No reprieve had arrived for Samuels. Whatever he said would make not a jot of difference. After a final minute of prayer, the signal was given for the cart to be removed. But Samuels' noose didn't prove up to the job. With a snap of the rope, he simply fell to the ground.

This proved troublesome for the executioner, who needed help to get the prisoner back on his feet whilst the cart was returned. Another rope was unexpectedly available and once again Samuels' neck was threaded through. The second attempt failed too, the rope unravelling until Samuells' legs hit the ground: not so much a hanging as a trailing. 'All

John Henry George Lee (John 'Babbacombe' Lee), 'The Man They Could Not Hang', on his wedding day in 1907. (Courtesy Ian Waugh, www.murderresearch.com)

that beheld were moved at his protracted sufferings,' said the *Gazette*. Other reports suggest the crowd was by now close to riotous. Hangings weren't meant to take hours. Miscreants deserved to die, of course, but their end should take only a minute or two. However, pleas to stop the unfolding travesty went unheeded, for the law dictated that the hangman must try again.

The third attempt fared no better. With guards holding back the baying crowd, the flustered executioner rushed his work. Up on the cart went Samuels and down through the 6ft of air he fell once more. In a re-run of the first drop, the rope snapped. At this point, the Provost Marshal, overseeing the execution, decided that the law could go hang. This, he agreed with the crowd, was divine intervention. Nothing was wrong with the ropes, which were of the same quality as those that had been hanging colonial convicts and Aborigines for years. With Samuels writhing on the floor, an official rode to the state governor requesting a reprieve. Within an hour, it was granted. God was on Samuels' side; so much so that he eventually made such a good recovery that he was able to go back to his job robbing people.

The law soon caught up with Samuels for another offence. Finding himself back in prison and facing a long stretch, this was bad news. Calling upon God once more, his prayers were answered with a boat that he chanced upon whilst on work detail with other prisoners. Rowing hard and fast, the convicts made their escape through shark-infested waters. Presumed drowned or eaten, they were never heard of again.

Eighty-two years later, Britain got its own prisoner for whom divinity thrice intervened. On 23 February 1885, a hangman called James Berry tested the gallows at Exeter Prison. Everything was in place so that he could dispatch John Lee, a murderer from Babbacombe who had pleaded not guilty to murdering his employer, Emma Keyse, some months earlier.

Miss Keyse had been found in the early hours of 15 November 1884 with her throat slit and axe wounds to the head. With evidence of attempts to burn her body, this looked like a premeditated act, and John Lee, her footman, was in the frame. Lee had form. He had been jailed for stealing from Miss Keyse's home previously but had been unexpectedly rehired. Lee was the only male in the house when Miss Keyse was murdered. Given an inexplicable cut to his arm, he was quickly arrested and tried.

Nothing went well for Lee from the morning of the murder until the day he stood on the trapdoor waiting for the floor to fall away. Forensic science still hadn't been thought of, and fingerprinting was still fifteen years away, so his protestations of innocence were hard to corroborate. The jury considered circumstantial evidence carefully: the cut arm, the fact that he had been in the house and that he hadn't gone to the rescue of his employer as her throat was slit and she was beaten about the head, which, presumably, must have caused a bit of commotion.

With no Provost Marshal to overturn the law, Lee couldn't be reprieved. But with a malfunctioning trapdoor, neither could he be hanged – not in Exeter, not on that day anyway. When the executioner tested the trapdoor, it worked. When Lee stood on it wearing a noose, it didn't, even though his executioners tried it three times.

As with Joseph Samuels in Australia all those years before, the word went round that God had played a hand. And in the nineteenth century, when divinity intervened, politicians took notice. Lee himself explained his calmness in the face of his death sentence to the judge: 'I trust in the Lord, and He knows I am innocent.' Home Secretary William Harcourt, announcing that Lee's sentence would be commuted to penal servitude for life, remarked, 'It would shock the feeling of anyone if a man had twice to pay the pangs of imminent death.'

John 'Babbacombe' Lee, as he became known, remained in prison for twenty-two years before being released into a life of obscurity.

48

HOW BLIGH SURVIVED THE MUTINY ON THE *BOUNTY*

Hollywood painted him as a villain, but Lieutenant William Bligh had one of the most remarkable escapes in maritime history. For not only did he survive a mutiny and months at sea, managing to get himself from the South Pacific back home to England, he also successfully negotiated his way through a court martial for losing his ship and went on to a moderately successful naval career.

Bligh's narrow escape was predicated on a plant whose fruit tasted like bread and that was coveted for its medicinal properties. At a time when sailors on long voyages were often stricken with scurvy, the tropical *Artocarpus incisa* tree's fruit helped, but the only place it could be acquired appeared to be the South Pacific. Aside from the opportunity of garnering a £100 reward, rich Londoner Joseph Banks wanted the plant for his botanical collection and eventually convinced Prime Minister William Pitt the Younger to finance an expedition. England, he explained, was falling behind France when it came to botany. As transportation of convicts to Australia had recently begun, Banks suggested that the two enterprises could be combined – convicts out, breadfruit back. However, as different types of vessels were required for the two distinct activities, eventually the government paid for a cutter called *Bethia*. Renaming it *Bounty*, Banks appointed Lieutenant Bligh, a man who, like himself, had sailed to Tahiti under the great Captain James Cook.

Disappointed at not being promoted from a lieutenant to a fully fledged captain, and being equipped with only a cutter rather than a more appropriate sloop of war, Bligh recruited his crew. Some officers were sons of gentlemen, but the rest were a mixed bunch. Henry Hilbrant's left arm was shorter than the right; Alexander Smith was pitted by smallpox and he had an axe scar on his right foot; John Sumner's lavish scar adorned his left cheek, whilst William McCoy's stab wound was across his belly; and William Brown, the gardener, bore 'a remarkable Scar on one of his Cheeks Which contracts the Eye Lid and runs down his throat.' All in all, they looked like pirates. And they had yet to set sail.

Trouble blighted the voyage, which left England in 1787, from the outset. Delays waiting for the Admiralty to give permission to leave meant the ship would hit dangerous waters at the worst possible time. Even the initial attempt to leave Portsmouth ended with three weeks on the Isle of Wight.

Eventually, progress was made and ten months later the *Bounty* reached Tahiti. Bligh's relations with his crew, however, had become strained. Breaking his 'no lash' ambition, a number of men had been flogged. One had died after being bled by the surgeon for an infection. Several suffered from scurvy, hopeful that the breadfruit might help. Almost everyone resented the three hours of mandatory dancing Bligh insisted on each evening. His off-handed manner upset both officers and men. 'You are a parcel of lubbery rascals,' Bligh yelled when things didn't go well. For Master's Mate Fletcher Christian, the commander's ways wore thin.

However, welcomed warmly by the Tahitians, the *Bounty*'s crew quickly fell in love with the relaxed way of life and the plentiful food. The men also struck up relationships with the Tahitian women and Fletcher Christian later married a local. Months elapsed and eventually the work transporting breadfruit plants to the *Bounty* was complete. However, by now some of the men had turned native. Three deserters, caught after trying to set up home so they could stay in the South Pacific, had been confined in irons for weeks, being unchained now and again for a flogging. After almost six months of heavenly existence, a long voyage in an inadequate cutter with a prickly commander was unappealing.

A row over coconuts sparked the mutiny. Not long into the journey, Bligh got it into his head that his nuts had been pilfered. Ordering everyone, men and officers alike, to produce their own hoard of hardy fruit and face cross-examination, he questioned forensically. 'How many Nuts did you bye [sic] & how many did you eat?' he demanded of midshipman Edward Young. When it came to questioning Christian Fletcher, matters became very tense indeed. 'I hope you don't think me so mean as to be Guilty of Stealing Yours,' snapped Fletcher. 'Yes you dam'd Hound I do,' Bligh retorted. Leaving for bed in a sulk, he ordered yam rations to be reduced by two-thirds until the culprit owned up. This was not a happy ship.

At 4 a.m. the following morning, 28 April 1789, the mutiny began. Bligh, sleeping with his door unlocked, awoke with a jerk as he was dragged him from his bed, his desperate pleas for reason going unheeded. Reminding Christian that Bligh's four children, who 'you have danced upon your knee', would be bereft had some impact, with Christian disturbed by the reminder. 'That, Captain Bligh, that is the thing. I am in hell. I am in hell.' But it made no difference.

Granted few resources – a compass, quadrant and broken sextant, together with measly rations and a small band of loyal men – Christian lowered Bligh into the South Pacific into a vessel just 23ft in length. With Fiji about 500 miles away and England halfway around the world, death appeared a certainty.

But for forty-eight days, starvation rations bolstered only by the capture of passing birds, Bligh's new crew survived. Sailing first to an island called Tofua, the nearest landfall, 10 leagues away, proved their gravest mistake. The natives proved so hostile they were forced into a sudden escape, quartermaster John Norton beaten to death as they fled. Shaken, Bligh made a bold decision: despite the perils at sea, they would visit no more small islands. Instead Dutch Timor, 3,600 miles away and from where they could catch a ship for Europe, was their heading. Bligh deemed New Holland (today's Australia) an island large enough to be safe, and at the Great Barrier Reef they were able to recuperate before heading off again on the 1,000-mile journey to Timor.

Against the odds they made it. So it saddened Bligh that, although he had already navigated such a journey and lost only one man to murderous natives, during the two months they remained on Timor, five died, including gardener David Nelson who had so assiduously collected the breadfruit plants. Bligh's letter from Timor to his own wife carried the first news about the mutiny to England. 'Know then my own Dear Betsy that I have lost the Bounty,' he wrote. 'I have been run down by my own Dogs.'

Relief at having survived so far turned to disappointment when the Timor governor turned Bligh down for the credit he needed to procure a schooner for the next stage. Credit from His Majesty's Government would normally be acceptable, but the Dutch feared that even if Bligh did reach England, the inevitable court martial wouldn't make him good for credit. Although the governor eventually relented, news reached Bligh that his own men had spread the rumour about his creditworthiness.

Tensions returned. Despite getting them so far, his authority was shot. At Surabaya, on the coast of Java, a second mutiny looked likely, the men openly accusing him of bringing the original mutiny upon himself. When two men said Bligh should be shot from a cannon or hanged, he had them arrested by the Dutch. Inviting others to step forward if they had any complaint against him, three did so. One of the arrested men was sent on by another ship, one apologised and the others agreed to obey orders, but the next part of the journey was tense indeed. When, after three weeks in Batavia, space came up for three people on a Dutch ship back to England, Bligh, by now tired of his tumultuous crew, claimed the space for himself, his servant and his clerk.

And so it was that almost a year after the mutiny, on 14 March 1790, Bligh finally arrived back at Portsmouth, capping an amazing journey and receiving a hero's welcome. *The English Chronicle* reported, 'In navigating his little skiff through so dangerous a sea, his seamanship appears as matchless as the undertaking seems beyond the verge of possibility.' As a returning hero, he sailed through his court martial for losing his ship, going on to publish best-selling memoirs. But although Bligh gained his longed-for promotion to captain, his career eventually stalled as he fell victim to the well-connected, well-heeled families of mutineer officers who laid the blame for the *Bounty*'s loss squarely with its commander. At one stage he was embroiled in what became known as the second Bligh mutiny, when the men of his fifty-four-gun vessel *The Director* took a dislike to him. Out of kindness, eventually his old benefactor Joseph Banks, the man who had commissioned him on the *Bounty*, arranged for him to become governor of New South Wales. Bligh accepted reluctantly.

Back in the South Pacific, the British Admiralty's ship *Pandora* sailed to capture the mutineers, finding several of them in Tahiti. Despite the fact that the ship sank on the way home, several were eventually returned to England. Three were hanged from the yardarms of a ship off Portsmouth. Fletcher Christian was not among them, having settled in the sunshine of Pitcairn Island with several other mutineers. Located in the Pacific where no land was indicated on charts until an American sealer ventured upon it in 1808, Pitcairn was the missing link in the eighteen-year puzzle of what had become of the mutineers. Remarkably, the Americans chanced upon a teenage boy, Thursday October Christian, who told them that having lost the support of the other men within four years of landing at Pitcairn, his father, Christian, was dead. Accounts depend as to whether Fletcher Christian had been murdered, committed suicide or died from natural causes.

49

RUSSIA'S *APOLLO 13*

When the astronauts aboard the *Apollo 13* reported to ground control, 'Houston, we've had a problem', it seemed unlikely that the Americans would make it back from space to Earth. An explosion had crippled their 1970 mission to the Moon. But, after much drama, the US crew managed to fix the problem and the story of how they survived became one of the world's most thrilling and well-known escape stories.

However, thanks to the Cold War, it took longer for Russia's own *Apollo 13*-style space escape to emerge. Beginning as a mission that was ostensibly scientific, in the race to become the first nation to put a man on the Moon, it was a stepping stone that in itself achieved a historic landmark – the first transfer of cosmonauts from one spacecraft to another via a space walk. But one of its other firsts was not planned – the first rear entry by a cosmonaut returning to Earth. This latter fact, and the extraordinary story of survival, was little known outside the Soviet Union for decades.

Based around a spacecraft known as *Soyuz*, the Soviet space programme was three years old when, on 14 January 1969, *Soyuz 4* took off from the world's first space launch centre in what is today Kazakhstan. Only one of the previous four *Soyuz* missions – the first one was unnumbered – brought a cosmonaut back alive. Two had been unmanned and a third had crashed. But this had not dampened Soviet ambitions to reach the Moon before the Americans.

With the space race escalating, the USSR's aim now was for two to become one. Two *Soyuz*es, launching on consecutive days, would link together in orbit and exchange personnel. Flying solo in *Soyuz 4*, commander Vladimir Shatalov would link his craft with *Soyuz 5*, carrying three cosmonauts, Boris Volynov, Aleksei Yaliseyev and Eugeni Khrunov. Successfully docking two spacecraft and transferring men would prove that the USSR had the talent and technology to thrash the Americans.

At first, the mission progressed faultlessly. Both *Soyuz*es launched without a hitch, both reached their intended position and both conducted their scheduled experiments perfectly. Finally, after numerous orbits of Earth, the two craft came together where, first, *Soyuz 5* steadied itself, before Commander Shatalov in *Soyuz 4* executed the manoeuvre that would make history: linking two manned spacecraft together. It was peerless.

The four cosmonauts ran tests for a time before the next critical phase. Whilst Shatalov had gone out into space alone, it was up to Commander Volynov in *Soyuz 5* to make the solo return journey. On 17 January 1969 Yaliseyev and Khrunov made the historic (but little noticed) walk from *Soyuz 5* and into *Soyuz 4*. Waving goodbye to Volynov, they wished him a safe journey back to Earth. He didn't get one.

Once the craft separated, *Soyuz 4* headed back to Earth more or less straight away, leaving Volynov to orbit Earth for another day. By the time he pressed the button to set the trajectory home, he had orbited Earth forty-nine times, completing one circuit more than Shatalov. He could now look forward to being back on Earth in less than an hour. However, somewhere way above the South Atlantic, heading north-east towards the USSR, a crisis of astronomical proportions unfolded. The *Soyuz*'s descent module – one of three parts that made up the spacecraft and the critical section in which the commander travelled back – failed to detach from the equipment module. The 'retrofire' designed to separate the two capsules, propelling the equipment module safely away, failed, leaving bits still attached to the accommodation module. For re-entry into the Earth's atmosphere, one of the most dangerous parts of an already treacherous mission, this was almost certainly fatal. Through the windows, Volynov could see antennas from the equipment module still attached to his capsule, unmoving, like barnacles to a rock.

The implications were obvious. First, the spacecraft was now the wrong shape – almost the wrong way round – for perfect re-entry, making severe turbulence inevitable. Second, when the explosive separation bolts had misfired, they had put the *Soyuz*'s trajectory out somewhat. This would mean coming down on the wrong part of the planet; inconvenient, but probably survivable. But most crucially, taken together, the two elements meant that heat shields that would prevent the *Soyuz* incinerating on re-entry were now blocked by parts of the equipment module that should have detached. This was the catastrophic element.

Worse, the heat-resistant protective tiles were now towards the back end of the vehicle, where they would serve no useful purpose, rather than at the front, where they were life-savers. The heat when a spacecraft re-enters the Earth's atmosphere is almost the same as at launch. For those inside the cabin, it is far preferable for that heat and the associated flames to shoot out behind the spacecraft, rather than coming face on. Now it looked like *Soyuz* would re-enter Earth like a meteor – with no protection. As compressed shock waves cause temperatures to reach 5,000°C on entry, most meteors burn to a cinder, lighting up the sky with flame. Very little of substance is usually left when they hit the ground. That was now the prospect facing Volynov. And he was getting hotter.

As re-entry began, Volynov could only wait for death as the flames made their way through the module to the escape hatch where he was dangling by his seat belt. Miserably but calmly, he reported the disturbing news to Mission Control and whispered 'No panic' to himself. Despite the inevitability of the situation and the fact that any evidence would be cremated with him, he recorded details into his voice recorder and flight log.

Volynov later recalled, 'There was no fear, but a deep-cutting and very clear desire to live on when there was no chance left.' His thoughts, he said, were of family and friends; of his recent birthday party in Moscow. Only when the walls around him became hotter and smoke began to fill the cabin did he accept that he was minutes from death. With flames blistering his skin (he was not wearing a pressurised spacesuit) and railing against any logic, Volynov stuffed the most recent entries from his logbook into a pocket so that it would be found if his body was recovered.

Then, a narrow escape – thanks to the laws of physics and chemistry. Flames and fuel don't mix well in most circumstances, but for Volynov the combination was a life-saver. As the fuel tanks overheated, an explosion rattled the spacecraft. With another jolt, the heat began to recede, the rattling subsided. Somehow the *Soyuz* had righted itself, the stress of re-entry completing the separation of the remaining elements of the equipment module from its descent equivalent. The mission was back on track, something of which Mission Control, having lost audio contact, remained ignorant.

Although relieved that he hadn't fried, Volynov then faced another substantial hurdle. The *Soyuz* continued to hurtle towards Earth and needed to slow down for a controlled landing. Just two years before, *Soyuz 1* had smacked into the surface after its controls had malfunctioned. After grappling with them for a whole day, the pilot, Vladimir Komarov, the sole crew member, managed to get his craft on a trajectory back to Earth. Then, whilst congratulating himself on re-entering the atmosphere without burning up, a parachute that was meant to slow down the capsule for a safe landing failed to open. It hit the ground at more than 300mph, giving Komarov the honour of becoming the first spaceman to die in active service.

Happily, *Soyuz 5*'s parachutes deployed, but not perfectly. The fiery re-entry and botched separation of the two modules had damaged the outer containers storing them. So although they performed the vital function of slowing the craft, the lines connecting the parachutes to the spacecraft tangled as the capsule continued to spin. Landing rockets designed to help smooth the landing also failed. To cap everything, as the *Soyuz* hit Earth, Volynov flew across the cabin and his teeth shattered. But, giving thanks that he needed only a dentist not a funeral director, he clambered from the capsule and blinked into dazzling whiteness. Snow! Lots of it. Unfortunately, where once he had expected to be greeted by beaming officials proffering garlands, he now found himself hundreds of miles away from his intended destination. And Mission Control wouldn't know where to look. Muttering a few choice words, he stepped out into the snowy Ural Mountains where temperatures were minus 38°C, pulled his jacket tighter and stomped off to find some peasants who would feed him, taking care not to grit his teeth for fear more may fall out. He was tracked down via a trail of blood from the spacedraft.

Although the Soviets decided to keep the botched landing under wraps, Volynov's career continued. It took seven years before he returned to space, as commander of *Soyuz 21*, where he repeated the walk his colleagues had pioneered in 1969. Heaving transferred from his spacecraft onto the Salyut space station, he enjoyed eighteen days in orbit before making a safe and uneventful return journey.

Disaster struck *Soyuz* again two years later when, after a successful mission in space, a three-man crew suffocated after an air valve opened prematurely, proving, if proof were needed, that danger is inherent in space travel. Today at least one *Soyuz* spacecraft is docked to the International Space Station at all times so that the crew can escape and head for Earth should an emergency arise.

50

WHEN THE MILLENNIUM BUG DIDN'T BITE

As the twentieth century hurtled towards its end and most people prepared for a party, the boffins of the IT industry were in no mood for celebrating. The landmark year 2000 was proving to be one enormous headache for people responsible for the world's computer systems. With just about everything run by computers as the twentieth century drew to a close, from microwave ovens and television sets through to nuclear power plants and guided missile systems, a frighteningly large number of experts forewarned that 1 January 2000 would bring computer Armageddon, with a potentially cataclysmic effect on how the world ran. Once the clock ticked over to 1 January 2000 – which would occur at various times across twenty-four hours of the world's different time zones – computers would be unable to cope. Planes would fall out of the sky. Nuclear reactors would go into meltdown. Microwavable dinners would go uncooked. Evasive action was necessary everywhere – and it would cost billions.

The issue had become evident only relatively recently. Although a number of computer scientists warned of problems as early as 1971, the Millennium then seemed an age away, so almost nobody noticed or listened. After all, computers were novelties. Few believed there was any rush to fix glitches decades hence, and the problem, if there was going to be one, seemed to revolve around something rather small – the two final digits of the year: zero zero. Surely it couldn't have been beyond the capabilities of scientists to add two digits so that when 1999 clicked over to 2000, computers could cope. Unfortunately, said the IT sector, it really wasn't that simple and please could they have about $100 billion to work it out?

The problem originated at the dawn of the modern computer age in the 1930s and '40s. In building machines that could execute multiple complex problems simultaneously, the computer pioneers overlooked one essential detail, the four-digit year – unintentionally planting a time-bomb that would not become apparent until they were all long dead. The reason was this: in the nascent days of computing, memory and storage space were sparse and expensive; the space for those extra two digits valuable. This flaw would eventually cost governments, businesses, citizens and consumers billions of pounds.

Confusion about 1 January 2000 went beyond the accepted shorthand of writing the date as the digits 01/01/00. Semantics and the Gregorian calendar on which Western time is based confused people too. So whilst most people believed that 1 January 2000 was the start of the new century, pedants pointed out that the centuries consist of 100 years, and 00 was the hundredth year of the twentieth century, not the first one of the next. Under this calculation, indisputably mathematically correct, the new millennium would not start until 1 January 2001. To universal disdain, pedants said that celebrations would have to be put on hold for twelve months. Sensible people threw parties both years.

Next came confusion about whether 2000 was a leap year. Whilst leap years usually arise every four years, the Gregorian calendar actually omits the additional day at the turn of each new century – with an exception: as the Earth takes 365 days, 5 hours, 49 minutes and 16 seconds to journey around the Sun, an extra day is required at the turn of centuries only if the year is divisible by 400, otherwise the calendar would creep ahead of the orbit. For the first time since 1600, the new century would also be a leap year. Computers would need to know this too.

But the essential problem remained the two-digit 00 date. Unless a solution could be found, when 1 January 2000 came around, computers would scratch their metaphorical heads and spend a nanosecond puzzling how to handle the abbreviation. Is it 1900? Is it 19100? If you were a computer approaching the turn of the millennium, you might be about to send yourself and the organisation you worked for into a terminal tizzy. The flaw was nicknamed the 'Millennium Bug' and a whole new industry, christened Y2K, arose to eliminate it.

For some, the bug was good news. IT consultants raised their fees and waited for the work to pile in. Politicians pontificated. Sermons were preached. And a new genre of literature sprang up: the Y2K self-help book. In the United States, Karen Anderson's seminal guide, *Y2K for Women: How to Protect Your Home and Family in the Coming Crisis*, was typical. 'The Y2K bomb is ticking. Here's the survival guide you can't afford to be without,' proclaimed the flap on Michael Hyatt's *The Millennium Bug: How to Survive the Coming Chaos*.

So serious was the bug thought to be that governments set up commissions to handle the pending catastrophe. In the UK, a lively logo was designed and a Cabinet minister appointed to lead the battle. The British Standards Institute created new criteria. For organisations to comply, they must prove that their computers understood that the year 2000 would be a leap year and that IT systems would present dates in which the century was 'unambiguous, either specified, or calculable by algorithm'. The Standard would not be awarded if the computer infrastructure wasn't clever enough to work out the correct date.

The economy was under threat too. If this bug wasn't eliminated, global meltdown was on the cards, with stock markets, unable to compute or trade, crashing. Bankers choked on their bonuses when US Federal Reserve chairman Alan Greenspan admitted he was 'one of the culprits who created this problem', having earlier written computer software 'and was proud of the fact that I was able to squeeze a few elements of space out of my program by not having to put a 19 before the year'.

With four months to go, the UK Parliament's science and technology select committee warned that the NHS and local councils remained unprepared. Elsewhere too it looked like preparations had been left far too late. Japan's prime minister, Keizo Obuchi, declaring a three-day emergency holiday, warned citizens to stockpile food and water. China also announced an emergency holiday to cover the transition to the new year, even though it uses a different calendar. By now, the airline sector was thought to be particularly vulnerable. American football teams flew to matches on 30 December so there was no chance of being in the air over the critical period. As the date drew nearer, even experts threw in the towel. A systems analyst responsible for Y2K compliance at a large American phone company decided all was lost and headed for a camouflaged bunker in Oklahoma, stocking up on tinned food and M-16 assault rifles.

During the final weeks of the old century, the US Government printed $50 billion worth of banknotes, just in case computers lost track of money. Then, as the clock ticked down on 31 December 1999, attention focussed on the Republic of Kiribair, a thirty-two-atoll nation that straddles the equator on the international dateline and that would be the first place to enter the new millennium. Although home to just 100,000 inhabitants, and with computers few and far between, this was the test. Around the world, people put their fingers in their ears and waited for the Apocalypse. Nothing happened. And over the course of the next twenty-four hours, in every time zone and every country, nothing happened either.

Pedants apart, as the world celebrated the start of the third millennium, IT experts raised a toast – to themselves. All the hard work they had put in had averted the crisis, they said. US aviation chief Jane Garvey was arguably most pleased. She had braved a flight from Washington to Dallas to be in the air at midnight, putting her survival down to the investment made in killing the bug. As IT consultants declared themselves heroes, *Computer Weekly* gushed, 'The absence of IT disasters is testimony to the sterling work of IT professionals over the past three years and on the night itself.'

Not everyone was overjoyed. The US Government pulped the £50 billion worth of new banknotes it had just printed and began to count the costs of complying with their own Y2K standards, estimating $4 billion of government spending alone. Businesses would have committed multiples more: British businesses spent £20 billion.

Arguments then began to rage. Had governments and companies had the wool pulled over their eyes? Or was the threat so serious that only an obscene amount of cash could avert the problem? After all, computers do confuse dates. Ten years after the Millennium Bug was squished with a whimper, German and Australian shoppers found their credit and debit cards rejected in shops and in cash machines. The problem? A faulty microchip on their cards that couldn't recognise the year 2010.

SELECTED SOURCES & FURTHER READING

CHAPTER 1

Churchill, Winston S., *The Hinge of Fate* (New York: Houghton-Mifflin, 1950).
Colvin, Ian, *Flight 777* (Evans, 1957).
Hastings, Max, *Finest Years: Churchill as Warlord 1940–45* (HarperPress, 2009).
Howard, Ronald, *In Search of My Father* (St Martin's Press, 1984).
Jenkins, Roy, *Churchill* (Pan, 2002).
Lavery, Brian, *Churchill Goes to War* (Naval Institute Press, 2007).
Thompson, Walter, *Beside the Bulldog* (Media Publishing, 2003).
The Independent, 21 May 1994.

CHAPTER 2

Gilbert, Martin, *Finest Hour* (Heinemann, 1984).
Jenkins, Roy, *Churchill* (Pan, 2002).
Roberts, Andrew, *The Holy Fox* (Phoenix, 2004).
Taylor, A.J.P., *Beaverbrook* (Hamish Hamilton, 1972).

CHAPTER 3

Beeson, Trevor, *The Deans* (SCM Press, 2004).
Gaskin, Margaret, *Blitz: The Story of December 29, 1940* (Faber and Faber, 2005).
Johnson, David, *The London Blitz* (Stein & Day, 1982).
Keene, Diane; Burn, Arthur; and Saint, Andrew, *St Paul's – The Cathedral Church of London 604–2004* (Yale University Press, 2004).

Owen, James, *Danger UXB* (Little, Brown, 2010).
Pyle, Ernie, *Ernie's War: The Best of Ernie Pyle's World War II Dispatches* (Touchstone/Simon and Schuster, 1986).

CHAPTER 4

Ostrom, Thomas P., *The US Coast Guard in WW2* (McFarland, 2009).
Popular Science, 167, 1955.
Sea History, 126, spring 2009.

CHAPTER 5

Mieszkowska, Anna, *Mother of the Children of the Holocaust: The Story of Irena Sendler* (Praeger, 2010).
Obituary, *Daily Telegraph*, 12 May 2008.
Obituary, *The Economist*, 22 May 2008.
Obituary, *Washington Post*, 13 May 2008.

CHAPTER 6

Collie, Craig, *Nagasaki: The Massacre of the Innocent and the Unknowing* (Portobello Books, 2012).
Ham, Paul, *Hiroshima Nagasaki* (Doubleday, 2012).
Obituary, *Daily Telegraph*, 6 January 2010.
Obituary, *The Economist*, 14 January 2010.
Daily Mail, 30 March 2009.
The Guardian, 25 March 2009.
The Sunday Times, 30 July 1995.
The Times, 6 August 2005.

CHAPTER 7

Costigliola, Frank, *Roosevelt's Lost Alliances* (Princeton University Press, 2011).
Hastings, Max, *Finest Years: Churchill as Warlord 1940–45* (HarperPress, 2009).
Reynolds, David, *From World War to Cold War* (OUP, 2007).

CHAPTER 8

Dobbs, Michael, *One Minute To Midnight* (Vintage, 2009).
Sagan, Scott, *The Limits of Safety* (Princeton University Press, 1995).
La Crosse Tribune, 30 January 2009.

CHAPTER 9

Daily Mail, 29 December 2007.
Washington Post, 10 February 1999.
http://news.bbc.co.uk/1/hi/world/europe/198173.stm, 21 February 1998.

CHAPTER 10

'Escape by Balloon', www.ballonflucht.de, Günter Wetzel.
Petschull, Jurgen., *With the Wind to the West* (Hodder & Stoughton, 1981).
Popular Mechanics, February 1980.

CHAPTER 11

Hindenburg, The Untold Story, Channel 4, 2007.
Mooney, Michael M., *The Hindenburg* (Mayflower, 1974).

CHAPTER 12

Burton, Walt, and Findsen, Owen, *The Wright Brothers Legacy* (Harry N. Abrams, 2003).
Crouch, Thomas, *The Bishop's Boys* (W.W. Norton, 2003).
Howard, Fred, *Wilbur and Orville: A Biography of the Wright Brothers* (Alfred A. Knopf, 1987).
Tobin, James, *To Conquer the Air* (Simon and Schuster, 2004).

CHAPTER 13

Bishop, Patrick, *Fighter Boys* (Harper Perennial, 2004).
McKinstry, Leo, *Hurricane: Victor Of The Battle Of Britain* (John Murray, 2011).

Olson, Lynne, and Cloud, Stanley, *For Your Freedom and Ours: Forgotten Heroes of World War II* (William Heinemann, 2003).
Wilton, Brian, *Hurricane: The Last Witnesses* (Andre Deutsch, 2010).

CHAPTER 14

King, Ross, *The Last Supper* (Bloomsbury, 2012).
Ladwein, Michael, *Leonardo Da Vinci: The Last Supper: A Cosmic Drama and an Act of Redemption* (Temple Lodge, 2006).
New York Times, 2 July 1995.

CHAPTER 15

Scotti, R.A., *Vanished Smile: The Mysterious Theft of the Mona Lisa* (Vintage, 2010).
Financial Times, 5 August 2011.
Time Magazine, 27 April 2009.

CHAPTER 16

Bridgeford, Andrew, *1066: the Hidden History of the Bayeux Tapestry* (Walker & Company, 2006).
Hicks, Carola, *The Bayeux Tapestry: The Life Story of a Masterpiece* (Vintage, 2007).
Musset, Lucien, *The Bayeux Tapestry* (Boydell, 2005).
Rud, Mogens, *The Bayeux Tapestry and the Battle of Hastings 1066* (Christian Eilers, 2004).

CHAPTER 17

Longmate, Norman, *Island Fortress* (Pimlico, 2001).
McLynn, Frank, *Invasion: From the Armada to Hitler, 1588–1945* (Routledge and Keegan Paul, 1987).
Wheeler, H.F.B. and Broadley, A.M., *Napoleon and the Invasion of England: the Story of the Great Terror* (Nonsuch, 2007).

CHAPTER 18

Jones, Stephanie, and Gosling, Jonathan, *Nelson's Way: Leadership Lessons from the Great Commander* (Nicholas Brearley, 2005).

Lavery, Brian, *Horatio Lord Nelson* (British Library, 2003).

Pocock, Tom, *Horatio Nelson* (Bodley Head, 1987).

Sugden, John, *Nelson, A Dream of Glory* (Pimlico, 2004).

CHAPTER 19

Elton, G.R., *England under the Tudors* (Methuen, 1955).

Guy, John, *Tudor England* (Oxford University Press, 1990).

Johnson, Paul, *Elizabeth: a Study in Power and Intellect* (Weidenfeld and Nicholson, 1974).

Kelsey, Harry, *Sir Francis Drake: The Queen's Pirate* (Yale University Press, 2000).

CHAPTER 20

Barker, Juliet, *Agincourt* (Abacus, 2006).

Curry, Anne, *Agincourt: A New History* (Tempus, 2006).

Mortimer, Ian, *1415: Henry V's Year of Glory* (Vintage, 2010).

CHAPTER 21

Fraser, Antonia, *King Charles II* (Phoenix, 2002).

Miller, John, *Charles II* (Weidenfeld and Nicolson, 1991).

Ollard, Richard, *The Escape of Charles II after the Battle of Worcester* (Robinson, 2002).

CHAPTER 22

Butler, Sir Thomas, *The Crown Jewels and Coronation Ceremony* (Pitkin, 1990).

Mears, Kenneth, *The Crown Jewels* (Historic Royal Palaces, 1994).

Strong, Roy, *Coronation* (HarperCollins, 2005).

CHAPTER 23

Fraser, Antonia, *The Gunpowder Plot* (Weidenfeld and Nicholson, 1996).

Robinson, Bruce, *The Gunpowder Plot* (BBC, 2011).

Schama, Simon, *A History of Britain 1603–1776* (BBC, 2001).

CHAPTER 24

Evans, Eric J., *The Forging of The Modern State: 1783–1870* (Longman, 1983).

Ward, J.T. (ed.), *Popular Movements 1830–1850* (Macmillan, 1988).

Wood, Anthony, *Nineteenth Century Britain 1815–1914* (Longman, 1982).

Woodward, Sir Llewellyn, *The Age of Reform 1815–1870* (Clarendon Press, 1962).

CHAPTER 25

Rappaport, Helen, *Queen Victoria: A Biographical Companion* (ABC-Clio, 2002).

Vallone, Lynne, *Becoming Victoria* (Yale, 2001).

Wardroper, John, *Wicked Ernest* (Shelfmark Books, 2002).

Wilson, A.N., *The Victorians* (Arrow, 2002).

CHAPTER 26

'Charles Lucas – The First VC', www.victoriacrosssociety.com.

'Crimea in Finland', *History Today*, volume 54, issue 8, 2004.

Crook, Diana, *The Ladies of Miller's* (Dale House Press, 1996).

CHAPTER 27

Cunningham, John, *The Last Man* (New Cherwell Press, 2003).

Macrory, Patrick, *Kabul Catastrophe* (Prion, 2002).

Norris, James, *The First Afghan War* (Cambridge University Press, 2010).

CHAPTER 28

Hay, John M., and Nicolay, John George, *Abraham Lincoln: A History* (Ulan Press, 2012).

Foreman, Amanda, *A World on Fire* (Penguin, 2011).

Jones, Howard, *Blue & Gray Diplomacy* (University of North Carolina Press, 2010).

Rawley, James A., *Turning Points of the Civil War* (University of Nebraska Press, 1989).

CHAPTER 29

Herndon, William, and Weik, Jesse, *Life of Lincoln* (Da Capo, 1983).

Sandberg, Carl, *Abraham Lincoln: The Prairie Years* (Harvest Books, 2002).

Schroeder-Lein, Glenna R., *Lincoln and Medicine* (Southern Illinois University Press, 2012).

van Natter, Francis Marion, *Lincoln's Boyhood* (Public Affairs Press, 1963).

CHAPTER 30

Clifford Larson, Kate, *Bound For the Promised Land: Harriet Tubman, Portrait of an American Hero* (Ballantine, 2005).

Clinton, Catherine, *Harriet Tubman: The Road to Freedom* (Little, Brown, 2004).

Humez, Jean, *Harriet Tubman: The Life and Life Stories* (University of Wisconsin Press, 2003).

CHAPTER 31

Bechtel, Stefan, *Mr Hornaday's War* (Beacon Press, 2012).

'Last of the Wild Buffalo', Hanna Rose Shell, *Smithsonian Magazine*, February 2000.

CHAPTER 32

Parkinson, Roger, *Hussar General: The Life of Blücher, Man of Waterloo* (Wordsworth, 2001).

Snow, Peter, *To War with Wellington* (John Murray, 2011).

Uffindell, Andrew, *Waterloo Commanders: Napoleon, Wellington and Blücher* (Pen & Sword, 2007).

Uffindell, Andrew, and Roberts, Andrew, *The Eagle's Last Triumph* (Greenhill Books, 2006).

Young, Peter, *Blücher's Army: 1813–1815* (Osprey, 2001).

CHAPTER 33

Ackroyd, Peter, *Charles Dickens* (Vintage, 2002).

Tomalin, Claire, *Charles Dickens: A Life* (Penguin, 2012).

Wolmar, Christian, *Fire & Steam* (Atlantic, 2008).

CHAPTER 34

Betjeman, John, *John Betjeman Letters, Volume Two, 1951–1984* (Methuen, 2006).

Bradley, Simon, *St Pancras Station* (Profile, 2007).

Lansley, Alastair, et al., *The Transformation of St Pancras Station* (Laurence King, 2011).

Daily Mail, 14 September 2007.

Evening Standard, 21 December 2009.

www.bbc.co.uk, 6 Nov 2007.

CHAPTER 35

Harriss, Joseph, *The Eiffel Tower* (Elek, 1976).

Herve, Lucien, *The Eiffel Tower* (Princeton Architectural Press, 2002).

Sagan, Françoise, and Denker, Winnie, *The Eiffel Tower* (Deutsch, 1989).

www.tour-eiffel.fr

CHAPTER 36

Beamish, Richard, *Memoir of the life of Sir Marc Isambard Brunel* (1862).

Buchanan, Angus, and Rolt, L.T.C, *Brunel: The Life and Times of Isambard Kingdom Brunel* (Penguin, 1990).

Gillings, Annabel, *Brunel* (Haus, 2006).

Brunel Jr, Isambard, *Isambard Brunel* (Longmans Green, 1870). www.brunel-museum.org.uk.

CHAPTER 37

Eaton, John P. and Haas, Charles A., *Titanic: Triumph and Tragedy* (W.W. Norton & Company, 1995).
Hyslop, Donald; Forsyth, Alastair; and Jemima, Sheila, *Titanic Voices* (Sutton, 1997).
McGreal, Stephen, *The War on Hospital Ships 1914–1918* (Pen & Sword, 1908).
Southampton City Archives.
Southern Daily Echo, February 1937.
The Times, 23 April 1917.
www.bbc.co.uk, 30 March 2012.

CHAPTER 38

Seedhouse, Erik, *Trailblazing Medicine* (Springer, 2011).
British Medical Journal, 339, 2009.
Soviet Antarctic Expedition Information Bulletin, 1964.

CHAPTER 39

Bud, Robert, *Penicillin: Triumph and Tragedy* (Oxford University Press, 2007).
de la Bédoyère, Guy, *The Discovery of Penicillin* (Gareth Stevens, 2005).
Meyers, Morton A., *Happy Accidents: Serendipity in Modern Medical Breakthroughs* (Arcade, 2007).
History Today, volume 53, issue 3, 2003.

CHAPTER 40

'Churchill's Forgotten Hero', www.bbc.co.uk.
Jones, Simon, *World War I Gas Warfare Tactics and Equipment* (Osprey, 2007).
Journal of the Society of Chemical Industry, volume 37, 1918.
www.rsc.org.

CHAPTER 41

Brown, Frederic J., *Chemical Warfare: A Study in Restraints* (Transaction, 2005).

Hammond, James W. Jr, *Poison Gas: The Myths Versus Reality* (Greenwood Press, 1999).

Harris, Robert, and Paxman, Jeremy, *A Higher Form of Killing* (Random House, 1982).

McCamley, Nicholas, *Secret History of Chemical Warfare* (Lee Cooper, 2006).

Mikesh, Robert C., *Japan's World War II Balloon Bomb Attacks on North America* (Smithsonian Institution Press, 1973).

Spiers, Edward M., *Chemical Warfare* (Palgrave Macmillan, 1986).

Tucker, Jonathan B., *War of Nerves* (Anchor, 2007).

CHAPTER 42

Arnold, Lorna, *Windscale 1957* (Palgrave Macmillan, 2007).

Patterson, Walter C., *Nuclear Power* (Pelican, 1976).

Pocock, Rowland, *Nuclear Power* (Unwin, 1977).

CHAPTER 43

Beard, Mary, *Pompeii* (Profile, 2010).

Radice, Betty, *The Letters of the Younger Pliny* (Penguin, 1969).

CHAPTER 44

Neave, Airey, *The Flames of Calais* (Pen & Sword, 2003).

Neave, Airey, *They Have Their Exits* (Pen & Sword, 2002).

Routledge, Paul, *Public Servant, Secret Agent* (Fourth Estate, 2002).

CHAPTER 45

'Brighton Bombing', *Hoddinott Report* (Hansard, 22 January 1985, volume 71, cc 866–78).

Clark, Alan, *Diaries* (Phoenix, 1993).

Spencer, Graham (ed.), *Forgiving and remembering in Northern Ireland* (Continuum, 2011).

Thatcher, Margaret, *The Downing Street Years* (Harper Press, 1993).

CHAPTER 46

Childs, Jessie, *Henry VIII's Last Victim* (Thomas Dunne, 2007).
Head, David M., *The Ebbs and Flow of Fortune* (University of Georgia Press, 2009).
Hutchinson, Robert, *House of Treason* (Phoenix, 2010).

CHAPTER 47

Holgate, Mike, and Waugh, Ian David, *The Man They Could Not Hang: the True Story of John Lee* (The History Press, 2005).
National Police Memorial of Australia.
Sydney Morning Herald, 26 September 1953.

CHAPTER 48

Alexander, Caroline, *The Bounty* (HarperCollins, 2003).
Hough, Richard, *Captain Bligh & Mr Christian* (Readers Union, 1974).

CHAPTER 49

Flight Journal, volume 7, number 2, June 2002.
Wired, 16 January 2009.

CHAPTER 50

Computer Weekly, 26 October 2000.
Time Magazine, 1 January 2000.

If you enjoyed this book, you may also be interested in…

Pigeon Guided Missiles And 49 Other Ideas that Never Took Off
James Moore & Paul Nero

This book tells of the fascinating stories of daring plans from history that could have radically changed the world - yet somehow failed to take off. Discover how Nelson nearly got a pyramid instead of a column, the scheme to cover Manhattan in a glass dome, and why the Victorian Channel Tunnel hit a dead end.

978 0 7524 5990 5

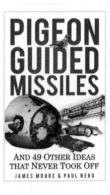

Ye Olde Good Inn Guide: A Tudor Traveller's Guide to the Nation's Finest Taverns
James Moore & Paul Nero

The essential handbook for the Tudor traveller. Packed with the finest hostelries to grace the 16th century and written with all the flavour of the language of the day, this witty and meticulously researched tome covers every county in the land and directs you to all the celebrated and charming pubs, many of which still exist today.

978 0 7524 8061 9

From 221B Baker Street to the Old Curiosity Shop
Stephen Halliday

London is unrivalled as a source of inspiration for writers from Geoffrey Chaucer to J.K. Rowling. Here we explore the capital both from the viewpoint of the writers who have used it as a stage for their plots and characters; and of the readers whose imagination is fired from knowing they are standing outside the home of David Copperfield on the Strand or Count Dracula's residence in Piccadilly.

978 0 7524 7024 5

**Visit our website and discover
thousands of other History Press books.
www.thehistorypress.co.uk**